The Why's of
Social Policy

THE WHY'S OF
SOCIAL POLICY

Perspective on Policy Preferences

HOBART A. BURCH

with the assistance of
Donna G. Michaels

New York
Westport, Connecticut
London

Library of Congress Cataloging-in-Publication Data

Burch, Hobart A.
    The why's of social policy : perspective on policy preferences /
    Hobart A. Burch, with the assistance of Donna G. Michaels.
        p.   cm.
    Includes bibliographical references and index.
    ISBN 0-275-94006-3 (alk. paper)
    1. Social policy.   2. Welfare state.   3. Human services.
    I. Michaels, Donna G.   II. Title.
    HN28.B87   1991
    361.6'1—dc20   91-10856

British Library Cataloguing in Publication Data is available.

Library of Congress Catalog Card Number: 91-10856
ISBN: 0-275-94006-3

First published in 1991

Praeger Publishers, One Madison Avenue, New York, NY 10010
An imprint of Greenwood Publishing Group, Inc.

Printed in the United States of America

The paper used in this book complies with the
Permanent Paper Standard issued by the National
Information Standards Organization (Z39.48–1984).

10 9 8 7 6 5 4 3 2 1

Every man will be thy friend
  Whilst thou hast wherewith to spend.
But if store of crowns be scant,
  No man will supply thy want. . . .
He that is thy friend indeed,
  He will help you in thy need.

Richard Barnfield, 1598
"Address to the Nightingale"

Contents

Preface

Major policy decisions turn not upon available facts but
upon judgment, with which policy makers are no better
endowed than the intelligent citizen.

—J. William Fulbright[1]

They suppose truth, justice, and temperance to be in
every man's power: the practice of which virtues,
assisted by experience and a good intention, would
qualify any man for service to his country.

—Jonathan Swift[2]

Social policy is everybody's business. It affects every member of our
society. In a democracy, it is equally the responsibility of government officials and ordinary citizens. And we are equally qualified to make
judgments about it.

Legend has it that in the eleventh century, King Canute, having con-
quered most of Scandinavia and England, ordered the ocean tide to go
back. It came in anyway. Kenneth Boulding referred to social policy as
a ''Canute complex'': ''We stand on the shore of an increasing tide of
human misery and disorganization and busy ourselves frantically in
sweeping it back, but for all our efforts, the tide seems to creep in and
in.''[3]

In Shakespeare's *Julius Caesar*, Brutus, plotting with Cassius, took the opposite approach: Go with the flow.

> There is a tide in the affairs of men
> Which, taken at the flood, leads on to fortune . . .
> On such a sea we are now afloat,
> And we must take the current when it serves
> Or lose our ventures.[4] (4.3.217-18, 221-23)

James Russell Lowell was more positive: "Truly there is a tide in the affairs of men, but there is no gulf-stream setting forever in one direction."[5]

This book recognizes social policy as a tide in human affairs. It is intended to help readers understand and respond to that tide with the guarded optimism of Lowell, the opportunism of Brutus, the sober humility of Boulding—and perhaps the qualities Jesus suggested to his apostles: "Behold, I send you out as sheep in the midst of wolves; so be wise as serpents and innocent as doves."[6]

When I became a teacher after twenty years in the "social policy business" (variously as a local and national church official, a federal poverty program planner, a social justice movement leader, and an executive of the national trade association for nonprofit social services), I found a gap in current literature. There were good books that offered

- the *history* of social welfare
- *descriptions* of current social welfare policies and programs and trends
- *technical* analysis of social policies, primarily from econometric models
- political and administrative action *strategies*

The missing link was an integrative overview on the *why's* of social policy, the foundation for making choices and predicting their effects. A doctoral student expressed her view on the "gap" rather forcefully:

Every policy text which I have read was successful only in one area—confusion. Muddling through is all most of us do. We need an opportunity to stop struggling through convoluted writing and dated examples and get on with the important business of learning a framework with which we can build or change social policy.[7]

The purpose of this book is to enable you to "determine" social policies and programs in relation to four different dictionary definitions of *determine*.[8]

- *Understand* policies: "to find out exactly; ascertain."
- *Evaluate* policies: "to reach a decision about, after thought and investigation."

- *Guide* policies: "to give definite aim or direction to."
- *Impact* policies: "to be the cause of; be the deciding or regulating factor in."

This requires *perspective* (from the Latin word for "to see through"): "the relationship of the parts of a whole, regarded from a particular standpoint."

If you care to, you can identify my "particular standpoint," especially when I use illustrations from personal experiences. I have chosen to follow my natural open style rather than attempt to sterilize and neutralize all material. However, this book does not offer The Truth. Just as I evolved mine, you have to develop your own "particular standpoint" and concrete applications in good faith, with self-awareness and a modicum of humility. All persons and human institutions, present company not excepted, are fallible. John Stuart Mill based his argument for academic, religious, and political liberty on this perception:

That mankind are not infallible; that their truths, for the most part are half-truths; that unity of opinion, unless resulting from the fullest and freest comparison of opposite opinions, is not desirable and diversity not an evil but a good, until mankind are much more capable than at present of recognizing all sides of the truth, are principles applicable to men's modes of action, not less than their decisions.[9]

This book provides frameworks for analyzing fundamental social policy issues and choices. Like ocean waves, policy issues seem to be "always changing, always the same." Concepts and choices are illustrated by both recent and past historical policies and programs. Current applications will soon be history, replaced by new ones. Yet the "timeless" issues will still be operating, albeit wearing different clothes. The goal of this book is to enable the reader to bring to each new situation insights and perspectives for developing creative responses without having to reinvent the wheel. To this end, each chapter identifies a different set of issues and the alternative values and principles that have been applied to it.

The flow of the book is from the general to the specific. The first chapter explains what social policy is and where it occurs. Chapters 2 and 3 address fundamental issues about ways of thinking, values and interests, and assumptions about the human condition that infiltrate every social policy issue.

Chapters 4, 5, and 6 address basic social choices involving "liberté, egalité, fraternité" and the tensions between central control and individualism.

A popular public health model identifies three points of intervention: hosts (the target beneficiaries), agents who affect them, and the environment in which it takes place. Chapters 7 and 8 address the macrodimensions of changing or enhancing the environment and the agents. Chapter 9 on the welfare state addresses the interaction of environment and hosts.

The next four chapters zero in on delivery of services and benefits to hosts. Chapter 10 discusses kinds of benefits, methods of delivery, and who is eligible. Chapter 11 addresses legal issues, including entitlement, appeals, and court decisions. Chapter 12 reviews the pros and cons of who delivers the service, followed by Chapter 13, which explores the question of who pays and how they pay.

Having completed the "substantive" part of the book, the last two chapters offer a brief, simplified approach to the *process* of analyzing policy choices. Chapter 14 summarizes the ingredients involved in making responsible choices, followed in Chapter 15 by a modest step-by-step model for analyzing the issue and reaching a decision. If you are interested in pursuing this in more depth, you will find no shortage of books that specialize in particular models of analysis and planning.

In Washington, where we referred to 100,000 separate, living, breathing, feeling human children on Aid to Families with Dependent Children (AFDC) as "zero point one" (0.1 million), it is easy to forget what social policy is about in the first place. To keep perspective under these circumstances, I consciously visualized specific families I had known as a welfare caseworker in Harlem.

As you read this book, with its broad perspectives and its conceptual frameworks, and deal with policy in the "real world," may you never lose sight of the only ultimate test of social policy: When all is said and done, who is the better for it? Alvin Schorr, who as deputy assistant secretary of HEW was deeply committed to "poor kids," quoted William Blake to me as we struggled to humanize federal programs: "He who would do good to another must do it in Minute Particulars. General Good is the Plea of the scoundrel, hypocrite, and flatterer; for Art and Science cannot exist but in minutely organized particulars."[10]

NOTES

1. Paraphrased by Barbara Tuchman, *The March of Folly* (New York: Ballantine, 1984), p. 336, from William Fulbright, *Vietnam Hearings* (New York: Random House, 1966), Preface.

2. Jonathan Swift, *Gulliver's Travels*, Pt I, Ch. 6, quoted in the concluding remarks of Tuchman, *The March of Folly*, p. 387.

3. Kenneth Boulding, "The Boundaries of Social Policy," *Social Work*, vol. 12, no. 1, January 1967, p. 9.

4. JC 4.3.217-18, 221-23.

5. James Russell Lowell, "New England Two Centuries Ago," 1888.

6. Matthew 10:16.

7. Donna G. Michaels, personal communication, December 1989.

8. Unless otherwise specified, definitions used in this book are from *Webster's New Twentieth-Century Dictionary of the English Language, Unabridged*, 2nd ed. (New York: World Publishing Company, 1971), or *The American College Dictionary* (New York: Random House, 1956).

9. John Stuart Mill, *On Liberty*, 1859.

10. William Blake, *Jerusalem*, 1804–1820, f. 55.

The Why's of Social Policy

Chapter 1

What Is Social Policy?

Bobby and Sammy, who live in the same Alabama town, have lost their fathers. Sammy's father died. Bobby's father just disappeared. Neither mother is employed. Both receive government support.

Aid to Families with Dependent Children (AFDC) and Food Stamps combine to give Bobby's family an income of less than half the official "poverty line." To be eligible, his mom must be willing to take a job rather than stay home with Bobby. Sammy's family receives triple that amount from Social Security. To be eligible for full benefits, his mom must *not* take a job. Social policy questions:

- Should Sammy be treated differently from Bobby? Why?
- Should mothers who choose to stay home with their children be rewarded like Sammy's or punished like Bobby's? Why?
- Does it "all depend"? On what?

Before Social Security, 3/4 of older people were poor and/or dependent. Now nearly 9/10 are above the "poverty line." Without Social Security, a majority would still be below the line. Social Security takes a dollar for every seven earned by the average American (counting both employee and employer shares). Social policy questions:

- Is the security and reduced poverty worth the taxes?
- Should workers be required to provide for their old age?

We buy our refrigerators at a competitive price in the free market. The electricity to run them is available only at a fixed price from a monopoly (a commercial business in San Francisco, a government business in Omaha). Social policy questions:

- When is the public interest best served by open competition?
- When is it better served by monopolistic "public utilities"?
- Should utilities be socialistic, as in "conservative" Omaha, or capitalistic, as in "liberal" San Francisco? Why?

This book does not answer these questions. What it does do is provide "tools" to help you understand—and develop *your* answers to—the "why's" of social policies:

- Where do you find social policies?
- What forms do they take?
- Where are they coming from, literally and figuratively?
- What are their expressed intents?
- What, if any, are their hidden agenda?
- How do their actual effects differ from their intents? Why?
- What choices are available, and what is a sound basis for choosing?

WHAT IS SOCIAL POLICY?

Policies are "courses of action, whether intended or unintended, that are deliberately adopted or can be shown to follow regular patterns over time."[1]

Social policies "have to do with human beings living together as a group in a situation requiring that they have dealings with each other."

Social policies may be good or bad. Slavery was a bad policy. Public education is a good one. What is the difference? The bottom line for every social policy is how it affects the welfare of human beings, collectively as a society and individually within it.

Welfare is "the state of being or doing well: the condition of health, prosperity, and happiness; well-being."

SORTING IT OUT: CONCEPTS AND FRAMEWORKS

Like all of human life, social policy is a potpourri of overlapping, inconsistent, and often contradictory intents and behaviors that affect different people in different ways. To help readers get a clear perspective on this complex mixture, this book uses concepts and frameworks that organize and distill key elements from the mass of detail.

- *Generalizations* are "concerned with the main or overall features; lacking in details."
- A *concept* is "a generalized idea of a class of objects."
- Concepts may be organized into a *framework*, "a structure serving to hold the parts of something together," or a *model*, "a representation of a social pattern."

This process is inherently selective and approximate. The apostle Paul, referring to himself and the early church at Corinth, spoke of receiving "the light of revelation" and then added, "but we have this treasure in earthenware pots."[2] All concepts and models are earthenware pots. They never exactly fit the messy reality you are dealing with. Hopefully the ones in this book contain a "treasure" of insight, but they are still pots. Neither accept them as "Truth" nor reject them outright for their imperfections. Use them—and develop ones of your own—as tools.

WHERE TO INTERVENE

During the building of the Panama Canal, health officers combating the scourge of yellow fever evolved a "systems" model that identified three interacting elements as points for possible intervention:

1. *Hosts*: workers who became "hosts" to the virus. Treat or immunize them.
2. *Agents*: carrier mosquitoes. Kill them before they bite.
3. *Environment*: swamps in which mosquitoes grow. Drain them.

Adapting this to social policy, hosts are the ultimate targets; they are the victims or intended beneficiaries. These may be persons or populations *at need* (those who already have a problem, such as unemployed adults); *at risk* of developing it, such as unmotivated students; *with potential* for enhanced well-being, such as disadvantaged youth whose employment future could benefit greatly from a college education.

Agents are people, organizations, or things that directly affect the hosts. Agents may be *causers of problems*, such as drug cartels and street pushers, or *potential helpers*, such as teachers and drug rehabilitation clinics.

The *environment* is the larger context in which the problem takes place. Thus, for example, the drug problem may be related to a setting in which poverty and racism give ghetto youth little hope for a "respectable" future, or it may be seen in the context of an affluent society in which a culture of self-gratification has displaced traditional social values.

Social policies usually address one or a combination of these three areas. In social welfare, interventions with hosts are often called direct services and benefits, whereas those aimed at agents and the environment are known by such terms as *indirect services, regulation, enforcement,* and *macroeconomics.*

WHEN TO INTERVENE

The traditional "medical model" addresses when to intervene by identifying three stages of "prevention": *primary prevention* means keeping the problem from ever occurring; *secondary prevention* refers to early detection and treatment, when it is cheaper and more effective; *tertiary "prevention"* is treatment after the condition has become acute. In regard to heart attacks, primary prevention might include a campaign against smoking. Routine screening for high cholesterol, with follow-up treatment, would be secondary prevention. The intensive-care unit provides tertiary care for heart attacks.

In child abuse, reaching out to high-risk potential future abusers, such as persons who were abused as children, is primary prevention. Training teachers to spot and report early signs of abuse in their students would be secondary. Tertiary interventions include public child protection services, medical treatment for abused children, and prosecution of abusers.

This model is limited by its negative definition of health as absence of ailments. Although it is fine as far as it goes, this definition stops short of the full scope of social policy. This can be remedied by adding two more "stages."

Enhancement is based on a holistic health perspective that defines health as positive well-being, not just the absence of specific problems. A good diet-and-exercise program increases your energy level and current quality of life. A mandatory family life course in high school may improve normal parenting. A bonus side effect of enhancement may be primary prevention.

Maintenance is a stage beyond tertiary treatment. Desirable as prevention and cure are, social policy must also deal with the sad fact of our inability to prevent or cure all problems. A permanently disabled heart attack victim may need long-term nursing care and income maintenance. Where abusive parents cannot be helped or punished into becoming nonabusive, the child may need long-term nurture in an alternative family through adoption or foster care.

With these supplements, our "stages of intervention" model includes

- enhancement of well-being
- primary prevention

- secondary prevention and treatment
- tertiary treatment
- maintenance

FORMS OF SOCIAL POLICY: THE THREE D's

Our definition of policy offers two dimensions: (1) "intended or unintended" and (2) "deliberately adopted or . . . follow regular patterns over time." These can combine in three ways, which we may call "the three D's."

	Intentional	**Unintended**
Adopted	de jure	(not possible)
Regular Patterns	de facto	default

De Jure

De jure means "from the law." It is official, explicit, "on paper," and legally enforceable in court. De jure public policies are rooted in some form of law (the Constitution, statutes, regulations, and/or court precedents). De jure private sector policy is written in articles of incorporation, agency bylaws, official manuals of procedure, and collective bargaining contracts. Mandatory participation in Social Security is a de jure policy by act of Congress. School integration is de jure by court interpretation of the Constitution. A corporation's board of directors enacts de jure policies on hiring, firing, and fringe benefits.

De Facto

De facto means "from what is done." Such policy is an unofficial but consistent pattern. Where no official policy exists, people use their own judgment. In time, common practices evolve. In turn, when courts are called upon to make decisions in the absence of a specific law, they tend to follow such "common practice." As a river gradually builds up new land in a delta from silt it has carried along, the courts gradually build de jure common law from accumulated deposits of de facto policy.

De facto patterns sometimes modify or subvert official policy. A supervisor's flexibility may permit workers to "bend" overly rigid rules in ways that increase their productiveness. In a business that has an official policy of hiring and promoting on "merit," the de facto "settled course of action" may in fact give more weight to age, gender, ethnic origin, height, weight, grammar, accent, dress, grooming, or upper-class manners than to job-related merit.

The Constitution and federal laws guarantee equal opportunity in education and employment. In the 1960s, the law as applied required corrective system changes to overcome the effects of past discrimination and current institutionalized inequities. In the 1970s and 1980s, with a de facto policy shift toward "benign neglect," the same law was limited to review of filed complaints alleging a direct personal discriminatory act.

De facto policy can subvert official policy. When Mississippi was "dry," I had occasion as a federal official to work with state human service programs there. Meeting me at the airport, a state agency director opened his trunk and pulled out a bottle of illegal whiskey, which he offered me "as a routine courtesy." A few minutes later my bellhop offered to sell me a bottle of the same brand. Reportedly, Mississippi bootleggers were billed by the state tax authority for sales tax, based on invoices provided by their Louisiana wholesalers. In my present community, illegal gambling is handled similarly. Bookies operate openly and are seldom bothered unless they make waves. Police officers and public officials are among their regular patrons.

A common policy dilemma is how to handle such discrepancies between the formal system (de jure) and the informal system (de facto)? There are three basic responses: (1) Conform the practice to the rules through enforcement; (2) change the rules to legitimize the existing practice; or (3) continue with a certain amount of deliberate ambiguity, keeping unenforced laws on the books to use on occasions when things "get out of hand."

Default

Default means "failure to act." Default policy results, paradoxically, from absence of policy. Typically, default tends to reinforce vested interests and the status quo.

Whereas some default policies, such as nonregulation, are intentional, many are unwitting results of ignorance, insensitivity, and indifference.

Unwittingness does not reduce their social consequences. The greater part of institutionalized racism and sexism is default policy. The General Confession in the *Book of Common Prayer* recognizes this: "We have done those things which we ought not to have done *and we have left undone those things which we ought to have done*" (emphasis added). Social ethics philosophers from Thomas Aquinas to Reinhold Niebuhr have stressed moral accountability for sins of omission and warned that they may be worse than sins of commission.

Default policy is difficult to deal with. How do you get a solid grip on empty air?

THREE POLICY SECTORS

The Public Sector

Public social policies exist at the federal, state, and local level. They are not difficult to identify. You can find them in the Bill of Rights and in statutes that regulate the safety of workers, set up Social Security pensions, allow tax credits for daycare expenses, and so on.

They are elaborated and applied by administrative regulations and guidelines (and modified by the de facto patterns of behavior of public officials). The public welfare agency I worked for had a manual of directives and guidelines a foot thick on exactly how the poor of New York City were to be aided.

When we disagree on what a public policy means or whether it is being properly carried out, our courts "clarify" the policy. Sometimes this can have a major social policy impact. Thousands of formerly "separate but equal" schools had to integrate in 1954 when the Supreme Court ruled that racial segregation was in itself inherently unequal treatment.

The Organized Private Sector

Private organizations such as businesses, labor unions, charitable agencies, and professional societies have social policies that apply within their orbits. Examples of internal social policies include

- a collective bargaining agreement with a union
- admission standards in an Ivy League university
- guidelines used by a United Way to allocate contributions
- refusal of a hospital to permit legal abortions within its facility
- a professional code of ethics requiring confidentiality

In addition to affecting the well-being of persons within their jurisdiction, private organizations may have an impact on the larger society. In the 1980s, decisions by Blue Cross/Blue Shield and other health insurance companies on what to reimburse and what to exclude had a greater effect than any new public policy on how mental health and chemical dependency services were provided.

There are also organized efforts within the private sector to influence public policy. Sometimes this is done through such formal associations as the Sierra Club, the Republican party, the American Civil Liberties Union, and the National Rifle Association. In other instances, the organization is more informal, such as the "military industrial complex" about which general-turned-president Eisenhower warned.

The Implicit Sector

Have you ever moved from your "roots" to a new situation—college, a job, a much larger or much smaller community, another part of the country, a different class or ethnic group—where "everybody" except you takes for granted a lot of unspoken things about what is proper and improper and about how things are done? Eventually you learned it too. Then did you return "home" and notice, with new perspective, what *you* had always taken for granted? If so, you are familiar with the implicit sector's nonorganized "courses of action" and "regular patterns over time." Classic portrayals of implicit policy include Sinclair Lewis's *Main Street* and Garrison Keillor's "Lake Wobegon" chronicles.

The implicit sector is sometimes powerful enough to overcome even coercive de jure public policies. The traditional Russian peasant commitment to individualistic enterprise and reward subverted Stalin's collective farms. Prohibition was unable to overcome Americans' implicit policy on the right to drink.

Implicit policy is the heart of institutionalized racism, sexism, and classism. While my son, whose PhD parents were a college professor and a national church executive, coasted with a B average into honors classes, his friend, the daughter of a blue-collar immigrant, was put in a secretarial "track" where the school said she "belonged" despite her straight-A average and her expressed desire to be a doctor. Eventually, faced with the prospect of a lawsuit, school administrators corrected their "error" and explained that "it wasn't personal" and "nobody meant any harm." This was true. They had simply followed Mamaroneck's standard implicit policy.

Because it is not organized, implicit sector policy is difficult to change. But it is possible. In the 1940s, when New York State passed the first fair employment practices law, opponents, citing Prohibition, insisted that "you can't legislate morality." In fact, by creating new experiences, the law *did* change the implicit sector, which came to treat workplace integration as normal and routine. (However, it had little effect at that time on another implicit sector policy against residential and social integration.)

THE SCOPE OF SOCIAL POLICY

What does social policy include? Everyone agrees that social policy affects the well-being of individuals. However, we quarrel over semantics. Some choose to restrict the term to direct health, education, and welfare programs. A more inclusive definition adds such areas as civil rights, employment, consumer protection, environmental protection, and fiscal policy that have a visible impact on individual well-being.

Dante described hell as a series of concentric circles. He worked his way in from the lesser reprobates in outer circles to hard-core sinners at the center. Perhaps without implying that "social policy is hell," we can use this model to look at the scope of social policy. Moving the opposite direction from Dante, we will start at the center with the most traditional direct-service core and move outward through progressively more indirect domains. This framework should enable you to define the boundaries of what you personally wish to address as "social policy."

The inner circles include provision of direct services and benefits to hosts. The middle circles add funding of services and benefits to be provided by others. The outer circles promote the hosts' interests indirectly through intervention with agents and the environment.

Circle 1. Direct Services: Public Welfare and Charities

The innermost circle is direct benefits to needy individuals, free or below actual cost, provided through the two social welfare institutions that have been in the "business" for thousands of years: *public welfare* and *charity*. Benefits fall into two basic categories:

- *material aid*: food, clothing, and shelter, as in Christmas food baskets and public housing projects, or the means to purchase them, as in AFCD grants, food stamps, and rent vouchers
- *personal services and care*: medical treatment, rehabilitation, family counseling, psychotherapy, education, and child care

Public welfare is offered through such government agencies as local public school systems, state welfare departments, and the federal Veterans Administration. Charitable services are dispensed by such not-for-profit voluntary agencies as parochial schools, Jewish Family Service, Girl Scouts, the Boys Club, South Street Settlement House, and the Salvation Army.

Circle 2. Direct Services: Mutual Assistance

Responding to the breakdown of feudalism, mutual assistance societies arose in the form of guilds, burial societies, and fraternal orders that took care of aged, widowed, and orphaned members. In the United States, this was a common nineteenth-century pattern among immigrants and other oppressed groups through Hibernian societies, black churches, and Jewish communal services, for example. More recently, mutual assistance may be found in union pension funds, credit unions, and co-op preschool programs.

Beginning in Europe at the turn of the century and in the United States in the 1930s, the government moved into mutual assistance on a large scale through public *social insurance*. Social Security, Unemployment

Insurance, and Medicare are collectively paid for by very large user groups through payroll taxes—and only "dues payers" are eligible for benefits. This contrasts with AFDC, Medicaid, and other Circle 1 services, which are normally financed by nonmembers of the benefit group.

Circle 3: Direct Services: Other Patterns

Other patterns for direct service include *commercial, occupational,* and *personal* welfare.

Not so many years ago, because they cost more than their users could pay, human services tended to be concentrated in public welfare and charity organizations (Circle 1). As public and private health insurance enabled users to pay in full, human service became potentially profitable. In a free-enterprise system, the natural response was development of a for-profit service industry: Businesses and private practitioners sell hospital, nursing, daycare, and psychotherapy services for a profit. This is *commercial welfare.*

A related response to the same forces has been the conversion of many public and charitable hospitals to quasi-commercial businesses. They remain nonprofit in the sense that they do not distribute their earnings to owners or sponsors, but they have become self-supporting from sales (fees and charges) with little or no subsidy from taxes or charity. Like a regular business, they turn away customers who cannot pay.

A second area of rapid expansion has been *occupational welfare,*[3] benefits provided to employees either as a noncash portion of their earned income or as an investment expected to pay off in worker productivity and loyalty. Employers may engage in this as a result of bargaining with security-oriented unions, enlightened self-interest, or old-fashioned paternalism.

Circle 3 includes services provided directly by the employer to employees. Historically, this was called welfare capitalism (not to be confused with commercial welfare). It dates back to Robert Owen's successful experiment in New Lanark in 1799. In its classic form, it has included (and still does in China and Japan) paternalistic direct provision of housing, recreational programs, and health clinics. Under attack from both the right and the left, it fell out of favor in the United States in the early part of the twentieth century. One side accused it of "coddling" workers, while the other side condemned it because it was usually associated with low wages and repression of worker freedom. In recent years it has reemerged in such areas as daycare, employee assistance programs (EAP), and fitness centers.

Another direct occupational welfare benefit is the company pension (which is actually deferred earnings to be paid after retirement). This includes civil service and military pensions, which are sometimes mistaken for public welfare (Circle 1) or social insurance (Circle 2) because the "company" happens also to be the government.

Often overlooked because it is not organized is *personal welfare*, which meets human need on a private individual level. Despite publicity about the decline of neighborliness and the extended family, there is still an immense amount of support and care provided personally to aged, disabled, orphaned, impoverished, or troubled relatives and friends, especially during crises.

Circle 4: Purchase of Services Provided by Others

Increasingly employers and government have found it easier to purchase services for their people from outside suppliers than to operate their own clinics and pension plans. Traditionally, the cost of a service was borne by the provider and/or the patient. In this circle, the purchaser is a third party to the transaction, hence the term *third-party payments*. In public welfare, Title XIX (Medicaid) and Title XX (Social Services) of the Social Security Act buy services for their clients. In the occupational welfare area, my university provides health insurance for its employees instead of treating them in its medical center, and it makes payments into their separate "equity accounts" administered by a national teachers' annuity fund in lieu of giving them a company pension when they retire. On the personal welfare level, my neighbor prefers to buy nursing services for her ailing father rather than give up her career to care for him full time in her home.

Circle 5: Tax Welfare

Let us say your sink clogs up, and you ask the landlord to fix it. The landlord tells you to call a plumber, pay him, and subtract the cost from your rent. Next month instead of $400, you send him $300 and the plumber's receipt for $100. The net effect is the same as if you paid your full rent and the landlord hired the plumber.

When the government does this, it is called a tax expenditure, as distinguished from a budget expenditure made after collecting the taxes you owe. *Tax welfare* subsidizes daycare by letting you pay for it and then reimbursing part of your expenditure. However, like the landlord, instead of sending a check, it subtracts it from what you owe (your tax bill). The overall tax rate is set high enough to cover these rebate subsidies. The outcome is the same either way: It is paying for selected benefits to certain citizens at the expense of other taxpayers. Because the cost is hidden in the tax rate, it looks "on paper" like less government spending.

There are three common forms of tax expenditure:

- After you have calculated your taxes, a *tax credit* is subtracted from what you owe. A $1,000 credit is a $1,000 benefit (provided you owe that much).
- A *tax deduction* reduces the taxable income *before* the tax is calculated. A $1,000 deduction nets you $280 if you are in a 28 percent tax bracket, $150 if in a 15 percent bracket.
- A *tax deferral* is like a deduction except that you must eventually pay the tax on that income. Meanwhile, you get to keep the interest earned on the government's share during the deferral period.

What does tax welfare look like in practice? Government can pay for a child's education in three ways. (1) It can collect taxes and pay for a public school (Circle 1). (2) It can collect taxes and give parents a voucher that promises it will pay the child's tuition directly to whatever vendor school the parents choose (Circle 4). (3) It can use tax welfare, reimbursing the parents' tuition payments through a tax expenditure (Circle 5).

Tax welfare is used primarily to provide middle- and upper-income welfare programs that parallel programs for the poor.

- Headstart is public welfare. The daycare credit for middle-income children is tax welfare.
- Rent vouchers subsidize low-income renters. Interest and property tax deductions subsidize middle- and upper-income homeowners.
- Retirement income from Social Security is a direct public program. Extra investment income in an Individual Retirement Account (IRA) is tax welfare.

Circle 6: Agents

The first five circles have involved host interventions, that is, direct benefits to the target individuals. British sociologist Peter Townsend says this is not enough:

Social policy is still conceived too narrowly. . . . . Any worthwhile social objective— for example, educational equality, the elimination of overcrowding and squalor, the reduction of ill-health, and social integration—depends on the use and control of institutions like the fiscal system and the wage and fringe benefit systems of industry and not just the conventional group of public social services (education, health, social security, housing, and welfare).[4]

The focus of Circle 6 policies and programs is to get agents to do less harm or more good to the hosts. Affirmative action rules require employers to give equal opportunity to their employees. Environmental Protection Administration (EPA) regulators and the police protect us from those who would do us harm. "Positive parenting" programs attempt to change child abusers into nurturing caregivers. Licensing restricts service provision to agents who meet high ethical and competence standards. Professional education is designed to supply persons who meet those standards.

Circle 7: Environmental Adjustments and Enhancements

The outermost circle addresses the social *environment* in which both the hosts and the agents function.

- A key environmental factor is the *economic system*: the patterns of production and consumption, of distribution and inequality, of division of labor, and of interplay among workers, employers, sellers, and buyers.
- A second one is *polity*: how the society handles democracy and authority, freedom and social control, centralization and decentralization.
- Closely related to both is *distribution of power*, which may involve a combination of economic, political, ethnic, gender, and social elements.
- Other environmental factors include patterns of beliefs, values, cultural practices, climate, natural resources, and demography.

Interventions range from *radical change* through *reform* to *enhancement*. *Radical change* involves major departures from the existing system, such as abolishing slavery, collectivizing peasants' farms, moving from a centrally planned economy to a free-market system, or overthrowing an oppressive government. Such fundamental changes may be called for where untenable situations or problems are so ingrained in the existing system that adjustments simply will not do the job. Another argument for radical intervention is urgency: The existing situation is so harmful to so many people that we cannot afford the damage done while gradual reform takes its slow course. Of course, there is usually disagreement on what is "untenable" and how "urgent" the situation is.

Reform is "the improvement or amendment of what is wrong." It takes a more moderate and incremental approach to the social environment. We added to civil rights by amending the Constitution to guarantee individual liberties (the Bill of Rights), assuring equal treatment under the law (Amendment XIV), and expanding the vote to all citizens (Amendments XV and XIX). We have also reinterpreted the Constitution on segregation and supplemented it with specific laws, such as the Civil Rights Act of 1964.

"Rules of the game" reforms have been initiated to restore a free economy threatened by monopolies, unfair labor practices, and stock market fraud. Game "referees" include the Securities and Exchange Commission, the National Labor Relations Board, and, of course, the courts.

Keynesian, monetarist, and supply-side government interventions, as well as international tariffs and quotas, are intended to *enhance* our nation's overall economy by tinkering with the law of supply and demand within our basic market system. (Some critics believe that this is fundamental change rather than enhancement. Others allege that it does not work and therefore is neither.)

SUMMARY

Social policies are settled courses of action that affect the well-being of people, individually and collectively. Policy may be officially adopted (de jure), or it may be an unofficial but regular pattern of behavior (de facto). Policies may result from both planned actions and default.

Within a society, social policies may intervene at the host, agent, or environmental level, or a combination. They may promote well being and/or address problems through preventive, treatment, and compensatory activity.

Clearly visible social policy can be found in both the public sector and the organized private sector. Less obvious are regular patterns of behavior guided by implicit norms.

The broad scope of social policy includes seven domains:

1. public welfare and charitable direct services
2. mutual assistance services and social insurance benefits
3. commercial, employer, and personal services
4. purchase of service by a third party
5. tax welfare for the middle and upper classes
6. influencing agents that can help or harm others
7. changing or enhancing the environment

NOTES

1. John Tropman, Milan Dluhy, and Roger Lind, eds, *New Strategic Perspectives on Social Policy* (New York: Pergamon, 1981), p. xvi.

2. Second Letter to the Corinthians, 4:7.

3. Richard Titmuss, "The Social Division of Welfare," in *Essays on the Welfare State*, 2nd ed. (London: George Allen & Unwin, 1958), identified occupational welfare and fiscal welfare domains. The latter, which I have retitled tax welfare, is Circle 5.

4. Peter Townsend, *Sociology and Social Policy* (London: Allen Lane, 1975), Preface.

Chapter 2

What Is Truth?

"Whoever belongs to the truth listens to me."
"And what is truth?" Pilate asked.[1]

They say, "You are what you eat." To a considerable extent, in social policy we are what we *think*: our *"facts"* about what is and why, and where various courses of action may lead; our *values* about what should be; how we *process* our ideas. To understand social policy, you must understand the *why's* of it, where those who made it or advocate it—including yourself—are "coming from" in their beliefs, values, and ways of thinking that affect social policy.

THREE SOURCES OF "FACTS"

Of history, Gerald Kennedy said, "Nothing changes more constantly than the past; for the past that influences our lives does not consist of what actually happened but of what men believed happened."[2]

In the television show *Dragnet*, Sergeant Joe Friday used to say, "Gimme the facts, ma'am, just the facts." It is not that simple in real life. In court, legal "facts" are whatever the jury determines them to be, which may or may not coincide with the actual truth. The facts that influence social policy are whatever each actor believes them to be. Their "facts" tend to come from three sources: preexisting beliefs about what is, direct experience, and collected empirical data.

A Priori Beliefs: I Already Know

A stage hypnotist tells his subject that the next thing that touches her will be very hot. When touched with a cool object, she reacts as if to a burn.

A seven-year-old ghetto child is reading poorly. Three people look at this "fact." One sees genetic inferiority. Another sees a "culture of poverty." The third sees institutionalized racism.

A priori means "prior to, and furnishing the basis of, experience." This includes *perceptions about reality* that color how we see the world. Is it a fact that there is equal opportunity for anyone willing to work hard? Are people really motivated to work primarily or exclusively by economic factors? Does the law of supply and demand actually operate as described by economists?

The problem is that because they are by definition "before the fact," a priori beliefs are inherently vulnerable to the fallibility of those who hold them. Of course, some may be purely right. John Knox, founder of presbyterianism, thought so when he asserted, "A man with God is always in the majority." The United States was founded on "self-evident" truths about our having been created equal with inherent rights. On the other hand, a priori "facts" have also justified slavery, subjugation of women, racism, terrorism, genocide, and blaming the victim.

To understand a social policy, we need to find out—and evaluate—the a priori "facts" on which it is based. Some can be tested empirically. If your facts are accurate, you should be able to predict future occurrences. Similarly, if your facts about causes (diagnoses) are correct, a treatment plan based on them should change future occurrences in a predictable way. If your predictions turn out to be incorrect, maybe your "facts" need to be reexamined. Unfortunately, however, even overwhelming empirical evidence may not convince a priori "true believers." Ask Galileo!

Unfortunately many beliefs, especially about values, are inherently beyond scientific proof or disproof and cannot be reliably measured by any "objective" criterion. A somewhat cynical and unscientific rule of thumb for judging their credibility is the extent to which they conveniently coincide with the self-interest of the holder. Those that do may still be true, but perhaps they should be taken with an extra grain of salt.

Projection—My Own Experience Is Universal

A second major source of "facts" is projection from personal experience. John Saxe's poem "The Blind Men and the Elephant" begins:

It was six men from Indostan
   To learning much inclined,
Who went to see the Elephant
   (Though all of them were blind).
That each by observation
   Might satisfy his mind.

One feels its leg and concludes it is like a tree; another feels its tail and says it is like a rope; a third feels its trunk and describes it as like a snake, and so on. Each is partly right but wrong about the big picture.

We often emulate the blind men by generalizing to the world from our limited personal experiences. This is exacerbated to the extent that a priori preconceptions have selected, slanted, and colored how we took in even that narrow information.

A look at recent history suggests that U.S. presidents may have projected "facts" about poverty in this manner. Is it pure coincidence that several twentieth-century presidents from "humble origins" ignored the plight of the poor and blamed them for their condition? Did these self-made millionaires, who boasted of how they had lifted themselves out of "poverty" by their own bootstraps through hard work and perseverance generalize that anyone with gumption can do the same? (Note: Their humble families *did* send them to private colleges.) Conversely, did the Roosevelts and the Kennedys project the existence of major external economic, social, and class contributions to inequality based on their life experience of inheriting wealth, status, and other advantages through an "accident of birth"?

Broad Empiricism—What Can We Find Out?

Another way of getting the "facts" is to draw information from every possible source—census data and other statistics, case studies, journalism, historical accounts, literature—and also one's own observations. The scientific method collects data systematically, projects conclusions, and then tests those conclusions experimentally.

However extensive and well analyzed, gaps and distortions remain. We never have all the data there is. All of our multiple sources of information are subject to some degree of a priori and projective bias. Widening the base and evaluating the sources give us a better chance to fill gaps and sort out the "real" facts. Still, there is no guarantee that pooling the data of all six of Saxe's blind men will guarantee an accurate description of that elephant, nor that by mixing colors we will achieve a rainbow. Comedian Allan Sherman, recalling the rinse water for his paint brushes in school, described a committee as a place where everyone puts in a different color and it comes out gray.

Each type of source has its merits and its limitations. For social policy purposes, our best shot is to test all three against each other.

• How do "objective" facts compare with our own personal experiences and observations. If they do not jibe, we need to look and think further.
• If empirical data conflict with our a priori beliefs about human nature, society, and the world, we must try to figure out why the discrepancy exists and how to reconcile them.

The result is a hybrid truth that blends scientific and other evidence with "common sense" and intuitive "truths." We do not accept what our leaders or opponents tell us on their authority alone. We test them against out imperfect but best available truth—with the humility, of course, to "stand corrected" when we encounter new insights or information.

TWO KINDS OF REASONING

As important as the source of our "input" is how we process it through *inferences* ("conclusions or judgments from premises and evidence"). This is done in two directions. *Induction* leads *into* general "truths" from individual instances (evidence). *Deduction* moves *from* general "truths" (premises) to specific applications. Both have an appropriate function in determining social policy. They are likely to lead to serious policy errors, however, when they are confused or used inappropriately.

Inductive Thinking

Induction is "the process of reasoning or drawing a conclusion from particular facts or individual cases; the process of generalizing about an entire class of facts." Policy makers may generalize from specific instances to a class of people. The base may be only one case, perhaps your own. Or the base may be millions of instances, as analyzed in census and financial reports. It may be based on systematic analysis of case histories or experimental research projects.

Induction is used to build theories that "explain" sets of observed instances. An apple falling on his head may not have done the job alone, but Isaac Newton's law of gravity was an attempt to explain many such observations. Sigmund Freud developed his ego psychology theory to explain his patients' behavior.

Diagnosis inductively infers causes from examining results. For instance, finding that most lung cancer victims were smokers and that few nonsmokers became victims, we concluded that smoking was a cause of cancer.

Deductive Thinking

Deduction is "reasoning from the general to the specific, or from a premise to a logical conclusion." It starts with a *premise* "a previous statement or assertion that serves as the basis of an argument." An old computer slogan is GIGO: "Garbage in, garbage out." However faultless its circuitry, a computer can be only as accurate as its input (data and program). Deductive logic is a powerful tool for setting social policy directions, but like the computer, it is as good—or as bad—as its input (premises).

From his premises that (1) God controls everything and (2) there is a heaven and a hell, John Calvin deduced "predestination": that God determines our destinations (heaven or hell) in advance. His Puritan followers, deducing further that God would treat hellbound persons badly in this life too, enacted social policies of harsh treatment for the (literally) damned poor.

From their premise of a benevolent, orderly Creator, "Age of Enlightenment" thinkers deduced natural laws and natural rights. Our nation's founders applied these "unalienable rights" to "life, liberty, and the pursuit of happiness," in their enactment of strong social policies on civil liberty in the Constitution and its Bill of Rights.

In their 1986 "Pastoral Letter on Catholic Social Teaching and the U.S. Economy," U.S. bishops started with a premise, "We believe the person is sacred, the clearest expression of God among us." From this they deduced a succession of progressively more specific inferences:

1. "Human rights are the minimum conditions for life in community."
2. "Society as a whole, acting through public and private institutions, has the moral responsibility to enhance human dignity and protect human rights."
3. "These . . . moral principles . . . give an overview of the moral vision . . . of economic life [which] must be translated into concrete measures. Our pastoral letter spells out some specific applications of Catholic moral principles . . . full employment . . . eradicate poverty . . . halt the loss of family farms . . . relieve the plight of poor nations . . . reaffirm rights of workers, collective bargaining, private property, subsidiarity, and equal opportunity."
4. The next 200 pages elaborate concrete applications.[3]

Using Both Kinds

We can see the blending of induction and deduction in antipoverty policies and programs:

1. Based on available data, the 1935 Committee on Economic Security inductively diagnosed the general cause of long-term poverty and dependence to be loss of income caused by retirement or death of the breadwinner.

2. From this it deduced a social policy treatment: Old Age and Survivors Insurance (OASI).

3. Evaluation of the results showed that the diagnosis was accurate so far as it went, but incomplete. Long-term poverty was reduced for retirees and widows, but persisted in other groups.

4. From data about the other groups, inductive inferences were made about additional causes, such as family breakdown, discrimination, low wages, chronic unemployment as an inherent part of the existing economic system, institutionalized racism and sexism, ill health, and disability.

5. Deductive applications of these general conclusions, further evaluation of results, and, as the King of Siam said to Anna, "Etc . . . etc . . . etc."

Potential Errors

Social policy thinking has been susceptible to several errors in reasoning. One is to generalize from *inaccurate or incomplete data*. GIGO again! President Hoover, a brilliant engineer, responded ineffectively to the Great Depression in part because his "facts" about how the U.S. economy operated were incorrect. The autonomous free-enterprise market he perceived had, in fact, been undermined by corruption and fraud, nonproductive speculation, monopolistic practices, wars, and international mercantilism.

A related error is for inductive conclusions to *exceed the data*. Herbert Spencer's harsh policy position known as Social Darwinism advocated that "the unfit must be eliminated as nature intended, for the principle of natural selection must not be violated by the artificial preservation of those least able to take care of themselves."[4] Darwin's findings applied to genetic physical differences among plants and animals. They did not support a generalization to nineteenth-century English society in which the key variables were economic, social, and political, not genetic.

The third great error is to *confuse a priori premises with empirical data*. Darwin described a "natural selection" of organisms best adapted to whatever the environment happened to be in a given time and place. He did not infer whether either the environment or natural selection was "good" or "bad"—only that it was a "fact." Social Darwinism advanced two a priori premises as if they were scientific conclusions derived from Darwin's data: (1) Natural selection represents the intent of a divine Creator. (2) The socioeconomic environment of nineteenth-century England is both permanent and desirable.

In making a policy choice, we properly may draw upon both empirical data and a priori beliefs and values. Indeed, it is probably impossible not to. However, confusing them may prevent either one from being examined critically on its own merit. The consequence for social policy can be disastrous.

TRANSCENDENT AND RELATIVE VALUES

Transcendent and Subordinate Values

When I was a young newlywed, my wife came home with a new hat and asked what I thought of it. I answered with painful honesty. She cried. I felt confused. Should I not have been truthful? From this momentous occasion, I learned that in a given situation, one value (truthfulness) may conflict with another (kindness). How do we choose? We do so by developing, consciously or not, a hierarchy of values in which one takes priority over another. (I decided quickly that in similar situations in the future, kindness would take priority.)

Transcendent values, based on a priori beliefs, are "superior or supreme" and take precedence over *subordinate* values and interests. An *absolute* value is supreme over all others.

A transcendent value can be narrowly specific or broad. This can be illustrated among antiabortion advocates. For both a national organization staff member and her spiritual leaders, "right to life" was supreme. But there the similarity ended. The former's value was narrowly restricted to embryonic and fetal right to life. Her group's policy position was concerned for their well-being before birth but did not support public policies to meet their special health, education, and welfare needs after they were born, not did it oppose such legalized taking of life as capital punishment and military combat. In an interview with *Mademoiselle*, this leader even defended life-threatening violence against adults in the cause of "right to life":

Elsie has a certain sympathy for those who have blown up clinics. She does not normally condone violence, but she feels that there were extenuating circumstances. . . . "I am not ready to spend the next twenty years in prison. But I don't condemn those who did," she says.

"But isn't this terrorism?" I ask. "What is the difference between bombing a clinic and blowing up U.S. Marines in Beirut?"

"They [terrorists] weren't killing [unborn] babies," says Elsie.[5]

In contrast, her bishops defined their transcendent "right to life" value broadly. With the exception of something they called a "just war," they opposed all taking of human life, from conception to natural death, including abortion, capital punishment, terrorism, euthanasia, and nuclear war. Further, as noted earlier in this chapter, their "right to life" value extended beyond the preservation of life to the economic, physical, emotional, and spiritual quality of that life as well.

Obviously, when one value is made transcendent, others become relative, at least to the extent that they may conflict with the "higher" one. This often occurs between *substantive versus procedural* values:

Substantive values relate to *ends*: homes for the homeless, a chicken in every pot, a secure old age, or healthy babies. *Procedural* values relate to *means*, how things are done: market economics, civil liberty, majority rule, collective bargaining, judicial due process, or trial by combat.

Does the end justify the means? Where the substantive end is transcendent over procedural values, it does. Elsie accepted terrorist bombings of clinics in her "right to life" cause. White House officials, accused of violating their oath of office, subverting the Constitution, and lying to Congress, argued that national security took precedence over these procedural issues. Admitting his illegal actions, one proudly called his criminal indictment "a badge of honor" and claimed to have divine support.

When procedural values are supreme, the focus is on how the game is played. A free-market advocate may regretfully accept the price of inequality, deprivation, and suffering for many of his fellow humans. A Jewish civil rights lawyer may go to court to protect freedom of speech and assembly for neo-Nazis whose antisemitism he deplores.

Value conflicts are not necessarily just between two values. There can be several levels. Malcolm X, our Founding Fathers, and Martin Luther King all agreed with the Declaration of Independence, which affirmed government and law and order but asserted human rights as transcendent value. Although they opposed it under normal circumstances, the Founding Fathers, justified violence (the Revolutionary War) in defense of human rights. The end justified the means. Malcolm X agreed:

I think there are plenty of good people in America, but there are also plenty of bad people in America and the bad ones are the ones who seem to have all the power and be in these positions to block things that you and I need. Because this is the situation, you and I have to preserve the right to do what is necessary to bring an end to that situation. . . . I am not against using violence in self-defense. I don't even call it violence when it's self-defense, I call it intelligence.[6]

At this point, Martin Luther King departed from Jefferson, Washington, and Malcolm X by restricting action to nonviolent civil disobedience against unjust laws that subverted human rights. Why? Because his Christian values transcended violence as a means, even in a just cause.

Violence as a way of achieving racial justice . . . is immoral because it seeks to humiliate the opponent rather than win his understanding; it seeks to annihilate rather than to convert. Violence is immoral because it thrives on hatred rather than love. It destroys community and makes brotherhood impossible. . . . It creates bitterness in the survivors and brutality in the destroyers.[7]

Relativist Ideology

Automatically, a value becomes relative whenever it is compromised by any higher value. In addition, relativism may also be an ideology in itself, based in "the theory of ethics of knowledge which maintains that the basis of judgment is relative, differing according to events, persons, etc."

One version of relativism holds that no single universal truth exists. (1) *Pluralism* affirms the validity of more than one truth. Said Henry David Thoreau, "If a man does not keep pace with his companions, perhaps it is because he hears a different drummer. Let him step to the music which he hears, however measured or far away."[8] (2) *Classical empircism* carries this further, holding that the only reality is each individual's direct experience. (3) *Nihilism* is most extreme. It "denies the existence of *any* basis for knowledge or truth."

Another view is that while there may be a "truth," nobody has it. (1) *Skepticism* believes "that the truth of all knowledge must always be in question and that all inquiry must be a process of doubting." John Stuart Mill expressed it this way: "Mankind are not infallible . . . their truths for the most part are only half-truths . . . diversity [is] not an evil but a good until mankind are much more capable than at present of recognizing all sides of the truth."[9] (2) *Cynicism* is "questioning the sincerity and goodness of people's motives; belief that people are motivated entirely by selfishness." Saul Alinsky asserts:

The purpose of the Haves is to keep what they have. Therefore, the Haves want to maintain the status quo and the Have-Nots to change it. The Haves develop their own morality to justify their means of repression and all other means employed to maintain the status quo. The Haves usually establish laws and judges devoted to maintaining the status quo.

Since any effective means of changing the status quo are usually illegal and/or unethical in the eyes of the establishment, Have-Nots, from the beginning of time have been compelled to appeal to "a law higher than man-made law."

Then, when the Have-Nots achieve success and become the Haves, they are in the position of trying to keep what they have, and their morality shifts with their change of location in the power pattern.

As an example, Alinsky reports that immediately upon achieving independence through passive resistance the Indian National Congress made it a crime. Prime Minister Nehru stated, "To tell the truth, I didn't approve of fasting as a political weapon even when Gandhi practiced it."[10]

INTERESTS AND VALUES

"What is 'welfare' for some groups may be 'illfare' for others," observed Richard Titmuss. One does not have to be a complete cynic to recognize that values are often closely related, sincerely or hypocritically, to the self-interest of those who hold them. For instance, it has been proposed that the United States follow the precedent of all other advanced industrial nations and guarantee adequate health care to all citizens. Those who identify with the interests of the 38,000,000 citizens with little or no health care resources cite such traditional American values as the sacredness of each human being, individual right to life, and commonality. Others, who have adequate private health coverage and would be taxed for a program they themselves do not need, stress another set of traditional American values related to liberty, property, and free enterprise.

When conflicting social policy positions reflect the competitive self-interest of one group versus another, how do you make an ethical choice among them? You cannot—*unless* you have a transcendent value criterion. One national church leader used an egalitarian yardstick: "God's will temporarily coincides with the self-interest of whoever is on the short end of the stick."

SUMMARY

Social policy is influenced by our beliefs, values, and interests. Three sources of facts are (1) a priori beliefs, (2) projection from personal experience, and (3) broad empirical data.

Conclusions are drawn by two kinds of inference. Inductive reasoning generalizes "truth" from specific instances, as in theory building and diagnosis. Deduction applies generalized "truth" to specific cases, as in hypotheses that predict future effects and programs designed to implement policy intents in a concrete, workable way. Evaluation tests the deductive conclusions and may lead inductively to new or altered generalizations.

Values are usually a priori beliefs and/or a rationalization of self-interests. Not all values and interests can be maximized at once, requiring a hierarchy of values, whereby transcendent ones take precedence over subordinate ones. The latter become to some degree relative, varying with the situation. In social policy, this is particularly evident where substantive ends are in tension with procedural means. Social policy values also become relative where the decision makers are either cynically self-serving or believe that there are no reliable universal truths.

Social policy inevitably reflects a mix of different kinds of "facts," conflicting or ambiguous values, and different ways of thinking. They are the most difficult to deal with, and most subject to error, when applied unawares or inappropriately.

NOTES

1. John 18:37–38.

2. Gerald Kennedy, *Of Heroes and Hero Worship*, 1943.

3. *Economic Justice for All* (Washington, DC: National Conference of Catholic Bishops, 1986).

4. Quoted in Walter Trattner, *From Poor Law to Welfare State*, 4th ed. (New York: Free Press, 1989), p. 83.

5. Judith Hennessee, "Inside a Right-to-Life Mind," *Mademoiselle*, April 1986, p. 261.

6. Quoted in the *Omaha World Herald*, August 12, 1989.

7. Ibid.

8. Henry David Thoreau, *Walden*, 1854, XVIII, "Conclusion."

9. John Stuart Mill, *On Liberty*, 1859, Ch. 3.

10. Saul Alinsky, *Rules for Radicals* (New York: Random House, 1972), pp. 42–43.

Chapter 3

The Human Condition

How much are you worth? Is it all right to sacrifice you for broad national purposes? If you are in need, do you have a right to expect help from your fellow humans?

To what extent do you control your own life? Should social policy shape your behavior, protect you, compensate for bad luck, or leave you alone?

Are you innately good? If so, should social policy facilitate fulfillment of your potential? Are you a sinner? If so, should policy coerce and control you? Or are you just a dumb animal? If so, should policy manipulate your instincts?

Conflicting beliefs and values in such fundamental areas as individualism, social responsibility, freedom, equality, fairness, and basic human rights profoundly influence specific social policies. These will be discussed in subsequent chapters. Underlying all of these is something even more basic: our beliefs about human nature, the worth of individual persons, and the extent to which we are self-determining or subject to external circumstances.

WHAT IS A PERSON WORTH?

High: The Individual Is Sacred

So God created man in his own image, in the image of God He created him; male and female he created them. And God blessed them.[1]

> Are not five sparrows sold for two pennies? And not one of them
> is forgotten before God. Why even the hairs of your head are all
> numbered. Fear not; you are of more value than many sparrows.[2]
>
> All men are endowed by their Creator with certain unalienable
> rights . . . among these are life, liberty, and the pursuit of hap-
> piness. . . . Governments are instituted among men . . . to secure
> these rights . . . in such form as to them shall seem most likely to
> effect their safety and happiness.[3]

Western societies, influenced by Judaeo-Christian beliefs, at least profess that the worth of each individual human being is extremely high.
Where people are highly valued as individuals, social policies tend to support civil liberties, civil rights, social and economic justice, peace, antipoverty programs, quality of life, and other *human*itarian objectives.

Low: Life is Cheap

Others place a low value on human worth. In 1798, Thomas Malthus
warned that overpopulation would resolve itself in unpleasant ways.
"Positive checks to population [include] all unwholesome occupations,
severe labor and exposure to the seasons, extreme poverty, bad nursing
of children, great towns, excesses of all kinds, the whole train of common diseases and epidemics, wars, plague, and famine."[4] Malthus
himself advocated birth control and moral restraint to avoid these consequences. His contemporaries, ignoring his proposed solution, treated this
gloomy prediction as a "natural" fact and put a cheap price on life. Among
them was Adam Smith, whose "classical" economic theory accepted the
misery and premature death of a majority of citizens as a routine cost
of free enterprise. Later, Social Darwinists carried it a step further, describ-
ing wholesale suffering, hardship, and premature death as a "beneficent
purging of the social organism."[5]

"Low worth" social policies comfortably sacrifice individuals for military
goals, political ideology, the business climate, or simply the self-interests
of those in control. Where social welfare exists at all, it is an investment
evaluated on the basis its *payoff* in productivity, profit, or social control.
According to Frances Piven and Richard Cloward in *Regulating the Poor*,
this is the function of AFDC (Aid to Families with Dependent Children).[6]

Conditional: I Love You But . . .

In the middle ground, individual worth is affirmed as a high value—except
where a transcendent value takes precedence. Some of these values are
"noble", such as honour, patriotism, the Faith, or the Cause. Richard Lovelace, forsaking human relationship while "to war and arms I fly," explained, "I could not love thee, dear, so much / Loved I not honour more."[7]

Others are as mundane as pelf. After Congress passed several laws to protect people by regulating environmental pollution, occupational safety and health, and air traffic safety, the United States Office of Management and Budget ordered enforcement agencies to subordinate human values to economic interests.

In evaluating a new regulation, an agency will try to estimate how many lives it will save, what it will cost to adopt the rule, and thus *the cost per life saved. This cost is weighed against the [dollar] value of those lives* as part of the "regulatory impact analysis" demanded by the Reagan Administration (emphasis added).[8]

Experts said that a 1985 airliner disaster in Dallas would have been avoided if a planned new Doppler radar system at the airport had not been disapproved after such a calculation.

Double Standards: Us and "Them"

Policy makers may apply different worth to different groups. In 1786, Joseph Townsend's *Dissertation on the Poor Laws by a Well-Wisher to Mankind* differentiated by class:

It seems to be the law of nature that the poor should be to a certain degree improvident, that there may always be some to fulfill the most servile, the most sordid, and the most ignoble office in the community.

The stock of human happiness is thereby much increased, whilst the more delicate are . . . relieved of drudgery and freed from those occasional employments which would make them miserable.

As for the lowest of the poor, by custom they are reconciled to the meanest occupations, to the most laborious works, and the most hazardous pursuits; whilst the hope of their reward makes them cheerful in the midst of all their dangers and their toils.

Our Founding Fathers asserted their own unalienable rights—but denied them to women and blacks. Thomas Jefferson copied his Declaration of Independence statement of human rights for "*all* men" from a John Locke treatise,[9] which explicitly and unequivocally applied these principles against slavery. Nevertheless, Jefferson personally continued to enslave black men and women for the next fifty years.

Distance may create double standards. When I was a national church social welfare official, I worked with "fifty-mile liberals," who espoused civil rights in Mississippi, Washington, D.C., and South Africa—all more than fifty miles away—but resisted integration of their own Massachusetts neighborhoods. Robert Pinker calls this "the law of telescopic philanthropy . . . that the further away the object of our compassion lies, the more intense will be the feelings of concern and obligation which it evokes."[10]

Another set of my church members had an opposite double standard. These "caring conservatives" were generous and compassionate toward people they knew personally while opposing social programs that extended the same treatment to people they did not know.

Double standards on human worth can be found in "two-tier" approaches to social welfare, such as the segregated public school systems that were legal before 1954 and the different provision for Sammy and Bobby described in Chapter 1.

AM I THE MASTER OF MY FATE?

Are you master of your own fate? To what extent do you control your life? How much of it is determined by outside forces? What we believe about this guides our determination of who (or what) is to blame for social problems, what is "fair," and how we should intervene if at all. American society is ambivalent on this point.

Preordination

Medieval religion believed that every person is born ("preordered") into his or her place, has God-given rights associated with it, and should not depart from it. It is all right to be rich or poor, male or female, black or white, so long as you *know your place*. This was the moral foundation for feudalism, monarchy, aristocracy, and the Elizabethan poor laws.

Cecil Alexander celebrated this view in a familiar nineteenth-century hymn:

> All things bright and beautiful,
>   All creatures great and small,
> All things wise and wonderful,
>   The Lord God made them all. . . .
> *The rich man in his castle,*
>   *The poor man at his gate,*
> *God made them, high and lowly,*
>   *And ordered their estate* (emphasis added).

"The song is ended, but the melody lingers on." Many modern hymnals have deleted the rich-man/poor-man verse because preordination is no longer respectable. It has rationalized U.S. slavery, racial segregation, subjugation of women, and tracking of school children. Yet it is alive and well today in such policies as inheritance, admission preferences for alumni children, and Social Security's basing aid to orphan children on the former income status of a father who no longer exists.

Although there is much upward, downward, and sideward mobility in the United States, a strong element of preordering remains in the implicit sector. My family has a four-generation "tradition" of being human service professionals. My in-laws have operated the same family farm for more than a century. Other families have multigenerational ties to plumbing, railroading, or banking.

Preordination offers stability and security at a price. The origins of both philanthropy and public welfare can be traced to its doctrine of *noblesse oblige*, that noble status carries with it a paternalistic responsibility for one's social inferiors. On the other hand, it restricts self-determination and equal opportunity.

Predestination

The Calvinist doctrine of predestination emerged about the same time that medieval feudalism was giving way to an individualistic and competitive market economy. Believing that God had determined in advance each person's destination (the elect to heaven, the damned to hell), it projected parallel divinely ordained differences in this life.

Preordination and predestination both rationalize inequality as God's will, but they differ in two important respects: (1) Preordination supports the status quo, for one's place in life passes from parents to children. Predestination legitimizes social mobility, for each individual's place in life is separately determined by God. (2) Preordination theoretically does not make moral distinctions about where your place happens to be. In Calvinism, poverty is divine punishment.

Social policy directions consistent with this set of beliefs include

- *Individualism.* Each person will find his/her own appropriate place in life. Let the chips fall as they may without government interference.
- *Acceptance of inequality.* After all, it is a precursor of even greater inequalities in the next life.
- *Blame the victim.* The damned poor do not deserve help.

Although next-world predestination is out of fashion today, many of our national leaders continue to attribute a secular elect and damned status based on wealth or poverty in this world.

The *Protestant Ethic* is a free-will descendant of predestination, through a very human thought process. Believing virtue and prosperity to be indicators of a *pre*determined election, anxious believers strived to achieve these indicators to reassure themselves and others that they were indeed among the preselected favorites. From *demonstrating* their election with these attributes, it was but a short step across the line to *deserving* it because of them (which implies some degree of self-determination).

One more step brought them to a de facto belief that one *earns* both worldly success and heaven through the *four Puritan "virtues"*: temperance, industry, thrift, and individualistic moralism.[11] These production-oriented virtues coincided with the qualities that emerging capitalism required from competitive entrepreneurs and a docile, hardworking labor force. Conversely, poverty was punishment for matching vices, the *Four I's*: intemperance, indolence, improvidence, and immorality.

Capricious Determinism

Unlike the orderly determinism of preordination and predestination, *kismet* (fate) is a divine intervention that is either haphazard or unknowable. We call it luck, the roll of the dice. My daughter, after several years in Saudi Arabia, attributed that nation's reckless driving, such as passing on blind curves at high speed, to the drivers' belief that they are safe until their time comes, *Insh'Allah*, and when it does, there is nothing they can do to avoid it.

While Americans profess not to believe in kismet, insurance companies and the popular press refer to seemingly capricious natural disasters as "acts of God." Combat troops fatalistically speak of "the bullet that has my name on it." Astrology, often only half-believed, is a popular method of trying to second guess fate. Even a recent president, after narrowly escaping death by an assassin's bullet, was reported to have consulted "the stars" before scheduling affairs of state.

United States social policy responses to fatalism have taken two very different directions.

- An individualism approach has been *nonintervention*. Tough luck!
- A collective social responsibility approach has been to *provide for misfortune* either through charity after the event or sharing anticipated risks through public and private insurance.

Secular Determinism

Determinism need not be divine. In the Depression, President Roosevelt attributed the suffering of individual unemployed persons to external economic forces beyond their control. He responded with a range of programs that included direct relief for current victims of circumstance, social insurances to compensate future victims, and economic assistance to business.

Environmental determinism is also well established in the behavioral sciences. Psychologists attribute many emotional, social adjustment, and psychosomatic problems to experiences in one's "family of origin."

Social policy positions differ according to what the determinist identifies as the external cause. In the 1960s, sociologists "discovered" a self-
perpetuating "culture of poverty," caused by a combination of social,
economic, ethnic, and psychological environmental factors. Michael
Sherraden counters that the cause is purely economic:

Many behaviors labeled "culture of poverty" are better explained by financial
inability to focus and specialize. Assets matter and people know it, and therefore,
when they have assets, they pay attention [to opportunities, to plans, and to their
own counterproductive behavior]. If they do not have assets, they do not pay
attention. Indeed, in a sense, assets are the future. They are hope in concrete
form.[12]

The first view calls for an array of services to reprogram poor people
to a middle-class lifestyle. The latter has a simpler conclusion: Lift them
out of poverty and let nature take its course.

Free Will: Self Determination

"I am the master of my fate; / I am the captain of my soul."[13]
American democracy is a free-will ideology based on John Locke's social
compact assumption that only a government created by, and answerable
to, the free choice of its citizens is valid. Individual self-determination
is the cornerstone of all John Stuart Mill's arguments for personal freedom
in *On Liberty*.

Social policy responses may be passive or activist. Classical liberals like
Charles Rowley and Alan Peacock take the passive view.

We believe that mankind marks out its true distinction from the animal kingdom
by exercising free will, by making choices and recognizing the responsibility that
such choices imply. We are concerned therefore to assist in the development of
a society that encourages individuals to want to exercise free will, which assists
them in their efforts to do so, and which confronts them with the responsibility
for their decisions. In this sense, freedom is not a means to a higher political end,
but itself the highest political end attainable by mankind.[14]

Another traditional approach to self-determination is the go-getter view
that "opportunity knocks but once." Free will is something that must
be exercised aggressively or it will be lost by default.

There is a tide in the affairs of men
Which, taken at the flood, leads on to fortune;
Omitted, all the voyage of their life
Is bound in shallows and in miseries.[15]

Special-interest groups see it this way. If the social order is not governed by a divine dictator or blind chance, then all social policy is the product of somebody's free-will choice. If they do not assert their self-determination, someone else will, at their expense. Their conclusion: Lobby to promote your interests or be "bound in shallows and in misery."

Advocates for the disadvantaged agree that these are the "facts of life." Therefore, *empowerment* of "Have-nots" has been a central theme of Saul Alinsky's Industrial Areas Foundation, the civil rights movement, and Poland's Solidarity—as a prerequisite for achieving self-determination in the competitive policy arena.

Free Will within Fixed Laws of Nature

In the Age of Enlightenment, the growth of science led to the "discovery" of impersonal *laws of nature*, which are "sequences of events that have been observed to occur with unvarying uniformity under the same conditions." Isaac Newton started it with his universal laws of physics, such as gravity and motion.

From this physics model, social thinkers inferred a similar constancy in the social sphere. You can make choices, but only within the inexorable dynamics of a fixed natural pattern that cannot be evaded or changed. You choose—and reap the direct consequences. If you smoke, your heart and lungs will be damaged. If you drop out of school, you will suffer in the job market. As my mother used to say, "You can decide for yourself, but . . . " There are several different social policy responses to this worldview:

1. *Blame the victim*. Disclaim social responsibility for smokers, dropouts, and others who "brought it on themselves."
2. *Preventive education*. Help citizens make good choices by warning them of the consequences of smoking and illiteracy.
3. *Protective controls*. Restrict free will by banning cigarettes and making education mandatory, to protect weak and foolish citizens from the consequences of unwise choices.

Some years after Newton, a physician-turned-economist named François Quesnay applied his knowledge of physiology to social policy. The human organism is a self-regulating system that balances many internal and external elements. He observed that the medical interventions of his day did more harm than good by disrupting the system's natural functioning. Calling himself a "physiocrat," he inferred that society, and specifically a free market, is a comparable self-regulating organism, integrating diverse free individual choices into an overall equilibrium that can be disrupted by "artificial" interference.

Quesnay reasoned that the proper public social policy was default. He called it *laissez-faire*, "let [people] do [as they please]". Modern followers of the biological natural law model oppose regulation, monetary interventions, and welfare state services on the grounds that they subvert the natural functions of a healthy social organism.

Free-Will Interventions Despite Determinist Beliefs

People who profess to believe in external determination often act in practice as if they really believe in free will.

- Puritans, who professed that God directly controls every action and outcome, aggressively sought political and social control and enacted public policies to repress a theoretically nonexistent freedom of choice.
- Karl Marx, after writing that historical determinism would inexorably bring capitalism down, spent his life exhorting workers to self-determining acts of revolution.
- Sigmund Freud, who attributed emotional problems to external causes (e.g., one's parents), developed therapies to help the patient achieve self-direction.
- The rhetoric of the 1960s War on Poverty was directed at social and economic causes of poverty, but most of its budget was spent for education and training programs to help the poor shape up individually.

How come? Some possible reasons for these apparent contradictions may be the following:

1. *Operating versus formal beliefs.* Perhaps Calvinists, Marx, and psychoanalysts intuitively leaned toward free will despite their intellectual ideologies. We have earlier observed how Calvinism evolved over time into the Protestant Ethic free-will doctrine.
2. *A mixed system.* It need not be all or nothing. One may believe in powerful external determinism and also that there is an element of self-determination. Therapists and poverty workers, powerless to control those external causes, may focus on what they can do.
3. *Goal displacement.* In an old Mutt-and-Jeff joke, Mutt finds Jeff crawling around under a street light. "What are you doing?" "Looking for the dollar I lost." "Where did you lose it?" "There," says Jeff, pointing to the middle of the block. "Then why are you looking for it here?" "Because the light is better here." Politicians who must face reelection may find it expedient to take the line of least resistance with little thought to accuracy or effectiveness. Such policies and programs usually succeed about as well as as Jeff's search.

NOBLE OR BASE?

Are human beings inherently noble and good or base and sinful? Perhaps they are neither, just instinctive dumb animals? Social policies vary markedly according to the answer.

Noble and Good

Optimism about inherent goodness influenced the emphasis on liberty in the birth of our nation. The Psalmist carried it a step further when he exulted that we are "little less than divine beings."[16]

Jean-Jacques Rousseau, appalled by human behavior in Paris and nostalgic for his home town in Switzerland, developed a "noble savage" perspective that preserved his optimism: "Man in a state of nature" is *innately good* but is corrupted by "modern" urban society—a view shared by many of my Nebraska neighbors as they observe New York, California, and Washington, D.C.

Protestant liberalism in the late nineteenth and early twentieth century optimistically sought to reform society through the personal conversion of inherently good business and political leaders. My father called this "moving the movers" when he urged me to pursue my humanitarian vocation within "the establishment." Despite recent disillusionments, this continues to be a strong article of faith for millions of Americans.

A number of policy approaches make the "noble" assumption.

- *Decentralization* is based on a premise that those closest to the situation will be better informed and more caring about the well-being of their neighbors.
- *Deregulation* assumes people do not have to be coerced into "playing fair."
- *Humanitarian opposition to public welfare* believes that private philanthropy and enlightened employers can and will voluntarily meet most human needs.
- *Democracy* expects voters and politicians to act in the best interest of all, not just their own narrow interests.
- *Populism* and other "power to the people" movements believe, with Rousseau, that even if the rich and powerful have become corrupt, the common folk are still innately good.

Base

Base means "morally low, without dignity of sentiment, mean-spirited, selfish."

The "sinful" version is that although we know better, "all have sinned and fallen short of the glory of God."[17]

The "brutish" version sees us as predatory animals following our natural instincts: "The natural man has only two primal passions, to get and to beget."[18] Thomas Hobbes, in his seventeenth-century defense of authoritarian government, gave *his* version of "man in the state of nature": "No arts, no letters, no society, and, which is worst of all, continual fear and danger of violent death, and the life of man solitary, poor, nasty, brutish, and short."[19]

The brutish view is not limited to cynics. It is also found in mainstream American ideology. Harold Wilensky and Charles Lebeaux described "great emphasis on the rational, acquisitive, self-interested individual" as being "of great importance to American capitalism":

Individualism is both a theory of human behavior and a doctrine in justification of *laissez faire*. As theory, it tries to explain man's conduct in terms of a pleasure-pain calculus. *Man, it is assumed, pursues his self-interest because of an acquisitive instinct or biological needs.* Self-interest is seen in economic terms: he acquires and consumes material goods (pleasure); he avoids economic loss (pain).[20] (emphasis added.)

Policies based on this pessimistic view of human nature apply social controls and sanctions to the first level of Maslow's hierarchy of human needs, physiological survival (an instinct shared with all other animals) and perhaps the second level of safety/security. They tend to overlook the three higher levels (social affiliation, esteem/recognition, self-actualization).[21]

Less eligibility, the cornerstone of the British welfare reforms of 1834, and of U.S. welfare reforms of the 1970s and 1980s, assumes that we are inherently lazy freeloaders who will not work unless relief is made more unpleasant than the worst job.

The first and most essential of all conditions, a principle which we find universally admitted, even by those whose practice is at variance with it, is, that his [the individual relieved] situation on the whole shall not be made really or apparently so eligible [desirable] as the situation of the independent laborer's of the lowest class.[22]

A different policy application is to protect us from the effects of base behavior through coercive control such as criminal justice, banking regulations, fair labor standards, and antidiscrimination laws.

A third policy response is to seek a *balance of power*, based on the assumption that "power tends to corrupt; absolute power corrupts absolutely."[23] This may include empowerment of disadvantaged groups, not as in the optimistic view because they are noble savages, but rather to enable them to compete for their self-interests on equal terms with "establishment" groups. Checks and balances attempt to keep any self-serving individual or group from gaining dominance, such as the American network of checks and balances between executive and legislative branches, national and state governments, government and business, and management and labor. The capitalist ideal, premised on the brutish view of human nature noted by Wilensky and Lebeaux above, relies on individual competition to balance conflicting interests.

A costly social consequence of the "base" view is the diversion of resources from social amenities to military security. During the cold war of the past few decades, the middle and lower classes of both the Soviet Union and the United States lost ground relative to their counterparts in countries that spent less for "protection" against an "evil empire."

HUMAN NATURE AND THE CAUSES OF POVERTY

Beliefs about the causes of poverty lie at the root of many of our most important social welfare policies and programs. These, in turn, are derived more from the views of human nature contained in this chapter than from any other source, including empirical data. They cluster into four categories: divine plan, moral deficiency, bad luck, and external forces.

Divine Plan

"The poor you will have with you always."[24] Preordination affirms that the poor are an integral part of an unequal society in which they faithfully serve their superiors, who in turn paternalistically take care of them (at a poverty level). In time of old age, ill health, disability, or natural disaster, the deserving poor (who know their place and have performed their subordinate functions obediently) are aided by the personal generosity and organized charity of their "betters." Since the passage of the English poor laws, public welfare has been an extension of organized charity.

Of course, practice may leave something to be desired relative to the ideal of noblesse oblige. Dante relegated such violators to the fifth circle of hell: "This was on earth a haughty personage; not any kindness gilds his memory. How many now up there [still alive] are held great kings who yet shall wallow here like swine in mire, leaving behind them hateful reckonings."[25]

Social policy is harsher when a double standard is attributed to the divine plan. Slavery of blacks (in North America and the Caribbean) and native Americans (in Latin America) was defended on the premise that they were created as a lower species of human, of lesser worth, to whom "natural" human rights did not apply. Through much of U.S. history, free Americans of black, Indian, and Asian ethnic identity were either ineligible for public health, education, and welfare services or eligible only for separate, inferior services.

Calvinism had a nonethnic double standard, based on God's differentiation between the elect and the damned. Since the poor are assumed to be among the latter, there is no social responsibility for their well-being.

Moral Deficiency

If we have free will, are we not responsible for our own condition? Protestant Ethic moralists see poverty as a just punishment for base behavior by persons who chose the Four I's instead of the Four Virtues. Enlightenment free thinkers more neutrally observe that under natural law, the price of freedom is to accept the consequences of your choices. Either way, the victim brought it on himself. "He made his own bed, let him lie in it."

In the 1970s and 1980s, the moral deficiency/low value perspective guided the direction of U.S. social policy toward the expanding poverty class, who would not be poor if they had been ambitious and self-disciplined, finished school, and behaved themselves sexually. It began as "benign neglect" and progressed to aggressive cutbacks in human services.

A different social policy response to the moral deficiency theory combines it with a higher value on each individual and a more optimistic view of the inherent goodness of the poor. Even though their condition is their fault, they are still precious human beings who have gone astray and need to be brought back into the fold by a good shepherd. Our social responsibility is to help them fulfill their potential.

This was the rationale for the Charity Organization Societies of the nineteenth century, which evolved into professional social work and a network of rehabilitative voluntary and public services, such as adult education, job training, therapy, counseling, programs for disadvantaged youth, drug and alcohol rehabilitation, and positive parenting support groups. This second-chance-opportunity approach, say "moderate" liberals and conservatives, is more humane—and promises a better cost-benefit payoff to society—than neglect or punishment.

Bad Luck

Although classical economics primarily embraces the moral deficiency theory, it admits that people do suffer unearned diswelfares in the form of natural disasters and some (but not all) ill health, disability, and accidents. Its policy response reflects low human value: "Let the loss lie where it falls."

On the other hand, when the bad luck view is linked with high human value, it fosters two complementary social policy responses. Traditionally, charity and public welfare provide needs-based special *assistance after the fact.* Victims of disaster receive emergency care and assistance in reestablishing themselves. The ill and disabled get medical care and rehabilitation. The impoverished get food baskets and relief. Special education and child welfare services are rendered to those who by an "accident by birth" have the unearned bad luck of genetic deficiencies or an abusive family.

A second positive response is to *anticipate bad luck* through no-fault insurance. We predict that some of us will suffer illness, disability, widowhood, or loss of parents, but we do not know which of us it will be. As a precaution, we all chip in premiums and/or taxes to pay for care of the unfortunate ones among us on whom those "acts of God" fall. (Social insurances are also used to share risks due to external environmental causes such as cyclical unemployment and to meet normal life-cycle needs related to old age.)

External Environment

The fourth perceived "cause" of poverty sees the poor person as a victim of circumstances beyond his or her control. The cause may be beyond anyone's control, such as technological unemployment. It may be the result of someone else's "base" behavior, such as an Oil Producing and Exporting Countries (OPEC) oil embargo, racism, exploitation of workers in a company town, or stock market fraud. It may be blamed on unwise decisions by leadership, such as the failure of a U.S. industry to remain technologically competitive or government policies that trigger a recession.

Combined with low value, the social policy response is the same as to bad luck: "That's the breaks, kid."

When external causation is combined with high value, social policy takes two directions. On a personal level, the focus is on *compensatory* measures, such as affirmative action, retraining, or unemployment insurance. On the macrolevel, policies are developed to *correct or enhance the environment itself* through such approaches as economic development, full-employment policies, supply-side tax cuts, regulation of business practices, tariffs, monetary manipulation of the interest rate, and environmental health interventions.

All of the Above?

The causes and the social policy responses may not be mutually exclusive. It is not unreasonable to believe that some instances of poverty are caused by each of the four. If so, no single policy response, however wise and effective, will eliminate poverty by itself.

A mix of policies may be needed. Perhaps a given individual's poverty is related both to the high national unemployment rate and to his or her decision to drop out of high school. The latter may require a "deficiency" intervention to make the individual employable. However, he or she will merely displace some other worker unless "external" economic development interventions increase the number of jobs so that all employable persons can find work.

AWARENESS

All the conflicting perceptions and values described throughout this chapter are "normal" in our society. How do you choose? There are no simple answers. In a lecture at Princeton University in 1951 sociologist Marion Levy, alluding to social policy advocates, observed that "good intentions randomize behavior," adding, "When good intentions are combined with ignorance, it is impossible to out-think them." Fallible as they may be, your *choices* will be better if you are at least aware of what your beliefs and values are, where they came from, and how they relate to the issue at hand. Likewise, your *strategies* will be more effective if you understand where others are coming from.

SUMMARY

A major determinant of social policy is whether high or low value is placed on each individual person. High worth tends to support humanitarian and justice-oriented policies. Low worth coincides with policies that subordinate individual well-being to collective goals, vested interests, and ideology. It supports social welfare only when there is a payoff in one of these areas.

How policy deals with social problems is influenced by the extent to which individuals are perceived to control their own lives. Determinist perspectives include (1) preordination (inherited status and role), (2) predestination (preplanned divine control), (3) fate (capricious divine control), and (4) external environmental factors. A passive policy response is acceptance of circumstances by default. An active response is to share risks through social insurance and to intervene in the operation of the overall political and economic system.

A contrary view is free will and self-determination, often perceived as operating within a predictable cause-and-effect pattern. The individual makes his or her choice and takes the inevitable consequences. This has spawned such disparate social policies as (1) denial of any social responsibility for others, (2) education and persuasion against bad choices, and (3) social controls that limit freedom by prohibiting bad choices.

Human nature is variously seen as noble and good, base and sinful, or animal. The optimistic view supports policies oriented toward democracy, individual freedom, and philanthropy. Pessimistic views lean toward social controls and primitive economic sanctions or, conversely, a diversified structure that has checks and balances among competing self-interests.

Perceptions of the causes of, and solution to, poverty and other social ills are profoundly influenced by one's beliefs and values relating to determinism and free will, the value of individual human beings, and their inherent moral character.

NOTES

1. Genesis 1:27–28.
2. Luke 12:6–7.
3. Declaration of Independence.
4. Thomas Malthus, *An Essay on Population*, 2nd ed., 1803, Ch. 2.
5. Quoted in Walter Trattner, *From Poor Law to Welfare State*, 4th ed. (New York: Free Press, 1989), p. 83.
6. Frances Piven and Richard Cloward, *Regulating the Poor* (New York: Pantheon, 1971).
7. Richard Lovelace, "To Lucasta: Going to the Wars," *English Poetry of the Seventeenth Century* (New York: Norton, 1942) p. 465.
8. Bill Keller, "What Is the Audited Value of Life?" *New York Times*, October 26, 1984.
9. John Locke, "Of Civil Government," Ch. 4, in *Two Treatises of Government*, 1690.
10. Robert Pinker, *The Idea of Welfare* (London: Heinemann, 1979), p.3.
11. These are adaptations of the four classical (Platonic) virtues of temperance, fortitude, prudence, and justice, with one major exception: that macro-justice is replaced by micro-individualized sexual and related moralism.
12. Quoted from a Corporation for Enterprise Development monograph by William Raspberry in his *Washington Post* column, March 20, 1990.
13. William Henley, "In Memoriam: R. T. Hamilton Bruce," 1888. Humorist Keith Preston responded to this exuberance in "An Awful Responsibility":

> I am the captain of my soul;
> I rule it with stern joy;
> And yet I think I had more fun
> When I was a cabin boy.

14. Charles Rowley and Alan Peacock, *Welfare Economics: A Liberal Restatement* (London: Martin Robertson, 1975), p. 80.
15. William Shakespeare, *Julius Caesar*, Act IV, Scene 3.
16. Psalm 8:5.
17. Letter to the Romans, 3:23.
18. William Osler, *Science and Immortality*, 1904, Ch. 2.

19. Thomas Hobbes, *Leviathan*, 1651, Pt. 1, Ch. 13.

20. Harold Wilensky and Charles Lebeaux, *Industrial Society and Social Welfare* (New York: Free Press, 1965), pp. 33–34.

21. See Abraham Maslow, *Motivation and Personality* (New York: Harper & Row), 1954.

22. Edwin Chadwick, *The Report of His Majesty's Commissioners for Inquiring into the Administration and Practical Operation of the Poor Laws*, 1833, p. 228. Quoted in Karl de Schweinitz, *England's Road to Social Security* (New York: A. S. Barnes, 1943), p. 124.

23. John Dahlberg (Lord Acton), in an 1887 letter to Bishop Mandell Creighton, quoted by Creighton in his autobiography.

24. Mark 14:7.

25. Dante Alighieri, *Inferno*, Canto VIII.

Chapter 4

Liberté and Fraternité

"This is a free country. I can do as I please!" Is it? Can you? Should you be able to? How does doing what you please affect other people? How does their exercise of freedom affect you?

When God asked Cain about his younger brother Abel, whom Cain had killed, Cain replied, "Am I my brother's keeper?" Was he? Are you? To what extent?

NEGATIVE FREEDOM

Liberty is "freedom to choose." In the tradition of John Locke, John Stuart Mill, and the Bill of Rights, classical liberals define liberty as the absence of outside interference with that choice. In addition to government, this may refer to intrusion by employers, "moral majority" movements, and others who want to proscribe what you can and cannot do in your private life. This is called *negative freedom*. Austrian economist Friedrich von Hayek explains:

It is often objected that our concept of liberty is merely negative. This is true in the sense that peace is also a negative concept or that security or quiet or the absence of any particular impediment of evil is negative. It is to this class of concepts that liberty belongs: it describes the absence of a particular obstacle—coercion by other men. It becomes positive only through what we make of it. It does not assure us of any particular opportunities, but leaves it to us to decide what use we shall make of the circumstances in which we find ourselves.[1]

Classical liberals have three social policy priorities according to British Liberal party spokesmen Charles Rowley and Alan Peacock.[2]

The first is intellectual and moral freedom, without which "the notions of political and economic freedom may be rendered meaningless, however wide they may seem to be in a superficial sense."

- Freedom of *religion and conscience* permits us to worship as we please or not at all and to refuse to do what we believe to be wrong.
- *Speech, press, and academic* freedom permits us to speak, read, hear, study, and teach without censorship or reprisals.
- Freedom of *privacy and nonconformity* permits us to conduct our private lives as we choose, regardless of the prevailing orthodoxy.

A second priority is to prevent "concentrations of political and economic power, whether in the hands of the State, of bureaucrats, of firms or of private citizens" because of the "difficulty of eliminating discretionary power and its abuses once established." *Political* liberty is derived from John Locke's social compact theory that government is a voluntary creation of free individuals for the sole purpose of protecting their lives, liberty, and property.[3]

- Freedom of *assembly and coalition* permits citizens to meet and deliberate on any subject or issue and to combine with others for common purposes.
- Freedom to *vote (secret ballot) and run for office* enables citizens to select and guide their government without intimidation.
- Freedom of *revolution,* says the Declaration of Independence (but not the Constitution), means that when a government deviates from the social compact, "it is the right of the people to alter or to abolish it and to institute a new government."

Economic freedoms are rooted in Adam Smith's economic theories.[4]

- *Market* freedom is the right to buy and sell both goods and labor at a price agreeable to all parties. This includes freedom of consumption and of contract (to enter into binding agreements).
- Freedom of *occupation and enterprise* permit unrestricted entry and open competition with others in all employment and business areas.

- Included in the above is freedom of *travel and migration* in pursuit of economic and social goals.

The third priority is *procedural protections*, especially "due process" and "equal treatment under the law," as expressed in the original Constitution, Bill of Rights, and Fourteenth Amendment.

POSITIVE FREEDOM

There is a second dimension to liberty. Negative freedom is the *absence* of external interference in making individual choices. Positive freedom is the *presence* of means to exercise the choice that negative freedom theoretically permits. Academic freedom is not worth much if you cannot read and write. Market freedom is useless if you are broke. Occupational freedom was a mockery in 1931 when 1/3 of the workforce could not find jobs.

Four key social policy areas affect positive freedom.

1. *Economic adequacy and security.* Lord Beveridge, architect of the British welfare state, pointed out that "liberty means more than freedom from the arbitrary power of governments. It means freedom from economic servitude to Want and Squalor and other social evils."[5] And Franklin Roosevelt, observing Nazi Germany and Fascist Italy, said, "Democracy has disappeared in several other great nations because the people of those nations had grown tired of unemployment and insecurity. . . . In desperation they chose to sacrifice liberty in the hope of getting something to eat."[6]

2. *Relative equality,* social, economic, and political. "Freedom rests on equality because if there are major inequalities of resources or power, some men are in bondage to others. The fundamental ideal of liberty . . . is power to control the condition of one's own life—and this means equality."[7] "Liberty can never exist 'in the presence of special privilege . . . [or] where the rights of some depend upon the pleasure of others.' . . . Freedom, in other words, without a substantial degree of economic security and equality is a hollow slogan."[8]

3. *Participation* in collective decisions affecting one's life. "Economic freedom means that men should have a voice in the conditions of their work, that they should be recognized as possessing certain rights in relation to it, that no one should be in a position to exercise arbitrary power of regulation or dismissal over them."[9] Collective bargaining, social development, organizing for political action, and "maximum feasible participation" of consumers and workers on governing boards are common positive freedom strategies.

4. *Personal resources,* such as physical and mental health, knowledge and skills, aspirations, self-esteem, and confidence. Among programs that contribute to this are universal health care, prenatal services, mental health, rehabilitation, and, perhaps most important of all, education. The United Negro College Fund has highlighted positive freedom with its slogan, "A mind is a terrible thing to waste."

People who have suffered inequality, deprivation, or disability appreciate the importance of positive freedom. On the other hand, "advantaged" groups, which already have positive freedom resources (education, skills, security, income, power, and status), often ignore or even oppose it. It makes sense. Freedom from outside intervention *is* all they need. From their British establishment vantage point, Rowley and Peacock charge that positive freedom is antifreedom:

[To] advocates of positive freedom . . . the demand for freedom is the demand for power to be attained and protected by legislation or by alternative coercive measures. . . . This is the philosophy of "bastard" liberalism as currently preached in the United States, which has developed subtly from a doctrine of freedom into a doctrine of authority and which, in other societies, has become a favored weapon of despotism. . . . The granting of this effective power brings with it the power of coercion for some individuals to wield over others and this is the negation of freedom.[10]

In practice, however, both sides turn to government for intervention. For instance, Rowley and Peacock advocate coercive government antitrust measures to protect their own market freedoms. The real issue seems to be not whether to intervene but, rather, where, how, and *for whom*.

The dual objectives of the civil rights movement illustrate how negative and positive freedom are complementary. Its *civil liberty* thrust seeks to regain lost negative freedoms by removing discriminatory barriers to voting, freedom of occupation, and free-market access to housing. Once negative freedoms are won, it works to equalize ability to benefit from them, through *affirmative actions* to restore positive freedoms that have been subverted by institutionalized racism, sexism, and classism.

LIMITATIONS ON FREEDOMS

If we had pure freedom, we could do anything without prior restraint or fear of subsequent reprisals. Every society puts some limitations on personal freedom to protect us from each other and, sometimes, from ourselves.

Each Other's Freedom

Even John Stuart Mill, a "pure" libertarian, would restrict your freedom to the extent that it interfered with another's freedom:

The liberty of the individual must be thus far limited; *he must not make himself a nuisance to other people*. But if he refrains from molesting others in what concerns them, and merely acts according to his own inclination and judgment in things which concern himself . . . he should be allowed, without molestation, to carry his opinions into practice at his own cost (emphasis added).[11]

When two freedoms are mutually exclusive, something has to give. We must determine the relative value of each, that is, which is transcendent and which is subordinated. This is an important policy dilemma.

- Does freedom of the press permit invasion of an individual's freedom of privacy in the area of consenting sexual behavior? Does the priority change if that individual is a presidential candidate?
- Can neighbors exercise their freedom of contract at the expense of market freedom for home buyers by entering into restrictive covenants against selling to specified minority groups?
- In order to protect the market freedom of his customers and competitors, is it proper for government to restrict a businessman's freedom of enterprise by prohibiting profitable monopolies and "sharp" practices?
- Can an owner-employer be denied the choice of following his or her personal prejudices or whims in order to protect the occupational freedom of women and minorities?

Protection

To what extent is it desirable to exchange freedom for well-being? How much and for what? John Locke described "man in the state of nature" as free but in constant danger from predatory fellow men. His social compact defined a minimum trade-off of freedom for security.

The great and chief end, therefore, of men uniting into commonwealths, and putting themselves under government, is the *preservation of their property*; to which in the state of nature there are many things wanting [lacking].

Firstly, there wants an established, settled, known law, received and allowed by common consent to be the standard of right and wrong, and the common measure to decide all controversies between them. . . .

Secondly in the state of nature there wants a known and indifferent judge, with authority to determine all differences according to the established law. . . .

Thirdly, in the state of nature there often wants power to back and support the sentence when right, and to give it due execution (emphasis added).[12]

The Preamble to the Constitution emphasizes the *protective* role of government: establish justice, ensure the domestic tranquility, provide for the comon defense, and secure the blessings of liberty. We go well beyond Locke's basic police protection and due process. Libel laws limit the use of free speech to hurt others. National security laws deny freedom of the press for information that might "give aid and comfort to our enemies." Consumer protection regulations restrict free enterprise.

Protection from others ia a well-established trade-off. What about protection from harming ourselves? John Stuart Mill insisted that we live and let live. Paternalists disagree: For your own good, we will limit your freedom to hurt yourself. Cocaine is illegal. Psychotics are committed for treatment. Children are required to attend school. Mandatory payroll deductions finance a secure old age.

In the tension between freedom and protection, what is important enough to control? When is the process of freedom more important than the consequences? Are there general guidelines, or it is a separate "judgment call" in each instance? American society remains divided and ambivalent about where to draw the line.

The General Welfare

The Constitution commits the government to "provide for . . . the general welfare." Health, education, and welfare services are financed by mandatory taxes that reduce our economic freedom to spend what we earn as we see fit. Although most Americans agree that some of this trade-off of freedom for well-being is desirable, they disagree on what and how much. Even the nearly unanimous commitment to universal public education has been undermined by taxpayer revolts, often led by childless taxpayers or older citizens whose children are already educated.

It gets confusing when the same people argue strongly for freedom in one situation and equally intensely against it in another. For instance, many of those who object to mandatory social security as an invasion of their personal freedom are eager to invade the privacy and bodily freedom of a pregnant woman. Is this inconsistent? A cynic might note that people tend to be cavalier about restrictions that force others to do what they themselves would choose to do anyway, while crying foul where a policy conflicts with their preferences.

On a more positive note, recalling the discussion of procedural and substantive values, a person who puts low value in one substantive value (universal old-age security) but high value on another (fetal right to life), is consistently following a hierarchy in which the procedural value of freedom is higher than the former and subordinate to the latter.

Exploitation

All examples given so far are limitations on freedom that the advocates truly believe is best for our society. Controls may also be imposed in bad faith for exploitive reasons, as in slavery, dictatorships, the oppression of workers by the old "robber baron capitalists," or, more subtly, the manipulations Frances Piven and Richard Cloward attribute to public relief policies in *Regulating the Poor*.[13]

FOUR KINDS OF LIBERAL

In his successful presidential campaign, George Bush scored major political gains when he implied a vaguely subversive un-Americanism to his opponent by accusing him of "the L word" [liberal].

This illustrates the confusion about the meaning of *liberal*, which, like *liberty*, comes from the Latin word for "free." The term is used to describe four applications of "free": open-mindedness, negative freedom, sharing and caring, and positive freedom. A given person may be liberal in one or all of these ways. In fact, both the "L-word" and the "anti-L-word" candidates presented themselves to the voters as liberal in at least the first three ways.

Liberal thinkers are creative and freely open to new ideas. Liberal education is committed to the free flow of ideas. Typically, this overlaps into negative freedom in the spirit of Voltaire, who reportedly said, "I disapprove of what you say, but I will defend to the death your right to say it."

Classical liberals embrace negative freedom. The British Liberal party is a champion of free-market economics. The American Civil Liberties Union exists solely to defend individual freedoms from coercive intrusion.

Humanitarian liberals are committed to individual well-being through giving freely. Private philanthropy, neighborliness, and volunteer service are expressions of this value, as are tax-supported public health and welfare services. President Bush espoused this in his campaign slogan, "a kinder, gentler America."

Social justice liberals emphasize positive freedom, equalizing the opportunity of each American to exercise his or her freedom in practice. This has been a theme of labor unions, civil rights and feminist groups, the settlement house movement, and social ministries. It was the rationale for establishing public schools and later for desegregating them.

FRATERNITÉ

In the slogan of the French Revolution, "Liberté, égalité, fraternité," the last word described "the people" as brothers and sisters within one family. Its marching song, the "Marseillaise," began, "Let's go, children of the fatherland."

Fraternité affirms that all members of a society (or a community, or the world) are one family, with mutual responsibility for each other. "No man is an island, entire to itself; every man is a piece of the continent, a part of the main; . . . any man's death diminishes me, because I am involved in mankind; and therefore, never send to know for whom the bell tolls; it tolls for thee."[14]

Benevolent Control

One approach to social responsibility has been *collectivist*, which stresses the overall best interests of the society rather than its effect on any given individual, as in the Federal Reserve Board's manipulation of interest rates to reduce inflation or stimulate demand.

Plato believed that the greatest common good would be achieved not by individual self-determination and democracy but by the rule of a "philosopher king" who operated with consistent wisdom and goodness. Skeptics doubt that any central authority could ever achieve the level of competence required. Human nature pessimists add that even if it did, it would soon be subverted by controllers who misuse their power to advance their own interests at the expense of the common good. One is hard put to find historical evidence to the contrary.

Nevertheless, most people prefer *some* social control, subject to checks and balances and democratic accountability. The issue is when and how?

Voluntary Responsibility

An anticontrol approach to social responsibility trusts the voluntary actions of individuals. Whereas social contract theory assumes that the predatory nature of human beings requires a trade-off of some freedom for welfare and security, voluntarism assumes the inherent goodness of people.

The most extreme application of this view may be *anarchism*. Derived from the philosophy of Zeno, it became a nineteenth-century political ideology "that formal government of any kind is unnecessary and wrong in principle." Free association of individuals and groups on the basis of equality and fellowship can and should replace both economic and political authority. Marx believed (incorrectly, it turns out) that communism would evolve into this. It has been practiced with mixed results on a small scale in communes of nineteenth-century Utopians and twentieth-century Hippies.

A more pragmatic approach builds on *commonality*. Recognizing that they are all in the same boat, people find it in their mutual interest to join voluntarily into cooperatives such as kibbutzim, farmer co-ops, condominiums, and credit unions. When human nature falls short of the ideal, these collaborations may experience internal divisiveness or evolve into fairly standard businesses, yet they usually retain a significant residual fraternité ethos. Cooperatives have proven to be viable in both a capitalist nation like the United States and in a mainline Communist nation like China.

A combination of altruism and freedom with responsibility is *stewardship*, Andrew Carnegie's rationale for philanthropy:

There remains, then, only one mode of using great fortunes; but in this we have the true antidote for the temporary unequal distribution of wealth, the reconciliation of the rich and the poor—a reign of harmony. . . . Under its sway, we shall have an ideal State, in which the surplus wealth of the few will become, in the best sense, the property of the many, because administered for the common good.[15]

Influenced by this ideal, the United States has a long and strong tradition of voluntary service and charity.

Individualism: Non-Fraternité

A contrary social policy approach is individualism, "the pursuit of individual rather than common or collective interests." Interestingly, this has been justified by both high and low opinions about human nature.

An optimistic rationale for individualism, based on the "natural law" of classical economics, assumes that "the good of all will best be served if each individual pursues his self-interest with minimal interference . . . unhampered by government restriction, unchallenged by labor organizations."[16] Carnegie expressed this view in *The Gospel of Wealth*:

The "good old times" were not good old times. Neither master nor servant was as well situated then as today. A relapse to old conditions would be disastrous to both—not the least to him who serves. . . . The poor enjoy what the rich could not before afford. What were the luxuries have become the necessaries of life. The laborer has now more comforts than the farmer had a few generations ago. The farmer has more luxuries than the landlord had, and is more richly clad and better housed. . . .

The price which society pays for the law of competition . . . is great; but the advantages of this law are also greater still than its cost.[17]

Vic George and Paul Wilding report that human nature pessimists espouse competitive individualism for a different reason, namely, as a bulwark against the greatest danger: centralized power in the hands of a corrupt and fallible few:

Individualism prefers to view man "not as highly rational and intelligent but as a very irrational and fallible being, whose individual errors are corrected only in the course of a social process." For this reason no one can have a panoramic view of society and can know what ought or ought not to be done on a grand scale. . . .

The spontaneous network of individual checks and counterchecks is enough to eliminate excessive demands, unworkable plans and so on by particular individuals. Any serious interference with this process by the State is bound to produce more harm than good.

Competition even by imperfect and irrational men is the ideal road to progress.[18]

Mixed Reality

Some ideologies emphasize one of these perspectives to the exclusion of the others. "Conservatives" stress voluntary altruism, while Marxists rely on collective approaches. British socialists endorse a combination of commonality and altruism: "By fellowship, the socialist means co-operation rather than competition, an emphasis on duties rather than on rights, on the good of the community rather than the wants of the individual, on altruism rather than on self-help."[19]

No major society today is a "pure" example of benevolent control, of voluntary responsibility, or of individualism. Total social control by fallible leaders would be as untenable as the unrestrained individualism of Hobbes's "state of nature." In the United States, individualism is in tension with social responsibility in an uneasy, ambivalent middle ground. Competitive individualism is softened by a frontier legacy of mutual assistance, a tradition of noblesse oblige, and a potpourri of human service programs. Benevolent control through regulation is kept in balance by judicial review, democratic elections, and division of power between the public and private sectors.

FREEDOM VERSUS CONTROL IN THE DELIVERY OF SERVICES

The balance between individual freedom and social control is a recurring and often controversial issue in social welfare programs. Which serves the best interest of the client? Which better serves society as a whole?

Those who favor freedom of choice take an optimistic view of human potential. Maximum liberty and self-determination should be allowed as a matter of principle, except when this is directly harmful to others. They argue further that it is cost effective for both the client and society. Clients make better use of services they voluntarily choose, and they develop self-reliance by exercising their freedom. This approach not only enhances the client's quality of life but also pays economic dividends to society by increasing the person's productivity and avoiding the long-term cost of induced dependency.

Where full freedom is not feasible, they advocate a client voucher system, as in Medicaid and Food stamps, to give clients some self-determination benefits within the prescribed limits. By enabling a healthy competition among providers, as opposed to a monopolistic direct public service, it preserves the free-enterprise market system.

Arguments for control do not trust clients to choose their own best interests. Because deviance causes problems, pushing clients into the mainstream will make life better for them—and more comfortable and secure for the rest of us. Clients will hurt themselves and their families by being irresponsible in such areas as nutrition, alcohol, money management, education, employment, and child rearing. Mandatory services may avert the future costs to both clients and society of chronic poverty, disability, or premature death. Similarly, ability to impose earlier intervention at primary and secondary stages of a problem prevents the need for more expensive care and maintenance later on.

Broad public programs are more cost effective than a collection of competing private-service providers, they say, because they eliminate the expenses of advertising, marketing, and wasteful duplication. Furthermore, standardized "off the rack" services can be provided more cheaply, by technicians, than "tailor made" services that require expensive professional staffs.

Clients with Impairments

Children, active psychotics, and the severely disabled have conditions that make them dependent. Others have lesser physical, mental, emotional, educational, or social disabilities. It would be convenient to draw a line and say, "These people need a protective and controlling level of care; these others do not." However, disabilities vary not only in degree but in kind. A person who is physically dependent may be fully competent and highly productive mentally.

In each program or situation, several policy questions must be addressed:

- What level of control is *unavoidable*? Why?
- What level of control is *best for the individual*? Why?
- What level of control is *best for society*? Why?
- What are the *civil rights and liberties* of persons judged by society to be dependent? To what extent does a mentally ill patient being institutionalized or a twelve-year-old being placed in foster care have a right to due process? Does an otherwise normal mentally retarded adult have the right to vote, to own property, to buy and sell freely?

In recent years, a consensus among libertarians, humanitarians, and fiscal conservatives has grown around the concept of *normalization*, the least restrictive setting possible in each case. Where effective community support systems have been developed, this approach may successfully combine the values of negative freedom, client well-being, and cost reduction. However, in other instances, the inadequacy of community supports (too much "freedom") has been harmful to the patient and costly to society in the long run.

SUMMARY

Liberty is the freedom to choose. Negative freedom is absence of outside interference in those choices. Positive freedom is having the means to actually make the choices that negative freedom theoretically permits.

Restrictions on freedom are imposed when they are seen as necessary to (1) prevent one person's exercise of freedom from depriving another of freedom, (2) protecting personal security and property, (3) protecting people from harming themselves, and (4) promoting the general welfare. Freedom may also be abrogated for exploitive reasons.

Liberal means free. Liberal values include (1) freedom of ideas, (2) individual negative freedom, (3) positive freedom, and (4) freely giving.

Fraternité is a community of mutual responsibility and caring. This may be promoted by benevolent controls, including regulation and tax-supported human services. Optimists about human nature look to natural altruism, integrity, and cooperativeness to maintain voluntary social responsibility.

Social welfare frequently encounters a freedom-versus-well-being dilemma in the treatment of patients, clients, and beneficiaries. A common rule of thumb is "normalization," the least restrictive circumstances compatible with the client's welfare and society's protection.

NOTES

1. Friedrich von Hayek, *The Constitution of Liberty* (London: Routledge & Kegan Paul, 1971), p. 19.

2. This discussion includes ideas and quotations from Charles Rowley and Alan Peacock, *Welfare Economics: A Liberal Restatement* (London: Martin Robertson, 1975), pp. 86–90.

3. John Locke, "Of Civil Government," in *Two Treatises of Government*, 1690.

4. Adam Smith, *The Wealth of Nations*, 1776.

5. W. H. Beveridge, *Why I Am a Liberal* (London: Jenkins, 1945), p. 9.

6. Quoted in Walter Trattner, *From Poor Law to Welfare State*, 4th ed. (New York: Free Press, 1989), p. 263.

7. Vic George and Paul Wilding, *Ideology and Social Welfare* (London: Routledge & Kegan Paul, 1976), p. 66.

8. Ibid., p. 86. (H. Laski, *A Grammar of Politics*, 1925, is quoted.)

9. Ibid., p. 66.

10. Rowley and Peacock, *Welfare Economics: A Liberal Restatement*, p. 85.

11. John Stuart Mill, *On Liberty*, 1859, Ch. 3.

12. John Locke, "Of Civil Government," Ch. 9.

13. Frances Piven and Richard Cloward, *Regulating the Poor* (New York: Pantheon, 1971).

14. John Donne, *Devotions*, 1624, Pt. XVII.

15. Andrew Carnegie, *The Gospel of Wealth* (New York: The Century Company, 1900).

16. Harold Wilensky and Charles Lebeaux, *Industrial Society and Social Welfare*, 2nd ed. (New York: Free Press, 1965), p. 34.

17. Carnegie, *The Gospel of Wealth*.

18. George and Wilding, *Ideology and Social Welfare*, p. 24. The internal quotation is from Friedrich von Hayek, *Individualism and Economic Order* (London: Routledge & Kegan Paul, 1949), p. 8.

19. George and Wilding, *Ideology and Social Welfare*, p. 66.

Chapter 5

Égalité: What Is Fair?

"Fair [fare] is what you get on the bus with." That is the only kind of "fair" you can count on, says a friend who has the experience to back it up. Perhaps after considering the complications of determining fairness, setting your standards of what should be, and comparing them with what is, you may be tempted to agree with her.

Nevertheless, Americans agree that there *should* be a "fair" distribution of income, wealth, opportunity, status, and rights. Philosopher John Rawls says, "Justice is fairness . . . a proper balance between competing claims" for these social goods.[1] But what *is* fair?

The French Revolution answered clearly, *égalité*! If so, which kind of equality?

Competitive individualists would substitute *equity*, what each person deserves. If so, what constitutes deservingness? How is it measured? Rawls's idea of fairness affirms equal liberty and equal opportunity, but "once these principles are satisfied, other inequalities are allowed to rise from men's voluntary actions in accordance with free association."[2]

Humanitarians argue that the bottom line is *adequacy*, a "fair" minimum standard of living and quality of life to which everyone is entitled. The question is: How much is "adequate"?

Is there one universal guideline for all areas of social, economic, and political life? Or can a society simultaneously choose, for instance, *equality* of rights to free speech and due process, *equity* of earnings according to the market value of work performed, and guaranteed *adequate* income below which no one falls regardless of earnings?

EQUALITY

Same or Equivalent?

If we want to treat each child in the family equally at Christmas, do we

- give *identical* toys to a two-year-old and a ten-year-old?
- give toys that provide *equal pleasure*?
- give toys of *equal dollar value*?

Narrowly defined, *equal* is "the same quantity, size, number, value, degree, or intensity; having the same rights, privileges, ability, or rank." However, this does not allow for variations in circumstances and preferences, as in the case of the two children at Christmas.

We can solve this problem by broadening it to mean *equivalent*, "equal in value, quantity, force, power, effect, excellence, or meaning." To compare, we must have a common denominator for value. A true measure would be *utility*, "the power to satisfy the needs or wants of a person," that is, how much pleasure or satisfaction it provides. This is theoretically the best approach. It worked with my children.

In dealing with most adults, this is not so easy. Try to find a way to measure utility that will satisfy everyone! For this reason, we usually compromise on dollar price as a flawed, but measurable, indicator of equivalence.

The difference between *same* and *equivalent* can be significant for social policy. Most of us profess to believe in equal pay for equal work. However, a 1980s social policy controversy rested on the definition used. In the 1965 civil rights law, "equal pay" referred narrowly to the same pay for the same work within the same company. This ignored widespread salary discrepancies between jobs predominantly held by males and those primarily occupied by females. The "equivalent" version redefines the policy as equal pay for work of equal value among different jobs. This is called comparable worth.

Input or Outcome?

Opposing policy positions may each claim to be based on the principle of equality. For instance, take two parallel groups of diverse six-year-olds, some of whom are at a more advanced learning level than others due to home environment and social circumstances. In the first class, you give them exactly the same teaching from the same teacher. At the end of the year, the advantaged children continue to score higher on achievement tests than the disadvantaged ones. In the second class, give them all the normal instruction, but add special education supplements for the less advantaged ones in order that they may, at least partially, catch up with the others by the end of the year.

Which is an equality approach? It depends on whether you are looking at what you put in or what comes out the other end. *Equality of input* means everyone gets the same but may end up unequal. *Equalilty of outcome* is the other way round. In order to end up the same, you make unequal inputs to compensate for different circumstances.

The Declaration of Independence talks about input equality. We are born with an equal right to the pursuit of happiness—but we do not necessarily end up equally happy. The basic Canadian Old Age Security program gives the same flat-rate pension input to all senior citizens. If you had no other income, you would live meagerly. If you were already well off, it could pay for a trip south in the winter.

Group health insurance, on the other hand, seeks outcome equality. It spends more on group members who become ill in order to restore them, as much as possible, to the same condition as members blessed with "natural" good health.

Is one of these always the correct approach to equality? If not, on what basis would *you* decide which to use in each particular policy situation?

Vertical, Horizontal, or Temporal?

Another point at which people differ on equality is "compared to what?" *Vertical* equality compares all people: whether anyone is higher or lower, better or worse off, than any other. According to the Constitution, Americans have vertical equality in voting and due process.

Horizontal equality makes the comparison only within subgroups that have like circumstances or similar needs.[3]

Temporal equality compares the same person or group at different times. After interpreting the pharaoh's dream of seven fat cows that were then eaten up by seven lean ones, Joseph in Egypt developed the first temporal equality social policy. He took grain from the people during seven good years and returned it to them to eat during the subsequent drought years. Unemployment insurance similarly reduces cyclical inequalities by providing income to workers laid off during recessions. Social security aims at lifespan equality. Its payroll taxes during working years pay for replacement of earnings during retirement years.

EQUITY

A hard-working student turns in excellent papers and is rewarded with an A. A party-boy classmate is less conscientious and settles for a "gentleman's C." This is not equality. You probably agree that it should not be. The first student *deserves* a higher reward. This is the principle of equity. An equitable "fair" share is *proportional* to what you have earned.

Most commonly this is measured by the *economic market value of output*, that is, how much a buyer is willing to pay for what you do. Is this fair? Is the output of a philandering third baseman worth more than one hundred times as much as that of the teacher who taught him to read and write? The market says yes, because he makes money for his employer, which is more than his teacher could claim!

If your idea of value goes beyond a commercial balance sheet, would it not be more fair to substitute *social contribution*? Farmers, teachers, and housewives will probably agree. The problem is that using this definition for equity requires

1. a *common denominator* to measure dissimilar contributions
2. *agreement* on the specific value assigned to each contribution
3. reliable *measures*, honestly and impartially applied
4. power to *enforce* the decisions

Realists argue that the first two are unachievable in a diverse society, and reliable measurement may be technically impossible. How do you measure the real effect on human lives of a pastor? Further, they distrust concentrating power in the hands of fallible and corruptible officials.

Merit pay systems are intended to provide outcome equity in noncommercial settings. However, they are frequently subverted by inability to measure that ouput reliably and by de facto displacement of deservingness from actual work performance to personal qualities that please superiors. Educators, nurses, social workers, and other human service professionals, who believe ideologically in equity rewards, end up bargaining collectively for egalitarian salary systems as a lesser unfairness than arbitrary and capricious pseudo-equity.

In the absence of commercial measures or consensus on how to quantify social contribution, military and civil service grades lean toward input measures—the length of training, effort, stress, and level of responsibility that goes into a job—as the best available indicator of true worth. Based on these criteria, professional social workers may earn the same as MBAs, and chaplains as much as lawyers. A variation on input is the "combat pay" concept. Should inherently risky or unpleasant jobs pay more than comfortable and satisfying work?

For all its flaws, advocates of market equity argue that it is the best system for producing social goods because reward and punishment are the dominant work incentives. Pure equality would make people lazy and irresponsible.

Not necessarily, say others. The strongest work incentives are self-fulfillment, satisfaction, and a sense of achievement. The materialistic preoccupation of commercial market equity undervalues and thereby subverts creative, artistic, and humanitarian contributions. Moreover, it diverts production from basic social needs to discretionary "luxuries." For instance, in a society where millions of citizens are homeless and ill-housed, construction of luxury vacation homes is more rewarding under market equity than building low-cost housing.

The "trickle-down" theory argues that everyone ultimately benefits from an equity approach because its incentives and rewards create a meritocracy in which the best rise to the top. There is some empirical support for this, but there are also many cases throughout history where the benefits did not trickle down to lower-income classes. In such circumstances, warns Richard Titmuss, "history suggests that human nature is not strong enough to maintain itself in true community where great disparities of income and wealth preside."[4]

Procedural Equity: "As Is" Equal Opportunity

Procedural equity is horizontal equality. It offers a "level playing field" to a cohort group of players who have "like circumstances": "Those who (1) are at the same level of talent and ability and (2) have the same willingness to use them, should have the same prospects of success, regardless of their initial place in the social system; that is, irrespective of the income class into which they are born."[5] "Pure procedural justice" calls for all admission, hiring, promotion, and salary decisions to be based solely on current merit as demonstrated by performance, testing, credentials, and other indicators. It is not concerned about where the actors came from nor how they got to where they are now. This is the *negative freedom side of equity*: absence of overt external barriers to success and reward. This has the advantage of simplicity: "Now the great advantage of pure procedural justice is that it is no longer necessary in meeting the demands of justice to keep track of the endless variety of circumstances and the changing relative positions of particular persons."[6]

Full Equity and Affirmative Action

Simple procedural equity works where the competitors have had comparable opportunity to reach their existing level of relevant competitive skills, experience, and credentials. When I was a student at Princeton University, which was located within sixty miles of a majority of all Jewish-Americans, the university had a reported 10 percent quota for Jews and admitted no women regardless of their ability. Since middle-class women and Jews already had comparable high school records, all they needed to succeed was "pure procedural justice." In fact, after the barriers were eliminated, my daughter enrolled in a Princeton that was half female and perhaps a third Jewish.

Unfortunately, this is not always the case. By happenstance, I was born into an affluent, stable, professional family that offered many social and educational advantages. Others with comparable inherent potential experienced deep poverty, racism, sexism, and other diswelfare. While tribulation can be overcome, and privilege may be dissipated, pure procedural justice gives some of us an unearned competitive advantage due to what Rawls calls "historical and social fortune."[7] To the extent that this exists, something other than equity is operating.

Full equity requires that the "like circumstances" cohort group be broadened to include all players, not just one subclass of them—in other words, vertical equality of opportunity. Since we are not born equal, if we are to have equal rights in the pursuit of life, liberty, and property, some form of *affirmative action to equalize opportunity is a prerequisite for equity*. The problem is *how* best to do this.

There are several basic approaches, which are not mutually exclusive. One is to *reduce advantages*. High inheritance taxes and elimination of private schools, for instance, would narrow inequalities of opportunity. You may not choose to run for Congress on this platform. Reducing the ability to pass on advantages to one's children would not win many votes from middle- and upper-class American parents.

A more widely supported approach is to *reduce disadvantages*. Affirmative actions that provide compensatory development opportunities for those on the short end of the stick are more consistent with professed American values. Rawls says, "Chances to acquire cultural knowledge and skills should not depend upon one's class position, and so the school system, whether public or private, should be designed to even out class barriers."[8] The 1960s War on Poverty, in its limited way, sought to supplement the school system with enrichment programs for the disadvantaged, such as Headstart, bilingual education, Upward Bound, and the Job Corps.

Another affirmative action equalizer is *compensatory preferences* to counteract the effect of past preferences or discriminations. World War II veterans received bonus points on civil service exams to offset career development advantages enjoyed by competitors who had stayed home. Quota systems open up opportunities for victims of past discrimination to "catch up" to where they would have been if it had not occurred.[9]

These have worked best when accompanied by enrichment and development programs that help such persons achieve their full potential, both
before and after they are admitted or hired.

Equity and Equality

Equity is a horizontal equality principle: It offers equal rewards within
subgroups that have "like circumstances" in relation to achievement. At
the same time, it conflicts with full vertical equality. Most nations have
stated social policy objectives that combine elements of equity and reduced
(but not eliminated) vertical inequality.

Modern industrial life, with its many demands, depends in large part on citizens'
believing that they are being treated fairly in the distribution of a nation's
resources. This equity . . . does not necessarily mean equality in incomes but some
understandable relationship between income and contribution to society, which
translates into a reasonable gradation between income classes at the bottom and
at the top of the ladder. Reducing disparities in income among classes of workers,
or between workers and the helpless . . . or redistributing income, are common
ends and objectives.[10]

There is evidence that *full-equity* policies, by reducing inequality caused
by discrimination and "historical and social fortune," do in practice lessen
vertical inequality. Between 1933 and 1980, statistical reductions in income disparities paralleled periodic extensions of equity policies in such
areas as expanded public secondary and university education, rehabilitation and remedial programs for the disadvantaged, equal employment
opportunity, affirmative action, equal-pay laws, and civil service comparable worth practices. This particularly benefited minorities and women
in a lower-middle to upper-middle range. During that period, the middle 3/5 increased their percentage of total national income, while the top
1/5 share dropped moderately.

Conversely, in the 1980s, new policies and de facto federal practices
that moved away from full-equity principles coincided with a reversal in
the trend. By the end of the decade, the top 1/5 regained all of the proportion of total income it had "lost" to lower- and middle-income sectors in the previous half century.

ADEQUACY

Although issues of equality and equity are common in many social
welfare programs, they are usually secondary to adequacy. As a fairness
principle it means assuring that people have "enough." If so, what is
enough?

What Is Enough?

The dictionary gives two definitions of *adequacy*: "barely satisfactory (subsistence)" and "fully sufficient."

The American "poverty line" standard uses a subsistence approach. Social Security researchers priced out an itemized "food basket" of inexpensive foods that provide full nutrition—if the buyer has the expertise of a professional nutritionist and exceptional self-discipline to make the same selection (no Twinkies, potato chips, pop, or beer!). Based on census information that poor people spent 25 percent of their income on food, the "barely satisfactory" standard became four times the food-basket price. (For political reasons, namely, to lower poverty statistics, the official poverty line was set in 1963 at a temporary subsistence level 25 percent below the researchers' standard. In 1984 and 1990, similarly motivated efforts by the government to lower it further were resisted by researchers and reformers.)

The Bureau of Labor Statistics (BLS), meanwhile, leaned toward the "sufficient" side in setting its "lower living level" standard. Using a comprehensive "market basket" of all needs, including a modest number of "normal" American amenities, it arrived at a figure about 50 percent above the official poverty line.

Programs that include middle- and upper-class beneficiaries are likely to use a "fully sufficient" definition of adequacy. For instance, in public education, the consensual standard of adequacy is not barely sufficient literacy (the ability to read simple workplace instructions and traffic signs) but rather a full high school diploma, including substantial history, literature, mathematics, and science.

Absolute or Relative?

Adequacy may be defined in *absolute* or *relative* terms. "Absolute" calculations are based on specifically defined "objective" standards, such as those used for the poverty line and the BLS lower living level. My local high school uses an absolute standard for adequate education: To receive the diploma, the students must not only take the required courses but also pass a battery of competency tests in reading, writing, and math.

Of course, the "absolute" list of necessities is influenced by time, place, culture, the economy, and politics. When asked to comment on the American poverty line in relation to his own country, a top social welfare official from India replied that it was too high. He would base a poverty line on "1400 calories per day, because my people need less food." In my father's day, the educational adequacy standards for working-class Americans was the eighth grade. Today, some national leaders assert that anything less than postsecondary technical or college education is inadequate to meet current labor force requirements.

Relative adequacy looks at social and psychological factors, such as self-esteem, satisfaction, status, respect, and social integration. It defines adequacy in comparison to the "normal" level of a community, region, or nation.[11] Suggestions for a relative poverty line have ranged from 50 percent to 75 percent of median family income. Using this measure, the poverty line would be well above our present one in the United States and well below it in third world countries.

While homesteading in northern Wisconsin, my mother's proud family lived well below any absolute poverty line but did not experience relative poverty because they were on a par with their neighbors and highly respected. By contrast, a recent president from modest middle-class origins who experienced a standard of living much higher than those homesteaders—or than what he proposed as adequate for AFDC children—described himself as growing up "poor." He was telling the truth according to the relative definition of poverty: If he *felt* poor, he *was* poor.

Adequacy and Equality

Occasionally, the standard for adequacy is *full equality*. According to the Fourteenth Amendment, nothing less than equal treatment under the law is adequate. The official policy objectives of all industrial nations (except the United States) define adequate health care to include all needed health services for all citizens, regardless of income, wealth, or social status.

Although equality is not the objective of most adequacy programs, their provisions nevertheless reduce inequality. While certain "elite" private colleges offer special advantages, fully sufficient public universities have dramatically reduced the educational difference between the "upper" and "middle" classes. Even AFDC benefits, which are below the poverty line in every state, redistribute some money from higher-income taxpayers to impoverished children.

Multiple Tiers: Adequacy plus Equity

Multiple tiers offer a floor but no ceiling. Most Americans believe that if you earn, deserve, or can afford something better, you should not be held back, so long it does not deprive someone else of adequacy. Sometimes the tiers are planned systematically. More often they evolve piecemeal. Three types of multiple tiers may be identified using the "Burch ice cream model."

Standard and premium brands: alternative tiers. My father was an ice-cream aficionado. Early in life I learned to distinguish between standard "store-bought" ice cream and premium hand-packed ice cream from the local dairy. The standard brands were all right, but they could not compare with the ice cream Dad brought home. It is like the difference between tourist class and first class on an ocean liner.

Sometimes both tiers are public. In New York City there were traditionally two tiers of public beaches. The common folk took the subway to a city beach at Coney Island. Jones Beach State Park was much nicer—for those who owned cars. Similarly, public schools are better in nearby suburbs than in the Bronx—provided you can afford to buy a house in Scarsdale.

Sometimes the premium brand is a private market alternative. Private school tuition may buy a premium you value, such as personalized attention, a proper religious perspective, socialization to the upper class, enrichment for superior students, or special services for problem children.

Double-dip cones: incremental tiers. By the age of four I had learned to ask for double-dip cones. They had more ice cream than regular ones. Incremental tiers let you keep the regular scoop and add a second dip besides. Swedish retirees have up to four scoops:

1. The Basic Pension System provides a flat-rate benefit at age sixty-five. One hundred percent of retirees receive this.
2. The National Superannuation Pension provides a Social Security type of wage-related pension to all employed persons. About 75 percent of current retirees qualify.
3. Most unionized workers have collective bargaining contracts for employer-financed pensions administered by a private insurance company. About 38 percent of retirees receive these benefits.
4. In the 1980s, private individual pensions tripled when the government began to subsidize them with favorable tax rules (tax welfare). About 10 percent of retirees have these.[12]

During World War II ice-cream scoops became smaller. We had to buy two scoops to get what used to be in one. This has happened to senior citizens. Originally, Medicare was intended as a single scoop to meet most of their health care needs. As inflation and political decisions eroded it, they had to add a second tier of private "medigap" insurance.

Ice Milk: the safety net. One sad day, I encountered ice milk. It looked like ice cream, but it was not creamy and smooth. It was thin and watery. The premium and double-dip methods offer a standard level with optional supplements *above* it. The "safety net" goes the other way. In the United States it is assumed that normal people should be able to "make it on their own." For those who fail, there is a thin ice-milk tier—the old poorhouse, modern AFDC, some state mental hospitals—*below* that standard level. Alfred Kahn has noted, "Services designed for poor people tend to be poor services."[13]

Opposition to multiple tiers is based on *equality* arguments:

- Unequal opportunity is reinforced and perpetuated when the privileged classes buy special advantages for their children.
- More lucrative second-tier rewards may "cream" the pool of personnel who would otherwise be teaching and healing "ordinary people" in the first tier.
- Private alternatives weaken support for basic programs. In communities where wealthy children go to public school, support for quality public education is much stronger than in communities where such children go to private schools.

Support for multiple tiers is not always ideological. In 1957, the British Labor party wanted to add a wage-related tier to the existing flat-rate old-age pension. Conservative Iain Macleod responded with amused irony that it was "pleasant to see our socialist opponents being converted to the capitalist system, and to a proposal which, in fact, intends to carry into retirement the inequalities of earnings in working life."[14]

NONFAIRNESS DOCTRINES

Social policies are not necessarily based on any of the three fairness criteria (equality, equity, adequacy). Some are openly predatory. Powerful interests cynically pursue their own interests at the expense of the majority. In other cases, vested interests are claimed to coincide with the collective good. In 1952, George Wilson, soon to become secretary of defense, was blunt and to the point: "What's good for General Motors is good for America." Still others profess to espouse the "ideal" of adequacy in income, housing, health, education, and so on—but regretfully "we" cannot afford it or "they" are unwilling to support our efforts.

Other nonfairness policies have an ideological base. Preordination affirmed a *nonequity inequality* built upon inherited wealth, status, and other advantages. A variation is the ancient idea of intergenerational personhood, that you live on through your "seed." If this be true, you yourself are enjoying the fruits of your labor when your children inherit advantages from you.

> Who is the man that fears the Lord?
> Him will He instruct in the way that he should choose.
> He himself shall abide in prosperity,
> And his children shall possess the land.[15]

A cynical justification for passing on wealth and advantages to your children brings us back to "fair [fare] is something you get on the bus with." All that idealism about equity and being born equal is fine, but "that ain't how it operates out there!" Equal opportunity is a myth. In the real world, what they call "equity" favors those with historic and social advantages. If you naively refrain from seeking every possible competitive edge for your children, someone less scrupulous than you will take advantage of them. In the hierarchy of values, taking care of "me and mine" and "the devil take the hindmost"[16] claims precedence over abstract equality and equity concepts.

Predestination, racism, and Social Darwinism each affirmed both inequality and inadequacy. For the first, inadequacy was an appropriate condition of someone destined for the ultimate in inadequacy: eternal damnation. Racism legitimized subhuman treatment of black slaves and native Americans on the grounds that they were inferior species created to serve the superior race. Social Darwinists carried this to its logical extreme. Assuming that the poor were genetically inferior, their "positive" policy to "improve" the human race was to let the poor fall below the subsistence level and die before reproducing a new generation of inferiors.

Combining the doctrine that a healthy economy requires a pool of low-wage laborers with a low view of human nature and worth, the principle of less eligibility frankly calls for deliberately inadequate public assistance. The rationale for the 1834 English poor-law reform states:

Throughout the evidence it is shown that in proportion as the condition of any pauper class is elevated above the condition of independent laborers . . . such persons, therefore, are under the strongest inducements to quit the less eligible class of laborers and enter the more eligible class of paupers. The converse is the effect when the pauper class is placed in its proper position below the condition of the independent laborer.[17]

In the 1970s and 1980s, less eligibility was used to justify punitive AFDC amendments. By 1990, while comparable aid to the aged and blind hovered near the official poverty line, the maximum AFDC grants in 2/3 of the states were more than 30 percent below that line even after federal food stamps were added, and 1/3 of states were closer to the 50 percent level.

REDISTRIBUTION

Distribution is *who gets what* within the society. While it may be applied to anything of value, including freedom, power, status, esteem, and opportunity, it usually refers to income (what you receive) and/or wealth (what you have accumulated).

Left alone, primary distribution has tended to increase the disparity between rich and poor in most times and places. Modern societies use two approaches to lessen the resulting inequality. One is to *regulate distribution*. This may be done marginally through "rules of the game" that limit predatory, fraudulent, and exploitive practices, or more extensively through central control of wages, prices, and profits.

The other method is *redistribution,* a second round *re*allocation through government taxing and spending. As discussed earlier in the chapter, redistribution may be horizontal among peers through private or public insurance, temporal through pension plans that return in "lean" retirement years what they took out in "fat cow" working years, and vertical through taxing "Haves" to pay for services to "Have-nots." Redistribution is said to be *progressive* if it reduces inequality, *regressive* if it increases inequality.

Taxes are progressive when the wealthy pay a higher percentage of their income than do the less affluent. In the United States, personal income taxes are progressive (except for loopholes). So are business profits taxes that tend to be "shifted backward" to wealthy stockholders in the form of reduced dividends.

Taxes that take a higher percentage from lower incomes are regressive. Sales taxes are levied on spending for goods. Low-income families spend much of their income immediately on taxed items. The wealthy save some of their income and spend more of the rest on nontaxed services. Because they spend a smaller percentage of their income on taxable items, their tax rate relative to income is lower. Social Security taxes are regressive between middle- and upper-income groups because they do not apply to unearned income (dividends and capital gains) nor to earned income over a specified amount (about $54,000 at the time of writing).

Government spending that tends to benefit lower-income persons, as in AFDC and food stamps, is progressive redistribution. Tax welfare such as mortgage deductions and expenditures for expressways that serve suburban commuters are regressive. Some benefits are difficult to classify. For instance, who gains the most from Medicaid, the low-income patient who receives the service or the upper-income physician who receives the money for services rendered?

The bottom line on redistribution is the net effect of taxation and expenditure combined. Means-tested welfare programs financed from progressive taxes and paying benefits only to low-income people are clearly progressive. Public education is less progressive, benefiting all income levels but at more cost to upper-income taxpayers. Government matching of gifts to private universities and the arts through tax deductions is regressive because it lowers the taxes of upper-income people and the services also tend to benefit that group.

SUMMARY

Three common measures of fairness in distributing social goods are (1) equality, the same or equivalent; (2) equity, earned rewards; or (3) adequacy, minimum human rights.

In addition to overall (vertical) equality, there are subcategories of equality within a like group (horizontal) and leveling of ups and downs over life spans and economic cycles (temporal). Although each is called equality, the policy implications may be quite different.

Equity provides rewards in proportion to what is earned on merit. "As is" equal opportunity is a limited equity approach that offers open competition (pure procedural justice) while ignoring past factors that have given some competitors unearned (inequitable) advantages over others. Affirmative action provides compensatory benefits that create "full equity" by equalizing opportunity to compete.

Adequacy can mean either bare subsistence or a fully satisfactory level. Multiple tiers typically provide for both minimum adequacy and inequality above that level. One form offers a standard level of service for one class and a higher level of service for more favored groups. A second form provides a basic service to everyone, with the option to add further benefits on top of it. A third model provides a subsistence-level safety net for those who "fail" in the "normal" world.

Nonfairness doctrines support nonequity and inequality based variously on God's will, the laws of nature, dumb luck, or cynical attitudes about self-aggrandizement and injustice. Deliberate inadequacy continues to be used as a punitive work incentive.

NOTES

1. John Rawls, *A Theory of Justice* (Cambridge, MA: Harvard University Press, 1971).

2. Ibid., p. 96.

3. Winifred Bell, "Analytical Tools That Are Useful in Evaluating Social Welfare Programs," mimeographed.

4. Richard Titmuss, "Social Welfare and the Art of Giving," quoted in Eric Fromm, ed., *Socialist Humanism* (London: Allen Lane, 1967), pp. 358–59.

5. Rawls, *A Theory of Justice*, p. 74.

6. Ibid., p. 87.

7. Ibid., p. 74.

8. Ibid., p. 73.

9. For contrasting arguments on compensatory preference, compare Justice Thurgood Marshall's dissent in *Regents of the University of California v. Allan Bakke*, 438 US 265, with Justice Potter Stewart's dissent in *Fullilove v. Klutznick*, 448 US 448.

10. Robert Morris, ed., *Testing the Limits of Social Welfare* (Hanover, NH: University Press of New England, 1988).

11. One cynic has a different relative standard: "10% more than whatever you have now."

12. For information about old-age pensions in Sweden and several other countries, see Morris, *Testing the Limits of Social Welfare*.

13. Alfred Kahn, *Social Policy and Social Services*, 2nd ed. (New York: Random House, 1979), p. 79.

14. Quoted in T. H. Marshall, *Social Policy*, 4th ed. (London: Hutchinson, 1975), p. 111.

15. Psalm 25:12-13.

16. Francis Beaumont and John Fletcher, *Philaster*, 1610, Act V.

17. Edwin Chadwick, *The Report of His Majesty's Commissioners for Inquiring into the Administration and Practical Operation of the Poor Laws*, 1833, p. 228.

Chapter 6

Socioeconomic Systems

We, the people of the United States, in order to form a more perfect union, establish justice, insure the domestic tranquillity, provide for the common defence, promote the general welfare, and secure the blessings of liberty to ourselves and our posterity, do ordain and establish this Constitution for the United States of America.

According to social compact theory, free men and women "unite in commonwealth" for mutual benefit.[1] Society exists to improve life for each of its members. The role of government is to protect the liberty and security of its citizens and promote the general welfare.

The key question is: How can the general welfare best be promoted? Even when there is consensus on an end, there may be intense conflict over the means. For instance, most industrial nations share the goal of assuring universal health care as a basic human right. The Soviet Union and Great Britain developed government-administered health services. Japan relied for many years on a consensual provision by all private employers, with a residual public program for those who fall between the cracks. The government of what was then West Germany took a middle role that provided incentives for employers to provide private health insurance that meets or exceeds an official federal standard. A residual government insurance program, financed by payroll taxes, was mandatory for those who do not choose the private route. All had the same destination. Which is the best way to get there?

The outermost of the seven circles identified in Chapter 1 involves the "social system," including overall social, cultural, and political institutions. To illustrate this immense and complex dimension of social policy, it may be useful to focus on one major subsystem, the economy. Economic choices are intertwined with just about everything else. They determine what is produced, how it is distributed, and to a great extent how we relate to each other. They are the cornerstone of equality—and inequality; of positive freedom—and oppression; of individualistic competition—and mutual support. Economic factors influence, and are affected by, nearly all political, legal, military, and individual decisions.

The fundamental system issue is the balance between centralization and decentralization:

- planning versus "natural law"
- regulation versus laissez-faire permissiveness
- control (by government or powerful business combinations) versus open competition

Robert Heilbroner has identified three basic approaches:

Societies can trust to the guiding hand of tradition for the maintenance of a fixed configuration of activities; this is the "system" of tradition by which primitive societies secure their continuance.

Tradition will not, however, arrange things when the environment changes, or when new technologies enter or when growth is sought (the latter two cases unlikely in a tradition-bound milieu). The coordinating mechanism then becomes "command"—the conscious direction of social energies by some individual or institution empowered to allocate effort, determine levels of consumption, etc.

Finally, the integrating and directing economic task can also be performed by the market. The market is actually a form of highly decentralized command in which each person is trained by culture and impelled by self-interest (or at the extreme, self-preservation) to "obey" the stimuli of the marketplace.[2]

TRADITIONAL

A traditional economy maintains things the way they "always" have been. It may be egalitarian or hierarchical.

Egalitarian economies tend to be small self-contained societies with a common identity, as symbolized by Indian legends about tribal origins and by the prophets addressing the Hebrew people collectively as Israel, their traditional common ancestor. They have relatively simple, consensual divisions of labor and share a modest production with little surplus for luxuries or accumulation of wealth.

No large modern society is egalitarian. However, a number of movements have established, with varying success, semi-autonomous communities along these lines, including utopian experiments and the Mennonite Amana Colony in the nineteenth century and, more recently, Hippie communes and Israeli kibbutzim.

Hierarchical economies have usually been relatively self-sufficient economic units, such as the feudal manor in the Middle Ages. They typically believe in some form of preordination that keeps people in their "proper place." A "just price," established by long usage, preempts individual bargaining. In practice, of course, feudalism was never purely traditional. There were always real-life MacBeths (ruthless aggressors) and Robin Hoods (marginal members) who deviated from these "givens." Remnants of this model still exist in some third world countries.

The traditional economy can thrive only where there is economic, social, and technological stability and high consensus about production and distribution. As a society advances in technology, size, and complexity, tradition must give way to some kind of coordinating mechanism. There is a centralized and a decentralized approach to such coordination.

CENTRAL CONTROL (COMMAND)

A command economy can be effective and socially responsible to the extent that it has three characteristics, without which there is a risk of chaos, "screw ups," or exploitation.

First, central planning requires high *technical competence*, which involves a comprehensive data collection and analysis system, reliable forecasts of noncontrollable elements, an ability to predict the direct and indirect effects of planning decisions, and a consistent basis for setting the price of each item in relation to all others in the absence of tradition or bargaining. Despite computer advances, these capabilities remain limited. Still, say advocates, imperfect planning is better than nonplanning.

Second, it must have *authority* to enforce the decisions. Heilbroner, an advocate of central planning, reluctantly admits:

An aspect of authoritarianism resides inextricably in all planning systems. A plan is meaningless if it is not carried out, or it can be ignored or defied at will. . . . Incentives may succeed where punishments fail. But planning will not assure a socialist society of a capacity to endure or adapt unless the planning is a system of effective *command*. From that conclusion I see no escape. . . . The economy must be concerted . . . and this coordination must entail *obedience* to a central plan.[3]

Third, exercise of such authority requires *wisdom, altruism, and impartiality*. Because capitalism assumes routinely that everyone is self-serving, it has a system of checks and balances among competing interests. Central control lacks such defenses. Its theory assumes that the planners and controllers are a moral and intellectual elite, akin to Plato's philosopher kings, who transcend their own narrow self-interest and resist others who seek special privilege.

Ideally, central control more fairly distributes goods among citizens, free from exploitation, special privilege, and individual aggrandizement, and it encourages a spirit of sharing and caring. Critics reply that decisions are actually made not by wise altruists but by self-serving leaders and/or unresponsive bureaucrats who neither know nor care about the real needs of the "little guy."

Another argument for a planned economy is that it uses capital and labor more efficiently by avoiding the costs of competition and the waste of economic cycles that periodically idle workers and equipment.

This is countered by the charge that it makes costly mistakes because decisions are based on incomplete and inadequate information. Further, central control is alleged to be inefficient because it squelches initiative and minimizes a strong incentive, individual gain. A common joke among Communist workers is, "They pretend to pay us, and we pretend to work."[4]

Private Sector Command

Although most discussion focuses on government, centralized control is just as common in the private sector. A business can dictate production, distribution, and price whenever it can put together two conditions to create a monopoly:

1. *necessity*: control of something people cannot—or think they cannot—do without, such as jobs, energy, or medical care
2. *exclusivity*: sufficient control of supply that the need cannot be met adequately from other sources

A loose form of this is a *cartel*, in which separate organizations collaborate to control their common market. In the 1970s, members of OPEC agreed to cut production, creating a shortage that enabled them to raise oil prices nearly tenfold.

In labor, the American Federation of Labor and Congress of Industrial Organizations (AFL-CIO), an association of independent labor unions, operates as a cartel when all of its unions agree to honor the picket lines of each member union or to boycott the products of employers who allegedly use unfair labor practices, as in the grape boycott of the 1970s.

An *oligopoly* achieves the same thing without formal agreement. In the 1950s, the U.S. auto industry was dominated by a few big companies and an industrywide union. The companies' costs remained similar because the union negotiated comparable wage agreements with each of them. By copying each other's price increases, they jointly passed along the costs of their high wages, high profit margins, and obsolescent technology to captive consumers. These monopolies weakened in the 1980s as outside competitors (new oil producers, nonunion immigrants, and Japanese auto makers) broke their exclusivity.

The Organization of Petroleum-Exporting Countries (OPEC) had a second problem. Some of its members cheated. They exceeded their production quotas and undercut the fixed price. This can be avoided by forming a *trust*, a holding company with central coordinating authority over its subsidiary corporations. Standard Oil and AT&T were trusts until the government broke them up into smaller companies to restore competition.

The labor counterpart is a *guild*, "a union of men in the same craft or trade to uphold standards and protect the members." A plumbers' union or a medical society can become a monopoly if it gains enough power to impose a "closed shop." That is, it (1) restricts employment in its field to members, and (2) controls entry into membership. (A "union shop" restricts employment to members but has an open policy on entry into membership.)

Although private sector control is motivated by self-interest, it may claim to coincide with the public interest. Businesses argue that a monopoly permits more cost-efficient production and marketing. Labor asserts that such control is necessary to equalize the bargaining between otherwise decentralized sellers of labor (workers) and a centralized buyer (the employer).

THE MARKET

An isolated family or small community may be self-sufficient at a subsistence level, meeting all of its needs internally and sharing the results. A *market* emerges as soon as there is a need or desire to trade some goods or labor for other items. All markets have three characteristics:

1. *division of labor* so that we have different things to trade
2. *a common medium of exchange* (money) so that we can compare the value of apples with oranges or an hour of work with a pair of shoes
3. *a method of setting prices* (including wages) so that we can agree on how many hours of work for those shoes

Not all markets are free. In the first two types of economies, tradition or a central authority regulates who does what, what is produced, how it is distributed, and the price/wage for each item exchanged. A *free market* has additional characteristics:

- *freedom of work, enterprise, and trade*; the right to produce and sell anything without restriction, favoritism, or discrimination
- *open competition* among suppliers (producers/sellers), without government restrictions or private "combinations in restraint of trade"
- *free and informed consumer choice* to buy what one wants from any seller in full knowledge of what one is buying, without coercion, constraint, or fraud
- *purely economic choice*, unaffected by social relationships, union loyalties, patriotism, or where one's physician has staff privileges
- *freedom of contract*; the right to make binding commitments with each other, except where they subvert the above.[5]

According to classical economics, a purely free market is regulated by the *natural law* of supply and demand, in which independent free choices of millions of individual buyers (demand) and sellers (supply) keep everything in balance. This will be elaborated in the next chapter.

Just as no existing economy is fully controlled, neither is any completely free. Some goods, such as cocaine, are illegal. Licensing and regulation, import tariffs and quotas, national unions and multinational corporations, each restricts competition to some degree. Consumer ability to evaluate goods and services is limited. Social inequalities restrict effective freedom of work, enterprise, and trade for some members of every large society. A relatively free market may approximate the law of supply and demand but will deviate from it to the extent that these conditions exist.

Advocates and critics differ on the effects of a free market system. Some key pros and cons:

Pro	Con
1. Stability	
Over the long run, the self-regulating system maintains approximate equilibrium and predictability.	Much undeserved hardship and suffering, in the form of unemployment and bankruptcies, is caused by the instability of recurring cycles.
2. Responsiveness to Needs	
Demand is the best determination of need as defined by consumers.	The human needs of those without adequate purchasing power are ignored.
3. Efficiency	
All production is based on demand; competition weeds out the inefficient.	Free markets are socially inefficient by diverting production from social priorities to affluent individuals' choices. They are economically inefficient because recessions waste both capital and human resources.

Pro	Con
4. Flexibility	
The market reacts automatically to change.	The market reacts slowly to change. It has problems coping with major rapid changes in environment and technology, and it typically does so only at great cost to individuals.
5. Fairness	
It is equitable, rewarding diligence and initiative.	It is inherently unequal, and it takes no responsibility for underserved disservices it causes.
6. Morality and Social Responsibility	
Dispersion and competition contain and limit the effects of unethical behavior and unwise decisions.	The system converts one of the seven deadly sins (avarice) into a cardinal virtue. Competition and conflict are rewarded at the expense of cooperation, mutual support, and commitment to public interest.
7. Liberty	
A free market offers negative freedom.	It subverts positive freedom, especially for the working classes.
8. Motivation	
Competitive self-interest is the strongest motivator.	It is a disincentive for noncommercial social contribution. It also discourages the majority who are not winners.[6]

British social policy expert Robert Pinker says, in effect, a pox on both your houses!

My own position is based on the view that both classical economic theory and its ideal state of capitalism and Marxist theory and its ideal state of communism offer attractive prescriptions for the maximization of human welfare which, when they are put into practice, also become instruments of oppression and diswelfare.[7]

VARIATIONS ON A CAPITALIST THEME

Most twentieth-century economic systems, even those with strong free-market or central control ideologies, are to some degree mixed. Not surprising, the results also come out somewhere between "natural law" and planned objectives.

Laissez-Faire and Monopolistic Capitalism

Classical economic theory assumes that left to itself capitalism will perpetuate the free market. The correct government role is laissez-faire noninterference. To do otherwise would upset the delicate operation of the self-regulating natural law of supply and demand. When Adam Smith wrote *The Wealth of Nations* in 1776, the primitive state of industrial and agricultural technology kept the economy relatively decentralized. However, even then, foreign trade was largely in the hands of government-sponsored monopolies; and since 1349, when the Statute of Laborers responded to the labor shortage caused by the Black Plague, English poor laws had restricted workers' freedom to move about and sell their labor to the highest bidder.

Discussing abuses in his industry, a business leader recently expressed strong support for corrective governmental regulation, then added, with a grin, "except of course when they are regulating me." He was only half joking. Maximum gain is the stated goal of capitalism. Is it not reasonable, then, for an entrepreneur to suppress competition when it pays to do so?

As the technical capacity to manage bigness increased during the nineteenth century, *monopolistic capitalism* (centralized private sector control) evolved. Through trusts and cartels, "robber baron" capitalists amassed huge fortunes by dictating lower wages and higher prices than would have been possible if they faced free-market competition. Ironically, the hands-off government policy of laissez-faire left society vulnerable to subversion of the very free market it was intended to preserve. Some modern economists fear that multinational corporations will similarly exploit the "no-man's land" gaps between national jurisdictions.

Pragmatism

In addition to monopolistic subversion of the free market, laissez-faire capitalism has been subject to cyclical depressions. For both these reasons, in every non-Communist industrial country there exists some form of pragmatic capitalism. While maintaining much of the earlier ideology, economic theory, and market structure of laissez-faire capitalism, it uses government intervention—usually a mix of regulation, social welfare supplements, and selective government ownership—to further social and economic objectives.

Faced with the threats of an out-of-control worldwide depression, unrest in the working classes, and an evangelical Communist outreach, John Maynard Keynes argued that this was the only way to save capitalism. In 1933 he praised Roosevelt's emergency New Deal measures: "You have made yourself the trustee for those in every country who seek to mend the evils of our conditions by reasoned experiment, *within the framework of our existing social system*" (emphasis added).[8]

Richard Tawney was more sanguine about selective government intervention: "Fools will use it, when they can, for foolish ends, criminals for criminal ends. Sensible and decent men will use it for ends which are sensible and decent. We, in England, have repeatedly remade the state, and we are remaking it now, and shall remake it again."[9]

Controlled Capitalism

Winston Churchill called democracy the worst possible form of government—except all others. In the same vein, moderate pragmatists on both the left and the right have concluded that for all its faults, capitalism is still the best available system, given judicious government regulation. They may, however, differ on the specifics of when, where, why, and how. Among the most common interventions are

- *enhancing the environment* through fiscal and monetary actions that counter the cycles, stimulate the general economy, and/or encourage specific development
- *refereeing the game* in financial transactions and collective bargaining
- *preserving free-market competition* with antitrust laws
- *setting a "just price"* for local utilities where free competition is not practical
- *preventing disservices* associated with capitalistic enterprise by setting standards for occupational safety and environmental protection
- *enforcing performance standards* through licensing of physicians, safety standards for autos, pure food and drug regulation, and so on

Compensatory Capitalism: The Welfare State

Whether out of altruistic charity, a sense of commonality, a belief in basic human rights under natural law, a desire for social stability, or a combination, the welfare state has emerged as a mechanism of pragmatic capitalism to handle diswelfares without changing the basic economic market system. This evolution was highlighted in comments by Flora Lewis following the 1990 decision of East German voters to switch from communism to capitalism:

No doubt there will be some jungle capitalism, speculation, and profiteering, as there was in West Germany's early days of economic reconstruction.

But the system established by Adenauer's economics minister, Ludwig Erhard, is a *social market economy* with a higher advanced benefit program, featuring universal health care, unemployment compensation, decent pensions (emphasis added).[10]

Selective Socialism: A Mixed Economy

Socialism is government ownership and operation of the means of production and/or distribution. Whereas Marxist socialism believes in government ownership of nearly all means of production and distribution, selective socialism is a mixed economy that permits governmental ownership for specific reasons within a predominantly private enterprise system. This view is ideologically represented by the British Labor Party and Western European socialist parties (but also quietly practiced to a lesser degree by conservative governments). According to Lord Beveridge, the mentor of British socialism, "We probably need public monopoly ownership in certain fields, private enterprise subject to public control in other fields, private enterprise free of any save the general controls in yet other fields."[11]

In a mixed economy, government ownership of business is usually based on one or more of the following judgments:

- *Unsuitabilitiy for private enterprise,* where the profit motive could subvert the primary objective, such as national military security or universalistic social welfare services.
- *Unprofitability,* where market revenues do not meet the full cost, such as a shelter for abused spouse or an expensive public transit system, leaving them by default to subsidized government and charity.
- *Need for a monopoly,* as in public utilities, where free competition is believed to be inefficient or inadequate. (Controlled capitalism is often used as an alternative to public ownership.)
- *Troubled industries.* When a number of U.S. railroads went bankrupt, the government took over the business through public companies called AMTRAK and CONRAIL. In other countries, "sick" coal, steel, and banking companies were "nationalized." Selective socialism may resell them to the private sector after getting them back on their feet. (In other cases, such as troubled automobile, defense, and banking corporations, government "bail-out" subsidies to commercial enterprise have been used instead.)
- *Strategic industries.* The people may choose government ownership of certain enterprises when they believe it will serve their own best interest. Mexico took over a highly profitable oil business in order to have the revenues for social programs. The State Bank of North Dakota was established because the state's wheat farmers were losing their farms due to alleged exploitation by "eastern bankers" (from Minnesota).

Except for subsidized social welfare services, a public business is usually expected to behave like a capitalistic enterprise within the market and either make a profit for the government treasury (as in national oil companies) or rebate its profit to the consumers (as in public utilities).

VARIATIONS ON A MARXIST THEME

There is disagreement on what is "true" Marxism. It appears that Karl Marx himself envisioned "dictatorship by the proletariat" (central planning and control) only as an interim stage to establish the new social order after the overthrow of capitalism. Gradually, the utopian new era of comradeship would make government authority obsolete, replaced by an anarchist society in which the workers would get together in decentralized groups to control their own means of production and engage in honest, egalitarian trade with other groups.

Twentieth-century Marxism has taken three different directions: a fixation at the "interim" central control stage, a compromise with capitalism and the market economy, and partial decentralization with worker control.

Stalinist Socialism

Under Lenin, Soviet communism established the basic pattern of central planning and control. Because of opposition, his compromise New Economic Policy of 1921 called for ownership and operation of "the commanding heights" (basic industries) while leaving peasants and small businesses alone and permitting limited foreign capital investment. Stalin completed the move to central control when he nationalized the rest of industry and commerce and combined peasant holdings into state-owned collective farms.

Except for a small profit-oriented "gray market," the Soviet economic system continued into the early 1980s as a "model" of central control.

Market Marxism

In the 1970s, Hungarians began making pragmatic compromises with free enterprise. They nicknamed it "goulash communism" because of its stewlike mixture of socialism and capitalism. A few years later, after leadership changes, China and then the Soviet Union followed suit. The Chinese called it "yin-yang communism," reflecting the Chinese tradition of balancing opposite forces.

Selective socialism, as noted above, is a mixed economy with incremental socialist modifications on a capitalist foundation. Market Marxism is a mixed economy with incremental capitalist modifications on an authoritarian central control foundation. China's premier, Deng Xiaoping, defined the limits on this partial return to a market economy: "In carrying on socialism, I think we should uphold two things. First, public ownership should always play a dominant role in our economy. Second, we should try to avoid [class] polarization and we should always keep to the road of common prosperity. Within these constraints, pragmatism was a guiding principle. It does not matter whether a cat is black or white so long as it catches mice.''

There were two dimensions to market Marxism in the 1980s. One was to permit self-employed individuals and local cooperatives to develop modest free-enterprise in services, light manufacturing, and market gardening. The other was to give more attention to profit and market considerations by state-owned industries. Some authority was decentralized to branch managers so that they could respond more flexibly to local market factors.

Central planning seriously hampered the initiative and creativity of [Chinese] enterprises and workers and to a great extent emasculated what would otherwise have been a vigorous economy. The more centralized, the more rigid; the more rigid, the lazier the people; the lazier the people, the poorer they are. To criticism that this was a sell out of true Marxism, Premier Deng replied, ''There are those who say we should not open our windows, because open windows let in flies and other insects. They want the windows to stay closed, so we all expire from lack of air. But we say, 'Open the windows, breathe the fresh air, and at the same time fight the flies and insects.' ''[12]

Some years later, the Soviet Union adopted ''socialist privatization'':

Beset by a sinking economy and rising discontent, Soviet lawmakers made a break with communist orthodoxy Tuesday by voting to let private citizens own small factories and hire their own workers. . . .

The law will permit Soviets for the first time in nearly seven decades to privately possess ''means of production,'' a notion at odds with classic Marxist thinking, which views private ownership as the root of capitalist exploitation.

Deputy Premier Leonid I. Abalkin said the law, to take effect July 1, would enable private citizens to own workshops, auto repair garages, farms and other small-scale ventures to supplement the ineffective state-run economy. . . .

Although the Property Law keeps large economic monopolies for the state-run sector, it declares all forms of ownership legally equal . . . and it says society gains by competition among them. ''This is an enormous step forward because it lays down the principle of pluralism in the form of ownership,'' said progressive lawmaker Alexei Yablokov. . . .

Abalkin said another key provision of the 23-page law would order state-owned factories and other businesses to allocate a share of after tax profits to workers. By providing them with a material stake in their enterprise's profitability, the law presumably will encourage Soviets to work harder.[13]

Post-Marxist Capitalism

At the time of this writing, rejection of both political and economic central control has been gathering momentum in Eastern Europe. This is *not* a Marxist variant. It is a radical decision to replace it with pragmatic capitalism.

SYNDICALISM: WORKER OWNERSHIP

Worker ownership of the means of production and distribution historically had two separate origins, one a radical socialist ideology and the other a capitalistic reform.

Marxist Syndicalism

Radical syndicalism, founded in nineteenth-century France by Pierre Joseph Proudhon, believed that (1) workers were being exploited by capitalists, who misappropriated the fruits of their labor, and (2) government was an instrument of that oppression. They sought to bring down the existing order by withholding their labor through a general strike. In the new order, workers would control the means of production through their unions (syndicates), which would also perform the few government functions needed in this utopian society. Many of their views were incorporated into the teachings of Marx, who lived through a short-lived syndicalist regime in Paris (1870).

In 1950, Yugoslavia's Tito broke away from Stalinist ideology and set up a form of Marxist syndicalism, which differed from original syndicalists by maintaining government ownership and an authoritarian political structure. Workers in each factory belong to a Basic Organization of Associated Labor that elects from its membership a workers council to be the factory's board of directors. The council hires and supervises management, sets wages and production targets (within limits), and makes other basic policy.

Socialist Bogdan Denitch praised the success of syndicalism's "communitarian and consensual rather than conflictual" approach in Yugoslavia.

It posits an economy run essentially by elected bodies of workers and other employees. These elected bodies have had ever-widening powers. They have acted—and this is crucial—not merely as institutions managing sectors of the economy, but as organs of political socialization creating a new nexus of values and links in an industrialized society.[14]

Time Magazine took a more cynical view: "In theory, says a Western diplomat in Belgrade, the self-governing councils are 'the purest form of Marxism.' " But in practice, 'the trade union and the management are all controlled by the local party in every big plant.' "[15]

Capitalist Syndicalism

Beginning about 1820, Robert Owen, an English factory owner who had earlier pioneered paternalistic welfare capitalism at his New Lanark factory, proposed the establishment of *cooperative communities* of producers. Although his fellow capitalists rejected his ideas, working-class groups and liberal intellectuals responded. Several short-lived utopian communities were developed in England and the United States as part of this ideology. In the twentieth century, Israel has used a similar approach in its successful kibbutzim.

Paralleling this was the cooperative movement, with roots in both inner-city settlement houses and rural populism. The "maximum feasible participation of the poor" movement associated with the Community Action Program of the 1960s was an ideological descendent, on the consumer side, of the cooperative movement.

Among better-known cooperatives today are mutual insurance companies, credit unions, campus "co-op" stores, and such farm marketing operations as Land o' Lakes and Dairylea. Although their structure of ownership is communal, they tend to function externally like any other business corporation.

In recent years, workers have become overt capitalists by buying stock in their corporations. This has taken place variously through stock options as a fringe benefit, emergency buyouts by employees to prevent a factory from being closed by its current owners, pressure on workers from financially hard-pressed management to take some of their compensation in stock instead of cash, and strategic stock purchases by union members and their pension funds to gain voting power on the board of directors.

ESOPs [Employee Stock Option Plans] were dreamed up in the 1970s as a way to tie employees' finances more closely to the fortunes of their companies.

That's considered a noble goal by many corporations and "public companies pay lip service to the idea of creating an ownership mentality," says Corey Rosen, director of the National Center for Employee Ownership in Oakland, Calif.

But experts say public companies find ESOPs far more appealing as anti-takeover armor. . . . An ESOP allows a firm's management to put a block of stocks in the hands of employees—a group that almost always backs management in a takeover fight. . . .

In 1989, public-company ESOPs borrowed a record $24 billion, up from $6.5 billion in 1988. . . . Companies recently announcing ESOPs: Chevron, Upjohn, Mobile, AT&T, Bellsouth, Sears Roebuck.[16]

MERCANTILISM

In the late Middle Ages, central monarchies developed some autonomy from their feudal vassals by controlling foreign trade. This was accelerated by the discovery of the New World, which was exploited by trading monopolies owned by, or paying commissions to, the king.

Mercantilism emerged as a central control system which accumulated national (royal) wealth in the form of gold, silver, and precious stones by (1) exporting more than one imported, (2) overcharging domestic consumers through monopolistic price fixing, and (3) plundering foreigners, through conquistadors, colonialism, privateers (royally commissioned pirates), and military aggression.

Modern mercantilism is economic nationalism. The central government restricts market freedom in ways that favor domestic industry and maintain a "favorable" balance of payments (export more than you import). It is practiced by both capitalist and Marxist countries in a number of ways:

- *Quotas*: limitations on the quantity of imports admitted.
- *Tariffs*: taxes that increase the consumer cost of imports, giving domestic industries a price advantage.
- *Export subsidies*: lowering the price to foreign buyers, therefore stimulating sales. The government may purchase the goods to resell abroad at a loss, give tax welfare or cash rebates to exporters, and/or provide free marketing services.
- *Industrial development*: direct or indirect assistance in building a new or strategic industry. These subsidies to private business lower the consumer price of their products.
- *Devaluation of currency*: by making the dollar worth less in foreign exchange for yen, marks, and francs, the dollar prices of our exports cost less in the buyer's currency, and the prices of their goods cost more dollars to our consumers, thus encouraging exports and discouraging imports.

The pros and cons of mercantilism are somewhat muddled ideologically. On a macrolevel, its nationalistic approach to the "community of nations" is equivalent to the classical capitalist ideology of competitive self-interested individualism. On the other hand, seen from the perspective of individual producers and consumers, it substitutes central control for a free market, a violation of that ideology. In practice bottom-line decisions tend to be pragmatic, not ideological. Nations tend to favor free trade where it results in a "favorable" balance of trade and to be mercantilistic if their free-trade balance would be negative.

Developing a national consensus on the balance between mercantilism and free trade is not easy. Restrictions give a competitive advantage to domestic manufacturers, such as steel mills. Free trade tends to benefit exporting industries, such as agriculture. The average person may be ambivalent, being for restriction when it enhances his or her job security, but for free trade when it lowers the cost of his or her clothes and cars. A consistent national policy on mercantilism is further complicated by inability to control the ever-changing circumstances and practices of other nations.

SUMMARY

The widest domain of social policy is the overall social environment, the major social, economic, cultural, and political institutions of a society. A recurring issue at this level is centralization versus decentralization. There are three basic approaches: The traditional society operates on the basis of established, consensual patterns and values. In the central planning and control approach, presumably wise and disinterested leaders base their decisions on comprehensive data analysis and enforce them with authority. The free-market approach relies on the interaction of millions of individual decisions to guide the economy.

Too complex for a traditional approach to be viable, most modern nations struggle to find a balance between the two theoretical extremes of total control and a purely free market. Encountering unfair practices and monopolistic subversion of competition, nations that espouse the decentralized free-market approach have added selective central planning and control elements, including manipulation of the monetary and fiscal systems, regulation of commerce and industry, public "social market" compensations for the gaps and diswelfares associated with a market economy, and government enterprise in selected areas.

Facing corruption, fallibility, and citizen resistance, nations that favor central planning and control have added elements of the free-enterprise market to increase efficiency and motivation.

Worker control of the means of production is both a Marxist ideal and a democratic ideal. In a Yugoslavian Marxist version, a workers' council performs functions similar to a corporation's board of directors. In the United States, worker control has taken such forms as farmers' cooperatives, stock options for employees, and union pension fund stock ownership in the employer's company.

A central control method used by nearly all nations is mercantilism, which seeks in various ways to give domestic businesses an advantage over foreign competition.

NOTES

1. See John Locke, "Of Civil Government," in *Two Treatises of Government,* 1690.

2. Robert Heilbroner, "What Is Socialism?" in Irving Howe, ed., *Beyond the Welfare State* (New York: Schocken Books, 1982), p. 176.

3. Ibid., p. 179.

4. An excellent discussion of command and free-market ideologies may be found in Vic George and Paul Wilding, *Ideology and Social Welfare* (London: Routledge & Kegan Paul, 1976).

5. This section is indebted to H. B. Acton, *The Morals of the Market: An Ethical Exploration* (London: Longman, 1971), Ch. 1; and to Charles Rowley and Alan

Peacock, *Welfare Economics: A Liberal Restatement* (London: Martin Robertson, 1975), Ch. 5.

6. This listing is indebted to Acton, *The Morals of the Market: An Ethical Exploration*; George and Wilding, *Ideology and Social Welfare*; and various writings of Richard Titmuss.

7. Robert Pinker, *The Idea of Welfare* (London: Heinemann, 1979), p. 235.

8. Quoted in George and Wilding, *Ideology and Social Welfare*, p. 42, who cited as their source D. Winch, *Economics and Policy* (London: Hodder & Stoughton, 1969), p. 221.

9. Richard Tawney, *The Radical Tradition* (London: Penguin, 1964), p. 169.

10. Flora Lewis, "East Germans Didn't Want Another Experiment," *New York Times*, March 20, 1990.

11. W. H. Beveridge, *The Pillars of Society* (New York: Macmillan, 1943), p. 118.

12. Quotations in this section are from *Time Magazine*, vol. 127, no. 1, January 6, 1986, pp. 29–38.

13. *Omaha World Herald*, March 7, 1990.

14. B. Denitch, "A Response to Heilbroner," in Howe, *Beyond the Welfare State*, pp. 192–93.

15. *Time Magazine*, January 6, 1986, p. 63.

16. *USA Today*, February 20, 1990.

Chapter 7

Changing the System

No existing society is perfect. Our original Constitution permitted slavery and did not grant voting rights for women or poor people. In a society that professes an ideology of equal opportunity, on the average men are "more equal" than women; whites, than blacks; affluent children, than poor children. Not all businesspeople are honest, nor politicians wise. Although our nation has the economic capacity to eliminate poverty entirely, 1/7 of all Americans and 1/4 of our children exist below an official "poverty line," which itself is 25 percent below the government's own calculations of minimum adequacy.

Interventions are called for to improve the general economic, social, and political environments, as well as the behavior of agents within them. Even if all systems were "A-OK," periodic adjustments would be needed as times change. Such interventions may involve (1) *radical* system change, (2) *reform* within the system, and/or (3) *enhancement* of the system.

RADICAL CHANGE

Radical means "going to the root or origin, fundamental."

- A radical *political* system change was the move from representative democracy to dictatorship in Germany under Hitler—and another back to democracy after his fall.

- A radical *civil rights* change was the Thirteenth, Fourteenth, and Fifteenth Amendments, which ended slavery and granted full citizenship rights to former slaves.

- A radical *economic* change after the Russian Revolution was confiscation of large estates (privately owned) and dividing them among individual peasants—and another was confiscation of those peasants' farms and recombining them again into large estates (state-owned collective farms).

Many people are cautious about fundamental change. One issue is *feasibility*. Can entrenched resistance or public apathy be overcome? If a revolution succeeds, are the new leaders technically competent to implement the "new order"? Another issue is *cost*. "You can't made an omelet without breaking eggs." The transition will inevitably disrupt the normal operation of the life in that society. Many individuals, including innocent bystanders, will be hurt materially, physically, and/or psychologically.

The process involves risks. One risk is a *loss of freedom*: Radical change often meets heavy resistance. Coercive control is usually needed during a transition period to impose and consolidate the new system—and it may become permanent. Another risk is *unplanned consequences*: In the best of circumstances, knowledge is incomplete and wisdom is defective. Every change creates economic, social, and/or cultural side effects. Small incremental changes have small effects. The greater the change, the heavier the impact of errors. Where radical changes are implemented by inexperienced leaders, the risk increases further. A third risk is *corruption*: The original noble goals of the change agents may be subverted by their own self-interests after they become the new "Haves."

Given the costs and risks, why would anyone ever advocate radical change? A response is: "Compared to what?" Cost-benefit analysis may lead one to conclude that under given circumstances, the probable benefit exceeds both the potential costs of change and the certain costs of non-change. The most conservative American probably approves such radical changes as the Thirteenth Amendment and of the reconversion of Eastern Europe from Marxism to capitalism and political democracy.

Generally, the worse things are, the more attractive is radical change because there is less to lose and more to gain. Indeed, social radicals often strategically oppose reforms that benefit the "oppressed masses" lest their improved circumstances make them reluctant to risk what they have in support of fundamental change.

REFORM

Reform means "to make better by correcting faults or defects." The difference between radical change and moderate reform is *how far* it goes, *how fast*, and *how disruptive*. Marxist socialism was radical in its call for total system change. Britain's Fabian socialists were reformers who counseled *gradualism*: Take a small step without disrupting the total system, digest it, and evaluate the results before taking the next step.

In the 1930s, the New Deal "reformed" capitalism, which was in precarious condition, with regulation of banking and labor relations, Keynesian economic interventions to stimulate consumer demand, supply-side assistance to businesses, and social insurance programs to fill the gaps. Some historians say that these reforms saved U.S. capitalism from the radical threats of fascism and communism. More recently, leaders with a transcendent priority on military security have "reformed" constitutional civil liberties by restricting freedom of speech, press, and information where military security is involved.

When is reform not reform? When it does not "make better." While any honest advocate of a reform believes that the change is for the better, you may disagree. Each example above had passionate opponents who asserted that it was not reform at all but rather subversion (undermining of existing good things) or regression (return to the bad old days). If you get into the "reform business"—and heaven knows there are enough things in our society that need reform—you must be prepared to defend, against both vested interests and honest diagreements, what you are "correcting" and how it "makes better."

RULES OF THE GAME

A popular reform method is to keep the basic system but to change the "rules by which the game is played."

Professional football has changed its rules periodically to make the game more attractive to the fans. When scoring was low, offensive linemen were allowed to do more things to protect their quarterback. When scoring became too easy, defenders were given more latitude. The goal posts were moved forward ten yards to encourage field goals, and when they became too frequent, moved back again to discourage them. It is the "same" game, run by the same people, but the changes have markedly affected strategies, scores, and style of play.

Similarly, in social policy, rule changes affect the behavior of the players and sometimes the score. Rule changes may *further* already-established intents, *correct* ongoing faults, or *respond* to new problems.

Furthering Established Intents

According to Harold Wilensky and Charles Lebeaux:

Large and influential segments of the American people (not just businessmen) believe strongly that:

1. The individual should strive to be successful in competition with others, under the rules of the game.
2. These rules involve "fair play":
   (a) everyone should start with equal opportunity;
   (b) no one should take unfair advantage through force, fraud, or "pull."[1]

Unfortunately, some people *do* try to take unfair advantage, so we have developed rules and regulations to enforce competitive "fair play" in the stock market, financial transactions, advertising, consumer protection, and so on.

We periodically extend and update existing rules. The Fourteenth Amendment (1868) guaranteed equal treatment "under the law." Originally it applied only to the legal system. The 1954 school desegregation decision updated it to include the vast array of public service programs that did not exist "under the law" in 1868. Later court interpretations, statutes, and executive orders extended "under the law" to include private organizations that benefited from "under the law" public grants, contracts, and tax welfare.

In the absence of specific measures, a "rule of the game" safety net is *equity law,* defined as "(a) resort to general principles of fairness and justice whenever existing law is inadequate; (b) a system of rules and doctrines, as in the United States, supplementing common and statute law, and superceding such law when it proves inadequate for just settlements."

Responding to Change

Adaptive reforms respond to emerging needs and problems. President Pierce's 1854 veto message, rejecting Dorothea Dix's bill for aid to state mental hospitals, declared that federal involvement in social welfare was unconstitutional.

I readily and, I trust, feelingly acknowledge the duty incumbent on us all as men and citizens, and as among the highest and holiest of our duties, to provide for those who, in the mysterious order of Providence, are subject to want and to disease of body or mind; but I can not find any authority in the Constitution for making the Federal Government the great almoner of public charity throughout the United States. To do so would, in my judgment, be contrary to the letter and spirit of the Constitution and subversive of the whole theory upon which the Union of these States is founded.[2]

This prevailed for nearly eighty years until the crisis of the Great Depression required a new approach. Hunger was widespread. Conventional charity and local public welfare were exhausted. States were near bankruptcy. Roosevelt responded with emergency aid. When he followed his crisis response with a long-term federal plan to meet social security needs in the mass industrialized society that the United States had become, he was careful to stress the continuity of this major reform with the nation's past: "Our task of reconstruction does not require the creation of new and strange values. . . . If the means and the details are in some instances new, the objectives are as permanent as human nature. . . . It is a return to values lost in the course of our economic development and expansion."[3]

Technology may create the need for adaptive policy reforms. The Industrial Revolution replaced small, diverse, personal employers with large, impersonal factories. The immense power advantage of the large-scale buyer of unskilled labor over individual sellers of that labor destroyed the free-labor market.

Marxism's radical solution was to replace the market system. In contrast, a reform response was the trade union movement, which attempted to restore parity between buyers and sellers of labor within the free market system by collective bargaining, which involved a single seller (the union) negotiating with a single buyer (the employer). The 1935 National Labor Relations Act set up "rules of the game" for collective bargaining. Since then, like the National Football League, the rules are changed periodically to reestablish the balance between employers and workers (as perceived by the rule makers).

Correcting Inherent Faults

Rule changes are also made to correct faults in the original intent itself. A flaw in British "democracy" of the early 1800s was that it limited the vote to the upper classes. Thomas Carlyle, dismayed at the failure of Parliament to take into account the needs and interests of the working classes in the Reform Act of 1832, started the Chartist movement to gain them the vote. They finally got it a half century later, leading to their own political party and to policies more favorable to their interests.

It took longer to correct male-only democracy in the United States. In 1787, Abigail Adams urged her husband, John, to provide for women's rights, including the vote, at the original constitutional convention. He did not. It took another 133 years, including nearly a century of work by women's suffrage movements, to correct this fault with the Nineteenth Amendment.

In each of these cases, the reforms did not update or extend an original intent. They changed it. The British power structure believed that only those who owned property should vote. Our Founding Fathers did not consider women competent to share in the government.

While most rule changes tend to be incremental, they can be extensive, as proposed by the British Communist party:

Instead of trying to reduce people's capacity to gain a competitive advantage on one another, we would have to change the rules of the game so as to reduce the rewards of competitive success and the costs of failure. Instead of trying to make everyone equally lucky or equally good at his job, we would have to devise "insurance" systems which neutralize the effects of luck, and income-sharing systems which break the link between vocational success and living standards.[4]

CHANGING AGENT BEHAVIOR

In the host-agent-environmental model, some of the above environmental changes affect the host directly. Others, especially many "rules of the game," benefit the host indirectly by changing the behavior of agents. Getting compliance (the desired behavior) from agents is not always a simple matter. There are a number of variables that influence the effectiveness of this approach. Among them are the following:

- *Attitude of the actors* (those responsible for getting compliance). How strongly are they committed to the objective? Is it a "sacred" mission? Are they lukewarm or ambivalent? Do they privately disagree? Implementation of the same civil rights laws has been very different under "liberal" and "conservative" administrations.

- *Identification of actors with agents.* Reportedly, until Mothers Against Drunk Driving (MADD) had its impact, police, prosecutors, and judges, many of whom themselves drove after having "a few beers," tended to be indulgent toward drinking drivers.

- *Relative status of the agent.* Agents who are higher status tend to be less compliant and to "get away with" more. While small-time thieves were serving prison terms, a leading brokerage firm that had deliberately defrauded millions from trusting associates continued in business without prosecution. Similarly, corruption that would put any ordinary small company on a black list has been "forgiven" for large defense contractors.

- *Relative status of the host.* The Environmental Protection Agency may be a bit less zealous on compliance with a company that pollutes miners' air in a West Virginia town than one that does it to executives in a wealthy suburb.

- *The agent's self-interest.* Regardless of its merit, we can expect resistance by most hospitals and physicians to any change in health care policy that lowers their income. Unions have been much more accepting of affirmative action when it is applied only to future hiring without affecting the job security and seniority of present employees.

Coercion

An external approach to changing agents' behavior is *coercion*, "to effect by force, especially by legal authority." *Eradication* of undesirable agents is a "final solution": exterminate mosquitoes, mass murderers, and terrorists; launch preemptive first strikes against security threats. A bit less extreme is to *block access* to the host: imprison muggers; separate abusive parents from their children.

Licensing is gentler coercion. Prevent undesirable agents by setting competence, performance, and ethical conditions for the privilege of entering (and continuing in) certain endeavors, such as practicing a profession, offering daycare, transporting travelers, or driving a car. If the agent is already in business, so to speak, *regulatory actions* may be used to compel nonpollution, fair labor practices, pure food and drugs, or equal employment opportunity.

Coercion tends to be more effective in prohibiting clearly defined negative behavior than in motivating positive behaviors. When it is used, Theodore Caplow's tough advice to administrators may be relevant:

What makes a manager feared is the reputation of acting decisively and ruthlessly when the interests of the organization, as he conceives them, are opposed to the interests of the individuals. . . .

The appropriate style is that punitive measures are imposed promptly and confidently, without any visible interest in the excuses of the offender. One or two harsh actions of this kind can make a leader more feared than a whole reign of terror conducted in a more capricious manner.

The best policy to follow in developing a reputation for severity is to make all decisions that involve conflicts between the organization and its members according to fixed principles announced in advance and applied so consistently that each application takes on a didactic character.[5]

Gentle Persuasion

An internalizing approach is to *persuade*, "to cause someone to do something, especially by reasoning, urging, or inducement." The behavior of agents may be changed without coercion by appealing to emotions, values, relationship, facts, or logical argument.

My varied experiences as a church social action leader, a federal poverty program planner, a corporate philanthropy consultant, and a university administrator suggest a common recipe for persuasion in any situation.

1. *Mutual respect.* Accept the "target" agents as honest and sincere despite issue differences. Conversely, earn credibility and respect by your behavior, value base, knowledge, and competence, so that even if they disagree, they trust you personally. Without these prerequisites, the opportunity to persuade rarely occurs.

2. *Rational argument*. People are seldom persuaded by rational argument, but on the other hand, they often are not open to change unless their rationales are dealt with.

The key facts must be presented truthfully and accurately, whatever they may be. (Some persuaders fabricate or slant the facts for greater effect. Apart from ethical questions, this destroys your credibility when the deception is exposed.)

The targets' own values and interests must be related to the behavior sought. In the Church, this included biblical, credal, and theological appeals. In the government, it was usually an economic cost-benefit argument. In the private sector, it involved enlightened self-interest: "doing well by doing good."

3. *An experiential element*. The first two "ingredients" "soften up" the target but rarely change feelings or social behaviors.

In the welfare rights movement, suburban mothers who were given a direct, personal relationship experience with welfare mothers unfailingly discovered that they had similar aspirations for, problems with, and worries about their children. Identifying with the welfare mother, they became active advocates of welfare reform.[6]

When Wilbur Mills was chair of the House Ways and Means Committee, he listened intelligently and openly to advocates for services to mentally retarded children but did not act. Then someone back home in Arkansas persuaded him to visit a state institution for retarded children, where he met them personally, even holding and hugging them. The proposed program was funded soon afterward.

Incentives and Sanctions

A popular middle ground in social policy uses incentives (promised rewards) and sanctions (threatened punishment) that exert external pressure in the desired direction while leaving some degree of free choice to the agent.

Incentives can be purely positive, such as tax deductions that encourage the wealthy to make charitable contributions, with no particular consequence if they do not. When the reward is needed or wanted enough, of course, incentives escalate to the level of an "offer you can't refuse": Work and earn—or go hungry. Practice equal opportunity and get government grants—or forego needed programs. Commit yourself to becoming a navy doctor—or you cannot afford medical school.

Many policies offer an explicit combination of carrot and stick. Said Isaiah to Israel: "Come let us reason together, says the Lord. . . . If you are willing and obedient, you shall eat the good of the land; but if you refuse and rebel, you shall be devoured by the sword."[7] Environmental protection laws threaten polluters with fines should they continue to pollute, but may offer direct or tax welfare subsidies to companies that cooperate.

The organized private sector may use incentives on agents too. When large California growers refused to bargain collectively with their farm workers, church, labor, and civil rights groups united in an effective consumer boycott of the growers' grapes and wine. Profits dropped. When the growers finally agreed to bargain with the workers, they experienced their biggest ever consumption boom.

Incentives are not always tangible. A common human need is the esteem of others. Public recognition and honor by religious organizations, United Ways, civic groups, and professional societies can stimulate a great deal of socially responsible behavior by agents. Conversely, recent candidates for high public office can ruefully confirm the effectiveness of public exposure as a sanction against such disapproved behaviors as slum landlordism, alcohol abuse, and "womanizing."

Enhancement of Agents

A final method of affecting agents is simply to help them. Abusive parents may be dealt with coercively, by separating them from their children or by putting them on probation with threats of punishment. However, for many the most effective intervention may be therapeutic, helping them to do better through counseling, therapy, and education in parenting.

Land grant colleges of agriculture improve farming and conservation practices not so much by persuasion as by offering education and technical assistance to already highly motivated student farmers. Similarly, a NIMH rural mental health grant to my school of social work enabled us to do better what we were already committed to.

SUMMARY

In an imperfect and ever-changing world, social policy changes in the way the society operates are both necessary and inevitable. Change may be fundamental (radical) or corrective (reform).

A major change method is government intervention to create or change the "rules of the game" that govern how the system operates. These changes may further established goals, correct inherent faults, or adapt to changing circumstances.

Another approach to change within the system is to influence agents, the organizations and persons who affect, for better or for worse, the well-being of individual hosts. Agent behavior can be influenced by coercion, persuasion, reward and punishment, and/or enhancement.

NOTES

1. Harold Wilensky and Charles Lebeaux, *Industrial Society and Social Welfare,* 2nd ed. (New York: Free Press, 1965), p. 34.

2. Franklin Pierce, veto message, "An Act Making a Grant of Public Lands to the Several States for the Benefit of Indigent Insane Persons," Washington, May 3, 1854. Reproduced in June Axinn and Herman Levin, *Social Welfare,* 2nd ed. (New York: Harper & Row, 1982), pp. 80–84.

3. Franklin Roosevelt, "Message to Congress Reviewing the Broad Objectives and Accomplishments of the Administration," June 8, 1934; reproduced in National Conference on Social Welfare, *The Report of the Committee on Economic Security of 1935, Fiftieth Anniversary Edition* (Washington, DC: NCSW, 1985), pp. 136, 139.

4. Communist Party of Great Britain, *People before Profits,* 1970, p. 9.

5. Theodore Caplow, *How to Run Any Organization* (Hinsdale, IL: Dryden, 1976), pp. 10–11.

6. See Guida West, *The National Welfare Rights Movement: The Social Protest of Poor Women* (New York: Praeger, 1981).

7. Isaiah 1:18–20.

Chapter 8

Enhancing a System:
The Economy

ENHANCING THE SYSTEM

Reform tends to be problem oriented, following the "medical model" of diagnosis and treatment. *Enhancement*, which seeks to improve the existing system's operation, often focuses on well-being and prevention. Building on Chapter 6, we shall use the economic system to illustrate enhancement.

Authoritarian countries seek to enhance their economies through central planning and control, as in Soviet Five-Year Plans and the Chinese Great Leap Forward. It is not so simple in a free market. How do you steer those millions of separate decisions by individuals and companies in the "right" direction? Under laissez-faire, you do not try, choosing instead to endure the cyclical vicissitudes of the law of supply and demand:

- *inflation*, a rise in prices that reduces purchasing power and undermines confidence in the system of exchange (money)

- *boom*, overresponse to demand by uncoodinated suppliers, creating an oversupply that triggers a production-cutting reaction

- *recession*, a reduction in production, which causes unemployment, reduces profits, increases business failures, and lowers consumption

- *depression*, a deep recession in which the lost buying power due to unemployment and business failures more than offsets the "normal" increase of demand caused by lowered prices, thus obstructing a recovery

The Law of Supply and Demand

Supply is what is for sale. *Demand* is the means and desire to buy. In a free market, the process is a continuous auction, akin to haggling in a Middle Eastern bazaar. Buyers and sellers are each making counteroffers. When the bids of a buyer and a seller agree, they fix a price and the sale is made. Meanwhile, the auction resumes for the next deal.

Price is the regulator that keeps supply and demand in equilibrium. If there are more buyers (demand) than available goods or services (supply), sellers hold out for higher prices. These prices discourage some potential buyers, reducing demand. At the same time, the lure of easy sales and higher profits encourages expanded production. Supply goes up, demand goes down, and balance is restored.

If it is the other way around, and the supply exceeds buyer demand, buyers get choosey. Production is cut to reduce inventory, and sellers compete for the available business by lowering prices. New shoppers, who could not afford the earlier prices or felt they were not worth it, are attracted by the bargains. Supply goes down and demand goes up, restoring balance.

That is how it works in theory. However, it never comes out quite right. There is a time lag between a production decision and the finished product. By the time the product hits the market, the circumstances have changed. Further, determining how much to produce is not a coordinated action but many independent, scattered choices. When there is under-supply, each optimistically hopes to win a larger share of the market from its competitors. Where there is oversupply, worried producers may pessimistically cut back too far. The aggregate result is that the responses tend to overshoot the mark and create a new imbalance in the opposite direction. Thus, a free market experiences a recurring cycle in which inflation and expansion alternate with deflation and recession. Here is how it might apply to home computers.

1. More people want computers. Not enough are available. Demand exceeds supply. This is *shortage*.

2. Prices on available computers rise. This is *inflation*.

3. Responding to the excess of customers and the prospect of high profit margins, current manufacturers increase production and new companies enter the field. Supply increases. This is *expansion*.

4. A year later, the flood of new computers reaches the market. Because production levels are decided by many different manufacturers, each of whom is eager and optimistic, many more are made than there are buyers for. This is a *surplus*, caused by *overproduction*.

5. In order to move their high inventory of computers, companies hold sales, offer rebates and special discounts, or lower the list price. One way or another, the "real" price customers pay for computers drops. This is *deflation*.

6. Lower prices reduce profits. Unsold inventories cause losses. Some companies go broke. Some drop their home computer line. The rest cut back production. All of them lay off workers. This is *recession*.

7. The cutbacks return us to shortage again, and we begin another round.

DEMAND SIDE (KEYNESIAN) INTERVENTIONS

Into this cyclical world came John Maynard Keynes. Responding to the crisis of worldwide postwar depression, he wrote *The End of Laissez-Faire* (1926) in which he came up with the idea of influencing the dynamics of supply and demand. Keynes's point of intervention was demand, on the premise that supply responds to demand: Someone will make what other people are prepared to buy. If more people are buying cars, more cars will be made. If fewer people are buying cars, auto makers will cut back. By manipulating the money supply in certain ways, you can encourage individuals and businesses to make *countercyclical* decisions about buying (demand) and producing (supply): You increase demand to stimulate production during recession; you reduce demand to counter inflation and overexpansion.

An early application of this approach, which appears to have been pragmatic rather than ideological, was Franklin D. Roosevelt's emergency measures in 1933, which gave farmers and laid-off workers money with which to buy necessities, thereby helping business (suppliers) as much as the individual recipients.

Since then, Keynesian economics has been a standard ingredient in the pragmatic capitalism of every Western industrial nation. It appears to have been most effective under relatively free supply-and-demand market conditions. It has been, predictably, less effective in dealing with such anti-free-market factors as wars, monopolies, and mercantilism.

DEMAND

Demand is "the desire to purchase and possess, coupled with the power of purchasing"; that is, it is how much money we are ready, willing, and able to spend right now. It is the product of two factors, "money" times "velocity."

Money

In the United States, the *"M1" money supply*, cash and checking accounts, is a measure of demand because it is immediately available for spending. There are other money supply categories that are not counted as part of demand because they are not considered to be immediately ready for spending. M2 includes M1 plus short-term investments like money market funds and savings accounts. M3 adds long-term investments, like stocks and bonds.

The M1 money supply (and thus demand) increases when money is transferred from M2 and M3 by withdrawing savings or cashing in assets. It also increases when we borrow money to make purchases. This is called putting money into circulation. Printing more money is a form of government borrowing. Read the bills in your wallet. They say "federal reserve [promissory] note."

Some people argue that because lines of credit, including charge cards, are as spendable as cash, they should be included in M1 all along. Officially, however, such promised loans become M1 demand only when the money is actually borrowed.

Money is taken out of circulation when it is invested or saved, thus moving to M2 and M3, or used to repay loans for past purchases.

Velocity

Velocity is turnover, how fast money is spent. Each time the same money is spent, it counts again as demand. Let us use a simple example, following two different $10 salary payments, paid on Monday afternoon by the same company to a worker and an executive.

The first $10 turns over thirteen times in five days.

1. Monday, salary is paid to the worker.
2. Worker pays barber for a haircut on the way home from work.
3. Barber buys groceries on his way home.
4. Tuesday, grocer pays neighborhood baker for homemade bread, which he will sell in his grocery.
5. Baker pays his assistant.
6. Assistant spends it on beer at a local bar after work.
7. Wednesday, bar pays its bartender.
8. Thursday, bartender buys a used table at a garage sale.
9. Seller buys gas for her car.
10. Gas station pays its part-time attendant.
11. Friday, attendant pays rent to his landlord.
12. Landlord pays teenager to mow the lawn after school.
13. Teenager goes to the movies and buys snacks.

Meanwhile, the executive deposits her $10 in a checking account, and on Friday night she writes a check to pay for groceries. That $10 is spent twice, once to her and once to the store.

D = MV

Demand (D) equals the money available for spending (M) times how often it is respent in a given period of time (V). In the above example the first $10 generated $130 of demand ($10 × 13), while the second created only $20 of demand ($10 × 2). To increase demand, you can either increase the money supply or how fast it is respent. To decrease demand, take money out of circulation or slow down its velocity. These factors are influenced by fiscal and/or monetary actions.

FISCAL INTERVENTIONS

The word *fisc* means the government treasury. Fiscal actions involve money going into and out of that treasury (that is, taxing and spending).

Money Supply

Some fiscal interventions affect demand by changing the money supply. Taxes take money out of circulation. Public spending puts it back into circulation. If the two are equal, the money supply stays the same.

The government increases the money supply when it puts more money into circulation through public spending than it takes out of circulation through taxes. This creates a deficit, which is covered by borrowing, which increases the national debt. This is like running up your credit card bill.

The government decreases money supply by running a *surplus*. That is, it takes more out in taxes than it spends. The difference is used to reduce the national debt. This is like paying off more on your Mastercard than you spent with it this month.

Keynesian countercyclical economics call for deficit spending to stimulate demand during a recession by increasing the money supply. In response to inflation and overexpansion, the prescription is a government surplus to "cool" excess demand by reducing the money supply.

Velocity

Fiscal policies may also change velocity. Money is respent more quickly under some circumstances than others. In general, lower-income families spend faster than weathier ones because more of their income must be respent immediately for current living expenses that cannot be deferred. Wages and salaries get respent faster than corporate revenues. Public spending appropriated for short-term purposes, such as military salaries, goes into circulation immediately, while money appropriated for multiyear projects, such as building a new aircraft carrier, trickles out slowly.

In 1981, a change in government fiscal policy reduced the velocity side of demand. Tax cuts for corporations and wealthy investors, combined with Social Security tax increases for low- and middle-income workers, redistributed some of the nation's after-tax income from high-velocity workers to low-velocity upper-income groups. Meanwhile, on the public spending side, expenditures were transferred from welfare benefits (highest velocity of all) and wage-intensive human services to long-term military hardware projects. This fiscal policy coincided with the substantial drop in demand that triggered a severe recession in 1982-83.

If the government had wanted to stimulate the velocity side, it might have curtailed tax shelters and deductions for upper-income taxpayers while raising the standard deduction for working families, and it could have shifted spending to social welfare programs at the expense of long-term space projects.

MONETARY INTERVENTIONS

As noted earlier, private sector *borrowing* also increases the amount of money ready, willing, and able to be spent (M1), and therefore it increases demand. *Repaying* has the reverse effect, taking it back out of circulation, as does *saving*, which moves money to the not-for-immediate-spending M2 and M3 categories.

Monetary policies manipulate the money supply by influencing millions of individual and business decisions about borrowing and saving.

The central bank regulates monetary policy. In the United States this is a semi-autonomous government agency called the Federal Reserve System (the Fed). The Fed acts as the banks' bank for all nationally chartered banks and most large state banks. Banks deposit money for interest with the Fed (by buying treasury bills and notes) and borrow money from it to relend to consumers at a profit. The Fed influences private money supply decisions by adjusting its terms for deposits and loans.

Interest Rates

The most visible monetary intervention is to raise and lower interest rates. High interest rates reduce demand in two ways: (1) increasing the "effective price" (item cost plus interest on loan) of buying on credit and (2) making it profitable for you to save (instead of spending).

If you have a gross monthy income of $2,000 and need a $50,000 mortgage to buy your dream house, the monthly interest alone on an 18 percent mortgage (a 1981 rate), costs you $750 per month, a precarious 38 percent of your $2,000. At 10 percent (a 1990 rate), the *same* mortgage costs only $417 for interest, a conservative 21 percent of your income.

At 6 percent (a 1964 rate), the cost is down to 12.5 percent of income. When the rates come down, sales go up.

The exact same thing happens to capital investment by business. When interest rates are high, smart businesses postpone buying new, improved machinery because they would need greater sales and/or higher prices just to meet the overhead, as compared with the same improvement on a low-interest loan. More than a few farmers went bankrupt in the 1980s because they bought land, tractors, and harvesters when interest rates were high and could not cover the payments when the price of corn went down.

The Fed influences interest rates primarily by setting the *discount rate*, which is the interest it charges the banks. The banks, in turn, must charge you more than that to cover their administrative costs and turn a profit. In 1981, when the Fed was discouraging demand to lower inflation, the discount rate was 14 percent and banks were charging 18-20 percent to their preferred customers (the prime rate). Two years later, needing to stimulate demand to overcome a severe recession, the Fed dropped its discount rate to 8.5 percent, and the banks were charging customers only 10.5 percent.

Reserves

Another Fed control is the reserve it requires in cash and/or deposits as a condition for loaning money to the bank. Like the down payment required for a home mortgage, its original purpose was to protect the lender (the Fed) from any reasonable risk of loss. While this is still a purpose, the reserve requirement may be raised to decrease, and lowered to increase, how much money is available for private sector borrowing.

If the reserve ratio were 10 percent, a bank with a $1 million reserve could borrow $10 million from the Fed to relend to businesses and consumers. If the Fed wanted to reduce demand, it could raise the reserve ratio to 20 percent. Then the bank's $1 million reserve would allow the bank only $5 million to relend. At this point, the bank must drastically curtail new loans and scramble to collect on old loans to get down to the allowed level. This creates a *tight money* situation, in which it is difficult to get a loan, so we put off spending and corporations postpone capital improvements. Anyone in your family who tried to buy or sell a house in 1981, when the Fed was reducing demand to fight inflation, may recall how difficult it was to get a loan at any price.

To stimulate demand, the Fed could reduce the reserve ratio to 5 percent. Now the bank's $1 million reserve would permit it to borrow and relend $20 million instead of $10 million. This creates a *loose money* situation, in which banks try to increase their profit by lending more money. In 1983, when the Fed was stimulating demand to counter a recession, those same banks that turned us down in 1981 had lots of money and were begging us to borrow—and spend.

SUPPLY SIDE ECONOMICS

In the early 1980s, supply-side economics was widely hailed as a replacement for Keynesian demand-side economics. *New York Times* economic columnist Leonard Silk reported that "leading proponents say it is really nothing but classical economics in modern garb."[1] In fact, both are rooted in classical economics supply and demand theory—and both use "artificial" interventions to manipulate it. Keynes argued that suppliers would respond to increased demand. Supply-side economists start on the other side, assuming that if suppliers invest in improved and expanded production, demand will follow.

In 1984, Silk described an American supply-side experiment:

The Economic Recovery Tax Act of 1981 slashed personal income taxes; cut business taxes . . . through accelerated depreciation and higher investment tax credits; made drastic allowances for savings through Individual Retirement Accounts and Keough plans, and reduced the marginal tax rate on capital gains to 20 percent from 28 percent and the marginal tax rates on individual incomes to 50 percent from 70 percent. All this added up to a tax cut of some $750 billion over five years. . . . Mr. Reagan unquestionably began a fiscal revolution in this country. . . .

The "supply-side" tax cuts, according to their advanced billing, were supposed to have stimulated economic growth so much that tax revenues would be thrown off sufficient not only to avoid swelling the budget deficits but actually to shrink them. This simply did not happen. . . . [Instead] they "opened up far bigger deficit gaps than he had inherited from the Carter and earlier administrations."[2]

A look at supply-side premises may help put those interventions and their apparent results in perspective.

Say's Law

Premise. Early in the nineteenth century, Jean Baptiste Say postulated that supply creates its own demand. The act of producing creates a demand by buying labor, supplies, machinery, and energy. This income in turn enables the workers and suppliers to buy what is produced. Put simply, employed auto workers can afford to buy cars.

Limitations. The recirculation is continuous—provided the product is sold. In 1981, while supply-side fiscal policies were encouraging new investment and production, monetary and social policies took buying power away from middle- and lower-class consumers. Without a market for new production, the circle was broken, Say's Law did not operate, and a recession occurred. On the other hand, supply-side economics *did* work in the 1930s (aid to banks and industries) and 1960s (upper-income and corporate tax cuts), when they coincided with social programs that increased low- and middle-income buying power at the same time.

Lesson. Supply-side economics may be effective as a partner with, rather than an alternative to, demand-side economics.

Pareto's Law and the Trickle Down Theory

Premise. In 1897, Vilfredo Pareto said that the distribution of income is essentially the same everywhere. Inequality is constant. When business and investors prosper, the benefits will trickle down proportionately to the middle and lower classes.

Limitations. This did not occur in the 1980s. The rich got richer and the poor got poorer. In comparative income, over that decade the top 1/5 income went from seven to ten times the income of the bottom 1/5 of the population. According to a news analysis of Census Bureau data:

In the 1980s, fast becoming a contrast between an economic recovery and a resurgence of poverty . . . the "new poor"—married couples with children, working families, young adults—have fallen below the poverty line in droves for the first time in recent history. Overall, since 1979, poverty has increased by 41%. That's the biggest, longest-lasting rise since poverty rates were first calculated, in 1959. Subsequent economic recovery made an unimpressive dent.

As a result, 8.4 million people have become poor. That's equal to the combined population of Oregon, Nebraska, Connecticut, and Maine. It virtually wipes out progress during President Johnson's "War on Poverty" and 20 years of rising social welfare spending.[3]

Lesson. If the intent is indeed to benefit all segments of society, supply-side economics may have to be supplemented by specific distributive social policies.

The Postulate of Rationality

Premise. According to the natural law theory of classical economics, businesses and individuals will pursue their self-interest in a way that optimizes the economic and social orders.

Limitations. In the 1980s, beneficiaries of the 1981 supply-side tax subsidies did pursue their self-interest rationally—maximizing their wealth and profit as they were expected to do—but in ways that did not achieve the assumed beneficial social and economic effects.

According to a study by Citizens for Tax Justice, a tax-reform organization, corporate-tax savings written into the 1981 tax law have not, contrary to Administration predictions, stimulated major new investments in plant and equipment by the companies who most fully enjoyed these breaks. . . . The 44 lowest taxed companies reduced their investments and payrolls, while the 43 highest taxed firms increased their plant outlays and their payrolls.

That reversal of the Reagan script should cause no surprise. For one thing, decisions on plant and job expansion are governed far more by market prospects than by taxes. For another, the tax law does not require a company to spend on new plant and equipment the money it saves from, say, highly favorable laws governing the write-off of old plant and equipment. A firm can spend its savings as it pleases: to give its executives a raise; to increase dividends to share-holders; to buy out another company. . . .

The 44 companies that paid no tax on their $57 billion of profits during the first Reagan term enjoyed an 11-percent increase in pre-tax profits. At the same time, capital investments by those 44 tax-free companies declined by 4 percent and their payrolls shrank by 6 percent. . . .

In 1980, corporations spent $44 billion buying out other companies. By 1984, the figure had tripled, and in 1985 it leaped to an estimated $180 billion. Such a buying mania hardly suggests that corporate America is cash-poor, requiring subsidies for new plant outlays.[4]

Lesson. Since supply-side subsidies benefit the economy only when they are used to improve and/or expand production, they should be applied selectively within a larger strategy. The U.S. approach gave unrestricted tax subsidies. Japan has had dramatic success in providing restricted subsidies, loans, and technical assistance, to industries targeted for special development. Perhaps more supply-side subsidies should be in kind rather than in cash. Government financed space research and alternative energy experiments have spun off knowledge and technology free to private enterprise. Research and technical assistance from land grant universities do the same for farmers.

LIMITATIONS ON ANY SUPPLY-AND-DEMAND STRATEGY

Political Expedience

"Virtue is its own reward." It had better be, for there may be no other reward for statesmanship. Politicians must stand for reelection every two, four, or at most six years. They are dependent on campaign contributions from wealthy donors, organized labor, and other vested interests, and they must be careful not to offend the majority of voters. Practical politicians, in the spirit of Neville Chamberlain's concessions to Hitler to achieve "peace in our time," find it expedient to please their most powerful supporters, focus on short-term appearances, and cater to popularity. It is not just a matter of individual ethics and vision. It is our system. President Kennedy's *Profiles in Courage* is about senators who submitted to abuse and rejection for the sake of moral principle, disinterested statesmanship, and broad, long-range societal interest. He found seven in 180 years!

Both demand- and supply-side interventions have a popular and an unpopular side. Keynesian economics calls for interventions to increase demand during recessions *and* to decrease it during periods of inflation and expansion. Increases are popular. They involve cutting taxes, expanding benefits to millions of citizens, fat defense and construction contracts, and easy credit with low interest rates.

The austerity appropriate to "up" times is, to say the least, somewhat less popular: higher taxes, fewer benefits, cutbacks in military and public works spending, tight credit, and high interest. If politicians are human, they will be tempted to do only the popular half of the job. If so, the result over time will probably be inflation, deficits, and an ever-increasing national debt. This is not necessarily the fault of Keynesian doctrine. It is a failure to follow it.

Similarly, supply-side economics calls for benefits to corporations and the wealthy, which they will use for socially beneficial investments. Given the ethos of capitalism and the realities of human nature, such benefits without careful restrictions and conditions cannot reasonably be expected to be used for society's best interests when other choices, such as corporate raiding, are more profitable.

Naturally, large campaign contributors and other powerful interests want unconditional supply-side benefits with no strings attached. Would you not want the same in their place? Supply-side politicians who need their support may, like their Keynesian counterparts, give the expedient half and avoid the unwelcome restrictions.

Cost-Push Inflation and Stagflation

In the law of supply and demand, there is *demand-pull* inflation. When there is a shortage, buyers will compete for the scarce item by offering higher prices. That is, demand pulls the price up. A dramatic example of this is what happens to the street price of cocaine when drug agents make a big bust that temporarily cuts off the supply.

According to the "law," when there are fewer buyers than there are cars for sale, smart buyers bargain hard as dealers compete to clear their crowded showrooms. Inflation cannot occur when there is an oversupply and weak demand—but during the 1970s, it did!

Faced with increased production costs beyond their control, suppliers *had* to raise prices. This was *cost-push* inflation. It had a predictable effect on sales. As prices went up, more and more people had to to revert to that World War II advertising jingle:

> There's a Ford in your future,
>> But the Ford in your past
> Is the Ford you have now,
>> So you'd better make it last!

As sales dropped, companies produced fewer cars; but pushed by costs, they raised prices again. Sales dropped more. Workers were laid off, further reducing demand, but not prices. Thus we had *stag*nation and *inflation* at the same time. We called it *stagflation*.

Traditional countercyclical responses did not work. Stimulating demand accelerated the inflation, while cooling demand deepened the recession. They were damned if they did, and damned if they did not.

Monopolistic Causes of Stagflation

How did this occur? *Somebody repealed the law of supply and demand.* Stagflation can occur in a market that has been subverted by the centralized private command discussed in Chapter 6. In the 1970s case, we can identify

- *Cartels.* Energy is a major cost in nearly all production. Controlling a majority of the world's oil production, OPEC unilaterally dictated a ninefold increase in the price of energy. This created the cost-push stagflation sequence described above. (When the cartel weakened in the early 1980s, stagflation diminished.)
- *Oligopolies.* Chapter 6 described how industries with a few big corporations and industrywide unions collaborate de facto in passing along parallel cost increases through parallel price increases. With nowhere else to turn, sales were down, but the remaining buyers had to pay the price or do without. (When foreign suppliers moved into the market, the oligopoly was broken and price competition was restored.)
- *Cost-plus regulation.* In regulated industries such as public utilities, transportation, and hospitals, cost-plus rate setting institutionalized inflation. The government approved rates (prices) based on the audited cost of production—plus a "fair" profit. Absence of competition minimized incentives to search for more efficient, less costly methods of production.

Alternatives

Where supply-and-demand interventions are ineffective due to the lack of price competition among suppliers, there are three choices:

1. *Restoration of free-market competition.* Deregulate, break up monopolies, and lower international trade barriers.
2. *Stronger central control.* In the absence of competition, establish "just price" controls on the finished product and on production costs, including wages.

3. *Laissez-faire*. Let the chips fall where they may and assume things will work out "for the best." Best for whom?

SUMMARY

Some macro social policies are intended to change the system. Others aim to maintain and enhance what is. One of the most far-reaching of the latter is intervention aimed at improving the functioning of the law of supply and demand.

Supply is what is available for sale. Demand is the ability and desire to buy. According to theory, supply and demand are kept in equilibrium by millions of separate buyer and seller decisions. The mechanism in a free market is negotiated pricing. Lower prices due to oversupply discourage production and encourage more buying. Higher prices due to undersupply encourage more production and discourage buying.

In practice, for various reasons, the system tends to overshoot a perfect balance, alternating between shortage-inflation-expansion and over-supply-deflation-recession. Keynesian economics lessens the extremes of these cycles by increasing demand during recessions and reducing it during inflation.

The primary method is to increase and decrease the money supply. In the fiscal approach, government spends more than it takes out of circulation through taxes to increase demand and does the opposite to decrease it. The monetary approach manipulates private sector behavior by making loans easier and cheaper to increase demand, and tighter and more costly to deter spending.

A secondary method is to influence velocity. Money that goes to the poor, to wage earners, and for labor-intensive services turns over faster, increasing demand. Money that goes to corporations, to wealthy families, and for long-term material projects is spent more slowly, lowering demand.

Supply-side economics seeks to expand the economy by giving benefits to those whose wise capital investments will increase production and create new jobs, which in turn mean more buying power for consumers. This is the trickle-down approach. It appears to work when carefully targeted and joined with policies that increase demand for the expanded production.

Both methods are frequently subverted by narrow interests, short-sightedness, and political expedience. They also tend to be ineffective to the extent that monopolies and/or other central control has eliminated the competitive free-market environment on which these methods are based.

NOTES

1. Leonard Silk, "Classical Laws Debated Anew," *New York Times*, December 23, 1983.

2. Silk, "Reagan's Shift on the Deficits," *New York Times*, February 1, 1984.

3. Thomas Moore, "Poverty Taints '80's Recovery," *Miami Herald*, January 20, 1986.

4. Philip Stern, "Big Business Is Subsidized," *New York Times*, March 19, 1986.

Chapter 9

The Welfare State

Sometimes it seems as if the welfare state is nobody's friend. It is damned for being too much or too little, too radical or too conservative. From one perspective it is "socialist" because it increases public intervention. From another, it is "a kind of ambulance service for capitalism"[1] that ameliorates without curing social costs of capitalism and the Industrial Revolution.

In another sense, it is everybody's friend. The dictionary calls it "a state in which the welfare of its citizens, with regard to employment, medical care, social security, etc. is considered to be the responsibility of government."

THE ECONOMIC MARKET AND THE SOCIAL MARKET

The *economic market* is the sum total of self-interested individual choices. The economic market approach to social welfare expects you to buy medical care, daycare, or psychotherapy instead of something else if you want it enough. If you do, human services providers will emerge in response to the profit opportunity. If you do not, why should anyone give it to you?

As a social welfare policy, this assumes three things: (1) You *know* what you need and have the sense to get it. (2) You can *afford* to buy it. (3) You are competent to *evaluate* providers and their products.

Unfortunately, this is not always the case. Young children, Alzheimer's disease patients, and unconscious accident victims may not be competent to decide. Tens of millions of Americans do not have enough to live on, let alone the extra income that enables them to choose between psychotherapy and a BMW. Few of us on our own can reliably judge doctors, marriage counselors, or hospitals in advance.

Social market approaches address these economic market deficiencies. Robert Pinker explains the difference this way:

In the *economic market* the criterion is one of utility, or price; in the *social market* the criterion is one of need. . . .

Within the *economic market* there is discrimination between like cases of need in terms of price. Those with an equal ability to pay can enjoy equality of provision. Within the *social market* the allocation of welfare provision is governed by the principle that like cases of need should be treated in a like manner (emphasis added).[2]

In pragmatic capitalism, the welfare state is a social market mechanism to fill well-being gaps while maintaining the basic economic market system. It is no more nor less than a collection of compensatory programs such as pensions, unemployment insurance, health care, public assistance, housing aid, and child care.

DISWELFARES AND THE ECONOMIC MARKET

In the normal circumstances of life, we may suffer harm that is completely or partially beyond our control to avoid. In economics this is called a *loss*; in social policy, a *diswelfare*. If it is caused by someone else or society as a whole, it is a *disservice*. Within the economic market, in order to obtain compensation for disservices, you must

- prove specific damage
- establish its dollar value
- prove specific parties to be responsible
- prove they were negligent
- prove you did not contribute to the loss yourself
- be willing and able to engage in adversary litigation
- not be outmaneuvered by an opposing lawyer.

Disservices Caused by Society

Many disservices cannot be compensated through the lawsuit system because they are within the normal operation of society. In a recent lawsuit, for example, the court found that the victim had indeed suffered disability and premature death caused by smoking cigarettes that the manufacturer knew full well were life-threatening. However, the tobacco company was held "not responsible" because making, advertising, and selling cigarettes are legal and normal in our society. Air pollution and resulting acid rain reduce your bushels of corn per acre, deteriorate your house, and aggravate your sinusitis. We all know their causes, but there are literally millions of industrial and auto-driving culprits, including you and me.

There is no place to turn for relief within the economic market system. Someone, somewhere, *is* at fault, but you cannot take us all to court, and you cannot prove that *one* of us specifically did it to *you*.

No-Fault Diswelfares

A similar problem exists when you suffer "acts of God" that seem to be nobody's fault, such as when a hailstorm destroys your wheat crop, a flood ravages your home, arthritis destroys your ability to work as a watch repairer, or a family wage earner dies of cancer.

Even our normal life cycle creates no-fault needs. Child rearing puts an extra financial burden on young families. In old age, earning power diminishes and medical needs increase.

Other Needs

What happens if you do have a legal right to damages from a clearly responsible party, but the company whose negligence damaged you has gone bankrupt, or the armed robber who crippled you is now a penniless jailbird?

What if it is your own fault that you became paraplegic in a drunk driving accident or developed emphysema from heavy smoking? The consequences are no less grim because you were unwise.

"Let the Loss Lie Where It Falls"

In all of these situations, the classical economics response is "let the loss lie where it falls" (and hope it does not happen to fall on you). "That's the way the cookie crumbles!" This is also called benign neglect.

WELFARE STATE OBJECTIVES

By the second half of the twentieth century, every industrial nation in the world had a package of welfare state programs to supplement the economic system. In 1988 Robert Morris, introducing a review of social policy in nine countries around the world, summarized this development:

Between 1950 and 1975, the major industrial nations pursued, with some national variability, a course of enlarging social programs to improve and to make more equitable the living conditions of all citizens. Conceptually, the welfare state, or a group of social programs, was seen as either a corrective or an amelioration for unevenness in the private economic world. . . .

Most governments have continued their commitments to the welfare of their citizens by retaining three purposes for [the welfare state]: the preservation of national stability and national community viability; equity in the use of national resources, including narrowing the gap between better- and worse-off citizens; and preference for work and more full employment as the best means for underwriting personal dignity and pluralistic choice.[3]

Welfare state objectives fall into two categories, well-being for individual citizens and collective societal interests. According to whom you talk to, these are complementary or conflicting.

Individual Benefit Objectives

One purpose of giving benefits to individuals is to achieve *adequacy* for all of its members. The welfare state may seek to assure a minimum standard of nutrition, housing, health care, and education. Our society, if it chose, could eliminate poverty entirely, as we define it today.

Another purpose is *equity*. If equity means getting what you deserve, a logical extension of the concept is not getting stuck with what you do not deserve. Said Richard Titmuss:

Services in kind and in cash . . . may represent not a benefit at all but a compensation for disservices caused by society and especially those disservices (or social costs) where the causal agent, or agents, cannot be identified, legally held responsible, and charged with the costs. When one examines in detail the social consequences in modern society of technological, industrial, economic and other processes of change it is evident that the problem of compensation is an immense one, and immensely complex.

Unless the social costs of these disservices are to lie where they fall (as they did in nineteenth century Britain and as they do to a large extent in the United States today) then we have to find ways and means of compensating people without stigma.[4]

Welfare state objectives often include *temporal and horizontal equality*. As noted in an earlier chapter, retirement pensions and family allowances are intended to equalize a person's standard of living over his or her lifetime, whereas unemployment, disability, and health insurances even out unpredictable risks among members of a group.

Because unemployed, retired, disabled, orphaned, and chronically ill beneficiaries usually have lower private income than the average taxpayer, a byproduct of welfare state benefits is to reduce overall (vertical) inequality. In the United States from 1933 to 1980 (but not thereafter), social market redistributions were just sufficient to offset the increase of pretax inequality occurring in the private sector.

Perhaps the most important objective of the welfare state is *security*, not only material but also psychological, knowing that these benefits are available if and when they are needed. A worker, for instance, may look forward to retirement with pleasant anticipation instead of fear.

Collective Interests and Social Control

Benjamin Disraeli, later to be prime minister of England, described current social conditions in an 1845 political novel:

Said Egremont, slightly smiling, "but say what you like, our Queen reigns over the greatest nation that ever existed."
"Which nation?" asked the younger stranger, "for she reigns over two."
The stranger paused; Egremont was silent, but looked inquiringly.
"Yes," resumed the younger stranger, "Two nations; between whom there is no intercourse and no sympathy; who are as ignorant of each other's habits, thoughts, and feelings, as if they were dwellers in different zones, or inhabitants of different planets; who are formed by a different breeding, are fed by a different food, are ordered by different manners, and are not governed by the same laws."
"You speak of . . . " said Egremont hesitantly.
"The rich and the poor."[5]

To Joseph Townsend, a contemporary of Adam Smith, this was good social policy:

When hunger is either felt or feared, the desire of obtaining bread will quietly dispose the mind to undergo the greatest hardships, and will sweeten the severest labours.[6]

Some critics accuse welfare state programs of subverting capitalism by weakening this "work or starve" social control.

A more common Establishment response to poverty, inequality, unfair disservices, and insecurity is pragmatic. Disraeli's dual society is a potential breeding ground for rebellion and revolution. By softening these sources of alienation and class conflict, the welfare state improves social integration and protects the status quo. Indeed, Morris reports that this is a primary rationale for the welfare state:

Stability in society is a recurrent theme; the differences among countries, other than in language are in the means to be employed to sustain such stability. The idea of a welfare state has popularly been treated as if it were an end in itself, but in actuality governments seem much more concerned with the production of welfare for their citizens by any means in order to preserve national stability. The welfare state is more reactive than proactive.[7]

Social justice advocates may oppose at least parts of the welfare state for this very reason:

As the uncritical servants of capitalist society, [social services] repair some of the ravages of the system, divert revolutionary ardor, and ingratiate the working class into the Welfare State. Instead of helping and being part of a wholesale reconstruction of society, they help to keep an outmoded contraption from falling apart.[8]

Frances Piven and Richard Cloward's classic critique of public welfare, *Regulating the Poor*, goes further and charges that some welfare programs are deliberate instruments of oppression.

This book is about relief-giving and its uses in regulating the political and economic behavior of the poor. . . .

Historical evidence suggests that relief arrangements are initiated or expanded during the occasional outbreaks of civil disorder produced by mass unemployment, and are then abolished or contracted when political stability is restored. We shall argue that expansive relief policies are designed to mute civil disorder and restrictive ones to reinforce work norms. In other words, relief policies are cyclical—liberal or restrictive depending on the problems of regulation in the larger society with which the government must contend.[9]

Even though a welfare state program serves individuals (hosts), its primary objective may be to benefit the collective economy. Although often obscured by altruistic rhetoric and fuzzy thinking, you can tell the tree by its fruits: If a program is evaluated by *cost-benefit* analysis (economic payoff to society), its objective is collective.

Mary Switzer, long-time head of vocational rehabilitation, gained her strong congressional support by stressing the dollar payoff from restoring disabled workers to economic productiveness. In this instance, collective and individual benefit coincided. Friedrich von Hayek, on the other hand, bluntly subordinated humanitarian interests to the collective economy:

It may seem harsh, but it is in the interests of all that, under a free system [of national health care], those with full earning capacity should often be rapidly cured of a temporary and not dangerous disablement at the expense of some neglect of the aged and mortally ill. Where systems of State medicine operate, we generally find that those who could be promptly restored to full activity have to wait for long periods because all the hospital facilities are taken up by people who will never again contribute to the [economic] needs of the rest.[10]

The ultimate collective social welfare policy was Jonathan Swift's satirical *Modest Proposal for Preventing the Children of Poor People in Ireland from Being a Burden to Their Parents or Country, and for Making Them Beneficial to the Public* (1729). He suggested that poor Irish families sell their year-old babies to the English to eat as a gourmet treat, thereby solving Ireland's dual problems of overpopulation and poverty, as well as improving the quality of life for English aristocrats.

HOW MUCH WELFARE STATE CAN SOCIETY AFFORD?

Even if we agree (which some do not) that (1) we share social responsibility for each other, and (2) government is a proper instrument to perform those social functions that are inadequately met by other institutions of the society, there is still a matter of how much caring we can afford.

The Pessimistic View

A traditional belief is that welfare state programs depress the economy. In 1983, Neil Gilbert, author of popular social policy texts, warned:

How much social welfare can society afford? . . . The welfare state is nonproductive. Social welfare provisions [may be] investments in human resources which are conducive to economic growth. But these welfare provisions are created and sustained by surplus produced in the market economy. This dependence on economic surplus places a practical limit on the size of the welfare state. Since the 1960s the American welfare state has been approaching this limit; some might say it has been crossed.[11]

If Gilbert is correct, how do we explain the European experience? In 1983, total United States federal, state, and local public social welfare expenditures (such as social security, public aid, health, veterans' programs, education, housing, institutional care, nutrition, and child welfare) added up to 19 percent of the Gross National Product (GNP). The same year, it was 33 percent in Germany, and above that in Belgium, Netherlands, Denmark, France, and Sweden.[12] Most of them had higher economic growth rates over the previous quarter century than the United States and had surpassed us in nearly every health statistic from the cradle (infant mortality) to the grave (longevity). Perhaps we should examine the premises more closely.

The Effect of Redistribution

Gilbert calls the welfare state, which transfers money from one person to another via taxation and social welfare benefits, nonproductive. This is technically correct but should *not* be misconstrued as meaning counter-productive. It is essentially a *neutral internal process* within the aggregate (collective) economy. It changes who spends the money but not how much money is available to be spent.

Economists argue that redistribution may have some marginal effects. On the average, it moves some money from middle- and upper-income groups to lower-income persons. Supply-side economists argue that this depresses the economy by reducing the pool of money potentially available for capital investment in favor of consumption by lower-income groups. Keynesian economists counter that the transferred money stimulates demand, for it is nearly all spent quickly (high velocity) for needed consumer goods. This in turn means higher sales and profits for business, thereby making further capital investment attractive and pro-fitable. They point out that a great deal of business investment comes from retained corporate earnings and borrowing against future earnings, both of which are enhanced by the stimulation of demand. Who is right? Perhaps a little of each, more or less offsetting each other?

Using Surplus Productive Capacity

The traditional definition of economic surplus is that which is produced over and above basic necessities. That surplus may be used in any of three categories:

1. *discretionary consumption goods*, such as videos and vacation homes.
2. *services* that contribute to quality of life, such as entertainment, education, and therapy.
3. *nonconsumption goods*, such as nuclear missiles. (At least we *hope* they will never be "consumed"!)

Due to technological advances, most U.S. production is in surplus categories. In 1985, manufacture of all goods, including discretionary and nonconsumption goods, accounted for only 20 percent of the GNP. Nearly 3/4 of all jobs were service producing. Social welfare benefits and ser-vices are choices in competition with luxuries, entertainment, military hardware, and all other possible uses of surplus productive capacity. Although the choices may be socially significant, it matters little to the aggregate economy whether meals and maid service are provided in a luxury resort or in a nursing home, or whether one buys the "product" of a psychologist or a rock singer.

The key elements in making the choice, then, are not macroeconomic but ethical and social. All consumption of goods and services, whether distributed through the economic market or the social market, have economic *utility*, "the power to satisfy the needs and wants of humanity," because they contribute to someone's perceived needs and wants.

- What *purposes* are better than others? Is a sports car for Dad as desirable as a year of college for Sis? Is health care as important as military strength?
- What uses are *effective* in achieving their purposes? Does a college education increase your earnings? Does cocaine make you happy?
- *Who* should get what, and why? To what extent should amenities be unequal due to merit? or aggressiveness? or luck? or inheritance?
- Who says so?

On the other hand, it appears that *nonconsumption* goods absorb resources without providing utility. This may explain why the average standard of living went up faster among our allies than in the United States. In his nine-nation study (which included Japan, Yugoslavia, and Israel in addition to the European democracies) Morris observed:

Except for the United States, where pressure to expand military expenditures are greatest, expenditures for defense represent a relatively small part of the GNP. . . . A marked diminution in international tensions could lead to a relaxation of pressure and a freeing up of more options for welfare.[13]

Morris made an oversight. There was one other nation in his study with a high military budget, Israel. It also had the lowest lower percentage of GNP for social welfare—and its economy was less prosperous than any of the others except Communist Yugoslavia. Although redistribution and human services, whatever their social pros and cons, have not turned out to correlate negatively with economic success, nonconsumption expenditures have. Premier Gorbachev thought so when he responded to a domestic economic crisis with disarmament proposals.

Stability and Inflation

A recurring problem of capitalism has been cyclical swings in supply and demand. During recessions, income goes down due to unemployment and reduced wages. This, in turn, reduces demand, which can worsen the recession by causing further cutbacks in production and employment.

Two kinds of welfare state programs stabilize the economy. Pensions, health care, and public education are *cycle proof*, remaining relatively constant during good times and bad. If you remove a major demand sector from economic swings, both the ups and the downs are moderated. A second set of benefits, such as unemployment insurance and food stamps, are *countercyclical*, increasing demand during recessions and decreasing in "good" times.

The welfare state has been accused of causing fiscal deficits and inflation. "It ain't necessarily so." Internal redistribution and substitution of one production-consumption choice for another are theoretically neutral, except for the countercyclical effects just mentioned.

And so it would be were it not for the human factor. If the government spends—whether for welfare or warfare—without offsetting taxes, inflationary deficits occur. You can have universal health service, daycare, and adequate welfare without inflation—so long as you raise taxes accordingly. Of course, what you *will* get is unhappy upper-income taxpayers who lose more than they gain on the transaction. For them—and politicians whom they vote out of office—the welfare state *is* depressing!

Work Incentive

The nineteenth-century principle of "less eligibility" assumed that people work only out of financial necessity. Modern believers have warned that improved social benefits will create a labor shortage because people will not work. This has not happened in any existing welfare state. Why not?

To begin with, the economic motive for work extends beyond subsistence. Work patterns in both the United States and Marxist countries suggest that most people want more than minimum adequacy and will work for it, as witnessed by the frequency of moonlighting, multiple-earner families, part-time work by retirees, and other efforts to supplement base incomes.

Second, "man does not live by bread alone," according to Deuteronomy 8.3. Work motivation is not just economic. Our jobs—or having none—make a big difference in how others view us and how we feel about ourselves. A millionaire heiress whom I know derives her primary identity from a job as a fashion buyer that contributes less than 10 percent of her total income. The will to work can be even stronger than that. I have worked personally with many former and potential welfare mothers who chose employment over relief even when doing so cost them net income and health benefits.

There is another social policy side to work incentive. Labor surplus, not shortage, is a chronic problem in most free-market economies. Varying with the economic cycles, there are between 8 million and 15 million unemployed Americans seeking work at any given moment, plus an equal number of "discouraged workers" such as youths and housewives who would seek work if they thought they could find a decent job. Our largest welfare state program, Social Security, combats this with an intentional work disincentive. To make room for younger workers, it confiscates benefits that older workers have already earned if they refuse to quit.

IDEOLOGY AND THE WELFARE STATE

The Real Issue: What Do We Choose to Afford?

How much welfare state can this society afford? There is sufficient surplus production to support far more social welfare than we have. The real question is: How do we choose to use that surplus? It is a matter of *social choices*. Social welfare is not a free bonus. It is a discretionary spending choice. Providing basic necessities for the poor reduces the net income taxpayers can spend on themselves. Social security pensions of retirees come out of the pockets of younger workers (who hope that in turn the next generation will pay for their pensions). Money spent for medical services is not available for movies, Mercedes, or MacDonalds.

Few Americans who are fortunate enough to have above-average incomes would accept pure equality. Yet few are so hard-hearted as to openly turn their backs on fellow citizens whom they personally know to be hurting. But where do we draw the line in between?

The answers come from our ideologies. What are our social values and beliefs? Do people have a right to a minimum standard of living? If so, at what economic and quality-of-life level? Are such rights absolute or conditional on certain behaviors?

Does society have a social responsibility to assure adequacy, security, and/or limits to inequality? If so, to what extent can they be achieved by purely voluntary charity and/or self-regulation? Should the government intervene in the original distribution, through regulation of wages, collective bargaining rights, and business practices? Should it redistribute by means of taxation and welfare state benefits after the economic market has found its "natural" level?

What are our individual interests? What social welfare benefits do *you* want? How much tax are *you* willing to pay? How do *you* personally gain or lose?

What are our beliefs about human nature? Are people lazy sinners who work only to survive—or do they work better if they already have adequate nutrition, health, security, and self-esteem? To what extent are people motivated by greed? social approval? self-fulfillment? altruism?

There are many ideological variations regarding the welfare state. Six somewhat simplified representative positions about a welfare state or its alternatives are listed below.

American Conservatives

The conservative position mixes individualism, free enterprise, the work ethic, and negative freedom, all in tension with an ambivalent humanitarianism. David Gil describes the result:

Conservatives believe, in spite of contrary evidence, that under the prevailing capitalist order everyone could provide for his own needs through work, savings, investments, and acquisition of property. They consider people who fail to do so unfit, lazy, and inferior, and hence deserving of blame rather than entitled to help from the government and honest, hardworking taxpayers. . . .

Policies derived from this position involve either "benign neglect" or measures to promote adjustment of individuals to prevailing realities, rather than adjustment of the social and economic order to the needs of people. Conservative policies will often also reflect authoritarian and punitive tendencies, and elements of crisis response, rather than prevention. Finally, conservatives prefer voluntary charitable aid to government programs.[14]

The welfare state of American conservatives includes tax welfare incentives, equity-based social insurances, general opportunity programs like public education, and minimal safety nets guarded by strict eligibility criteria.

American Liberals

The American liberal position reflects social justice and humanitarian liberalism in tension with the negative freedom of classical liberalism.

Liberalism now suggests . . . a fair, sympathetic, and humanistic attitude toward deprived population groups, and support for comprehensive government action to alleviate suffering and deprivation . . . [including] a wide range of health, education, and welfare services as well as transfers of purchasing power to population segments that fail to secure these services and a minimal income through conventional market mechanisms.

Liberals, during this century, have gradually come to acknowledge the roots of poverty and other social and economic problems in the unequal distribution of wealth and income. However, in spite of such understanding, liberals usually do not suggest strategies to overcome the social-structure roots of these problems. They tend to promote instead reforms aimed at ameliorating the symptoms through government-administered social services and financial assistance to those directly affected.[15]

The welfare state of American liberals, who are ambivalent toward centralized power, is a pragmatic, piecemeal, sometimes inconsistent set of social insurances, needs-based adequacy programs, and services to enhance individual opportunity, social adjustment, and rehabilitation. They often include an element of decentralization to states, localities, and the private sector.

European Labor Parties

European socialist labor parties had their origins in working-class experiences of economic oppression, from which government interventions partially liberated them. Their welfare state model tends to be less individualistic, more security-oriented, and supportive of comprehensive national programs.

Welfare Capitalism

In Japan, consistent with its tradition of paternalism and mutual obligation between employers and workers, benefits provided by the welfare state in other societies are often provided instead by employers, with the government providing residual public benefits for those who fall between the cracks. Corporate leaders prefer this approach because they believe it reduces administrative costs, avoids the dangers of big government, and reinforces employee loyalty. However, even Japan has found itself steadily expanding its public social programs.

Communism

In theory, because the centrally controlled economy is supposed to prevent or correct diswelfares, it does not recognize the need for a welfare state. As part of the general control, a number of services are provided either universally, such as health and general education, or selectively on merit, such as higher education and retirement pensions. Specific individual needs may go officially unrecognized and unmet.

Laissez-Faire

A number of ideologies do not believe in either a welfare state or its alternatives. "Pure" classical capitalism takes the position that the collective welfare is best served in the long run by letting the "natural" system operate without "artificial" interventions.

Radical anarchism and utopian Marxism believed that in a truly communal society, selfishness will have been replaced by a mutuality that makes governmental regulation or provision unnecessary.

A harsher ideology, as exemplified in such philosophies as Social Darwinism, believes the victims of diswelfares *should* suffer and/or die unaided.

Although they are alive and well in some circles, these extreme laissez-faire approaches are essentially nineteenth-century ideologies that are not the actual policy of any major nation today.

SUMMARY

The economic market of capitalism has no provision for mutual assistance to deal with diswelfares individuals experience, whether caused by the social and economic system, irresponsible actions of others, bad luck, the normal life cycle, or one's own imprudence.

The welfare state is a social market device to fill some of these gaps. It is a collection of public insurances, services, and financial aid that offer some degree of adequacy, equity, and security to all citizens. In the process, it moderates the inequality that is part of every private enterprise system and contributes to political and economic stability in the overall society.

It has been argued that welfare state programs depress the economy and that the United States has reached or exceeded the limit of what it can afford. However, several European democracies that spend up to twice as high a percentage of their GNP on social welfare (but devote much less to military expenditures) have outperformed the United States on economic and individual well-being measures over the past twenty-five years.

Only about 1/4 of the U.S. economy is devoted to producing basic material necessities. How the remaining, surplus productive capacity is used is a social choice in which human services compete with optional consumer goods, pleasure and convenience services, and nonconsumption goods such as military hardware. The net effect on the aggregate economy of such internal distribution choices is marginal. However, since these are choices for one set of goods and services instead of another, and for one individual's gain at the expense of another (as are private sector choices as well) the individual and social effects of social welfare choices, whether made actively or by default, can be significant and controversial.

NOTES

1. Peter Townsend, *Sociology and Social Policy* (London: Allen Lane, 1975), p. 28.

2. Robert Pinker, *The Idea of Welfare* (London: Heinemann, 1979), p. 224.

3. Robert Morris, *Testing the Limits of Social Welfare* (Hanover, NH: University Press of New England, 1988), pp. 1, 3.

4. Richard Titmuss, *Commitment to Welfare*, 2nd ed. (London: George Allen & Unwin, 1976), p. 117.

5. Benjamin Disraeli, *Sybil*, 1845. Quoted in Karl de Schweinitz, *England's Road to Social Security* (New York: A. S. Barnes, 1961), p. 128.

6. Joseph Townsend, *A Dissertation on the Poor Laws by a Well-Wisher to Mankind*, 1786 (Berkeley: University of California Press 1971), p. 28.

7. Morris, *Testing the Limits of Social Welfare*, p. 7.

8. Townsend, *Sociology and Social Policy*, p. 28.

9. Frances Piven and Richard Cloward, *Regulating the Poor* (New York: Pantheon, 1971), p. xiii.

10. Friedrich von Hayek, *The Constitution of Liberty* (London: Routledge & Kegan Paul, 1960), pp. 299–300.

11. Neil Gilbert, *Capitalism and the Welfare State* (New Haven, CT: Yale University Press, 1983), p. 139.

12. Morris, *Testing the Limits of Social Welfare*, statistics located throughout the book.

13. Ibid., p. 14.

14. David Gil, *Unraveling Social Policy* (Cambridge, MA: Schenkman, 1976), pp. 151–52.

15. Ibid. pp. 150–51.

Chapter 10

Kinds of Benefits

A *benefit* is "anything that is good for a person." It may be a service ("helpful activity") or material aid.

Let us assume that you want to provide "appropriate" social welfare benefits. So far, so good. Before you can carry out your good intentions, however, you must answer several questions. What benefits, and why? What are they supposed to accomplish? Who gets them, and how do you decide? How much control will go with them, and what methods of control?

These decisions may be de jure, de facto, or by default. They may be open or covert. They may be conscious or unwitting. But one way or another, they *will* show up in your final package. Key sets of choices include the following:

1. *Objectives*: How are they supposed to help the recipient?
2. *Societal function*: Do they meet normal needs or special deficiencies?
3. *Eligibility*: On what basis do people get them?
4. *Freedom*: How much do they control the recipient?

OBJECTIVES: MATERIAL, THERAPEUTIC, OR OPPORTUNITY?

A social welfare benefit may have a material, therapeutic, or opportunity objective. Benefits may be combined to accomplish multiple objectives. For instance, the Job Corps program provided financial aid, counseling, and vocational training in one package to disadvantaged youth.

Material objectives relate to adequacy or equality of food, clothing, and shelter. Social Security, AFDC, food stamps, and public housing are material programs.

Therapeutic objectives aim to cure personal problems through treatment, as in surgery, rehabilitation, marriage counseling, or remedial education, or to ameliorate them with supportive assistance, as in a hospice or a community support program for the mentally ill.

Opportunity objectives focus on helping people to succeed better in the world around them. One area is individual development, through such means as education, job training, or physical fitness. Related to this is empowerment of people to obtain rights and opportunities on their own, through assertiveness training, network building, political organizing, or community development. A third area is enabling access to existing rights and opportunities through such means as advocacy, legal aid, guidance counseling, employment services, and referral.

SOCIETAL FUNCTION: INSTITUTIONAL OR RESIDUAL?

A widely used social systems model sees society as analogous to a biological organism. In the human body, each organ—the stomach, the heart, the liver, the brain, the pituitary gland—contributes a function essential to maintain normal life and health of the total organism, which in turn must support each organ so that it can continue to perform its function.

Social institutions, "organized patterns of group behavior well-established and accepted as a fundamental part of a culture" (not to be confused with bricks-and-mortar institutions), perform the social functions necessary to maintain a "normal" and "healthy" society. Examples of societal functions are

- *material provision*, such as production, distribution, and consumption
- *reproduction and child rearing*
- *socialization*, creating internalized common identity, shared meaning and values, and mutually accepted behaviors toward each other (norms)
- *social control*, external enforcement of prescribed behavior, rewarding conformity and punishing unacceptable deviance
- *mutual support*, meeting special needs that occur in the course of life in that society, such as old age, illness, and disability

Traditionalists yearn for the "good old days," before urban, industrial mass society, when a few simple institutions like the extended family and the church took care of all the necessary functions. This nostalgia may be a myth, "a traditional story, ostensibly with a historical basis, but serving usually to explain the customs, institutions, religious rites, etc. of a people". Says Peter Townsend:

First, historical. Laslett and others have shown that there were in fact few extended families living as households in pre-industrial England, France, and America. The nuclear family was by no means cohesive, since many children went to work and lived in the households of strangers at the age of eight, nine or ten. Such education as children received from the family or church rarely resembled anything in the modern sense of the word. And the relatively flimsy data on occupation suggest that only about 40 percent of employed or occupied adults could be said to be within the field of family production or the "domestic" economy.

Secondly, there is evidence from contemporary pre-industrial societies, much of which suggests, depending crucially on the size of population of such societies, that usually there are embryonic "modern" organizations not strictly tied to the kinship structure, and a more specialized role-structure than is suggested in the differentiation model.[1]

In any case, today basic functions are performed, well or poorly, by a wide range of social institutions. An increasing share of child rearing is performed by daycare centers. Socialization is done by public schools, 4H clubs, Little League, "Sesame Street," the playground, and street corner gangs. Control is exercised by courts, police, and regulatory agencies. Mutual support is provided through social insurance, employee assistance, clinics, and welfare departments.

Institutional and Residual Social Welfare

Harold Wilensky and Charles Lebeaux identified two distinct approaches to social welfare, institutional and residual. *Institutional* social welfare meets *normal* needs of *normal* people under *normal* circumstances:

Social welfare becomes accepted as a proper, legitimate function of modern industrial society in helping individuals achieve self-fulfillment. The complexity of modern life is recognized. The inability of the individual to provide fully for himself, or to meet all his needs in family and work settings, is considered a "normal" condition and the helping agencies achieve "regular" institutional status.[2]

Residual social welfare meets *abnormal* needs under *abnormal* circumstances:

There are "natural" channels through which an individual's needs are properly met: the family and the market economy. . . . However, sometimes these institutions do not function adequately: family life is disrupted, depressions occur. Or sometimes the individual cannot make use of normal channels because of old age or illness. In such cases, a third mechanism is brought into play—the social welfare structure. This is a residual agency, attending primarily to emergency functions, and is expected to withdraw when the regular social structure—the family and the economic system—is again working properly. Because of the residual, temporary, substitute characteristic, social welfare thus conceived often carries the stigma of "dole" or "charity".[3]

Government's Roles

Since World War II, the institutional approach has become dominant in most modern industrial nations. In this view, government is a primary institution for performing such functions as mutual support (e.g., social security, health care), child rearing (e.g., foster care, daycare), and socialization (e.g., public schools). It has a further obligation to encourage and support private social welfare, such as organized philanthropy, occupational welfare, and colleges.

In the residual view, the government is a third-string reserve player on the bench, backing up the first team of family and market and the second team of private charity. It gets into the game only as a last-resort safety net when all else has failed.

From our colonial origins through the Hoover presidency, U.S. social policy was overwhelmingly residual. After facing the crisis of the Great Depression, President Roosevelt used a historical perspective on societal functions to persuade Congress that a shift to the institutional approach was necessary.

Among our objectives, I place the security of men, women, and children first. . . . Security was attained in the earlier days through the interdependence of members of families upon each other and of the families within a small community upon each other. The complexities of great communities and of organized industry make less real these simple means of security. Therefore, we are compelled to employ the active interest of the Nation as a whole through government in order to encourage a greater security for each individual who composes it. . . .

Fear and worry based on unknown danger contribute to social unrest and economic demoralization. If, as our Constitution tells us, our Federal Government was established among other things, "to promote the general welfare," it is our plain duty to provide for that security upon which welfare depends.[4]

Which Benefits Are Institutional and Which Residual?

What is considered to be either institutional or residual reflects what is considered normal in any given time and place, based on perceptions (accurate or not) about the facts and a priori values. Worldwide, perceptions of human need and policy responses have moved in an institutional direction throughout the century. While part of this trend, U.S. society has consistently retained more residual views and policies than most other countries.

In the late twentieth-century United States, institutional approaches to meet human needs attributed to normal circumstances and risks have included retirement income from Social Security and from private pension plans subsidized by tax welfare; employee insurance benefits covering death, disability, and illness; unemployment insurance related to cyclical economic recessions; workmen's compensation for occupational injury and illness; and education at the elementary and secondary level.

Traditionally treated as residual have been services to meet needs blamed on personal failings, such as chemical dependency; emotional and social adjustment problems; family breakdown, abuse, and unwanted pregnancy; chronic unemployment and underemployment; and poverty related to any of the preceding categories.

Services such as face-lift cosmetic surgery and treating minor neuroses, which are popularly regarded as neither basic enough to require institutional provision nor dire enough to qualify for residual treatment, are usually left to the economic market.

Changing Perceptions

Treatment of benefits as institutional or residual is influenced by changing beliefs, ideology, circumstances, and self-interest.

Relief was defined as institutional by President Roosevelt in the 1933 Depression crisis but was made residual again two years later in the Social Security Act on the assumption that with the "principal" causes of poverty (retirement, widowhood, and cyclical unemployment) covered by social insurance, the need for it would "wither away" to a very small safety net. Although the premises turned out to be faulty, relief—now AFDC and Supplemental Security Income (SSI)—has been treated as residual ever since.

Because alcohol abuse has traditionally been seen as individual deviance ("Just say no!"), treatment has tended to be residual. As awareness has grown about genetic predisposition, psychological vulnerability, and the environmental impact of a society where drinking is an integral part of the majority culture, employers are increasingly providing treatment as a normal employee benefit, both directly through employee assistance programs and by inclusion within their general group health insurance coverage.

Perhaps the most dramatic change has occurred in regard to daycare. When most mothers of young children remained in the home full time, daycare was often seen as a residual problem of irresponsible mothers.

Although the statistical reality changed during World War II and kept changing every year thereafter, daycare remained clearly residual until the 1980s, when it suddenly shifted:

American corporations, coming to grips with a drastically changing workforce, have increased the number of firm-sponsored or -paid child-care programs from 110 in 1978 to 2,500 in 1985. . . .

Employers are responding to the need for child care mostly by setting up a range of new employee benefits in addition to the traditional benefits package that includes life, medical, and disability insurance.

These new benefits can include maternity and paternity leave, subsidies for adoption expenses, flexible benefits for dependent care and flextime or job sharing arrangements.[5]

By 1990, daycare was officially institutional:

"This may be the most important issue we will deal with this year," said Richard A. Gephart, the House majority leader. "The world has changed. When parents go off to work, they want to know their children are safe."

Child care became a hot political issue in the 1988 election year, with measures introduced in both the House and the Senate and with both Vice President Bush and Gov. Michael S. Dukakis pledging to put child care at the top of their Presidential agendas.

According to the National Research Council, 57.7% of women in the work force have children under 13. By the turn of the century, 80% of all school-age children and 70% of pre-school youngsters will have working mothers.[6]

The Role of Self-Interest

Why did Social Security largely escape the draconian cuts received by other human service programs in the 1980s? Because 15 million *voters* were already receiving benefits, and the rest of us had a vested interest in future benefits. This did not happen by chance. Roosevelt planned it that way. Liberals in his own party criticized him for using a regressive payroll tax instead of the progressive general income tax to finance Social Security. He replied that he was giving the workers a feeling of direct participation and ownership of *their own* retirement program in order to prevent his Republican opponents from gutting it after he was gone.

In general, social welfare programs for "us" (the "respectable" middle class), such as Social Security, Medicare, public schools and universities, and now daycare, tend to be set up as institutional, whereas benefits for "them" (anybody else), are made residual.

ELIGIBILITY: UNIVERSALISTIC OR SELECTIVE?

Who gets the benefit: everyone? anyone who asks? whoever needs it? only those who deserve it? If we do not have enough to go around, how do we decide who gets it and who does not: those who want it most? those who need it most? those who offer the best economic payoff? your brother-in-law?

Universal means "used or intended to be used by all." Universal benefits, such as public education and city parks, are equally available to everyone without distinction. Even if you choose to use a parochial school or not to take a picnic, the benefit is still available should you change your mind.

Many programs that are not absolutely universal have general universalistic qualities. Canadian Old Age Security and family allowances offer universal benefits—within specific age groups (over sixty-five, under eighteen). Social Security serves almost all citizens but leaves out families who never had a steady wage earner in a covered occupation. Universal health insurance provides security to everyone but limits actual benefits to those with a diagnosed need for medical care.

The *selective* approach targets hosts. Rather than serving an entire population, it sets criteria for choosing some people over others. The criteria may be based on need, justice, deservingness, payoff for society, or rejection of certain categories of people.

Pros and Cons

An institutional view of social welfare tends to support universal programs to meet needs *all* "normal" people have, such as education, health care, retirement income, cultural stimulation, and recreation. On both ethical and pragmatic grounds, Richard Titmuss, coiner of the universal-selective terminology, expanded the institutional perspective to include diswelfares caused by flaws in the economic system, harm done by others' behaviors, and unfortunate acts of nature:

One fundamental historical reason for the adoption of this principle was the aim of making services available and accessible to the whole population in such ways as would not involve users in any humiliating loss of status, dignity, or self-respect. . . . Hence the emphasis on the *social rights* of all citizens to use or not to use as responsible people the services made available by the community in respect of certain needs which the private market and the family were unable or unwilling to provide universally. If these services were not *provided for everybody by everybody*, they would either not be available at all, or only for those who could afford them, and for others on such terms as would involve the infliction of a sense of inferiority and stigma.

Avoidance of stigma was not, of course, the only reason for the development of the twin-concepts of social rights and universalism. . . . The idea of *prevention*—the prevention and breaking of the vicious descending spiral of poverty, disease, neglect, illiteracy and destitution—spelt. . . the critical importance of early and easy access to and use of preventive, remedial, and rehabilitative services. . . . If such services were to be utilized in time and were to be effective in action in a highly differentiated, unequal and class-saturated society, they had to be delivered . . . without loss of self-respect by the users and their families. . . .

National efficiency and welfare were seen as complementary. The sin unforgivable was the waste of human resources; thus, *welfare was summoned to prevent waste*. Hence the beginnings of four of our present-day universalistic social services: retirement pensions, the Health Service, unemployment insurance, and the school meals service.[7]

This view is echoed by U.S. doctors:

In a break from the long-dominant position of organized medicine, the American College of Physicians, the nation's largest group of specialists with 68,000 members, called Thursday for a radical restructuring of the nation's costly health-care system to guarantee equal access for all Americans.

"The current situation is intolerable for patients, their families, and physicians," said the college's board, whose members are specialists in internal medicine. "We have concluded that nothing short of universal access to a level of basic health care will be fair in the long run." . . .

The statement argues that by ensuring wider access to health care services, Americans would have better health in general, with lower incidence of many of the diseases that could easily be avoided through regular medical care.[8]

The primary argument against universalism is *seepage*. Scarce resources are "leaked" to persons who do not need them at all or who need them much less than others. Says Alfred Kahn:

When programs are universal, the very poor do not get their fair share. It is held that the educated and informed, or those with some resources to employ, are guilty of "creaming" what is intended as general public provision. The more advantaged permit services to reach the poorest only after skimming off the best for themselves. As evidence, one may cite how, historically, the very poor do not get a fair share of the best public secondary schools and colleges; . . . how expensive tax-supported beaches can be reached only by private car owners; how the very poor mentally ill may be incarcerated in state congregate-care facilities while the more advantaged receive ambulatory care and outpatient clinical service—and so on.[9]

On the other hand, he adds, selectivity may shortchange the poor even more: "Services for poor people tend to be poor services."[10] Middle-class voters favor universalistic programs like Social Security and public education in which they have a vested interest. Programs targeted for relatively powerless groups, such as poor female-headed families and the chronically mentally ill, are inferior to universal programs in benefit level and quality of service, and they are politically vulnerable to cutbacks under conservative administrations.

Yes, reply residualists, selective programs for the poor are inferior— and should be! People are needy because of their own laziness or irresponsibility. Universalism subverts the work incentive by divorcing benefits from production. You do not improve the lives of the poor by shielding them from the consequences of their unsatisfactory behaviors. Services for failures and laggards *should* be less desirable. That, and the ordeal of the means test, makes people face their need to shape up.

Another issue area is *freedom*. Universalism intrudes on negative freedom. Mandatory public retirement and education programs deprive individual taxpayers of free choice in how to spend their income. On the other hand, these same universal programs promote positive freedom by increasing adequacy and reducing class-based unequal opportunity— and there are few things more intrusive on negative freedom than a means test investigation.

After the smoke clears, although differing widely on how much of each and in which areas, nearly everyone accepts some universal social welfare and some selective programs.

SELECTIVE CRITERIA

Eligibility to receive a benefit may be decided by one or more of a variety of criteria. For instance, college financial aid may be based on need (a Basic Educational Opportunity Grant), deservingness (a merit scholarship), residence (reduced tuition for state residents), payoff for the college (athletic scholarship), or something unrelated to any of these (a scholarship for children of Elks Lodge members). Criteria may be as objective as the computer record of past Social Security taxes paid or as evaluative as a psychosocial diagnosis.

Means Test: Economic Need

Economic need is measured either by *income* alone or by *means* (income plus assets). In common usage, both methods are called a means test. This antiuniversal, residual approach seeks to limit benefits to the ''truly needy,'' who do not have enough money to pay for needed goods or services on their own.

Whether, when, and how to apply a means test are among the most controversial issues in social policy. It may *restrict eligibility*, on a yes or no basis to those poor enough to meet the test. Either you get Medicaid or you do not. There is no middle ground. In other cases, it is used to determine a *variable benefit*, which fills the gap between what you need and what you have. If you qualify for AFDC, your grant is the difference between the state's standard benefit and any income you have from other sources, such as employment, child support, or an annuity. Where a clinic charges a sliding-scale fee, your charitable benefit is the difference between the actual cost of the service and what the agency determines you can afford.

A means test is always intrusive. This was carried to an extreme in the AFDC full field investigations required of me when I was a New York City Department of Welfare social investigator:

- obtain and file documentary proof of income, expenses, and assets in the form of pay stubs, rent receipts, insurance policies, and so on
- cross-check each item with the employer, landlord, and so on.
- require mothers to file suit for child support against absent and putative fathers, and verify that they did so
- investigate and document the income of "legally responsible relatives" (parents, grandparents, or adult children) to determine how much each must contribute
- interview "socially responsible relatives" (siblings, aunts and uncles, etc) for the purpose of persuading, shaming, or intimidating them into "voluntary" contributions
- interrogate neighbors to determine whether a mother's lifestyle coincided with her declared income, whether she had a boyfriend who could be compelled to contribute, and in general what her moral character was

At the other extreme, a minimal means test may require you to fill out and sign a *declaration* comparable to a loan application.

In general, the lower the social class of the applicant, the more adversary and less respectful the means testing becomes. The suspicious, punitive approach of my Harlem Welfare Center was a far cry from the friendly helpfulness I received from the financial aid officer at my Ivy League college.

Means tests deter eligible applicants. In a society where the mere fact of economic need defines you as a failure, going through any means test is painful. A full field investigation is deeply humiliating. In my public assistance experience, many mothers would endure anything to feed their children, but elderly persons, responsible only for themselves, often preferred death before dishonor—and subsequently did die prematurely from illnesses related to malnutrition and exposure. A majority of all persons eligible for AFDC and SSI benefits opt to do without rather than endure the process. To the extent that this occurs, the program has failed to accomplish its legal mandate. Of course, in so doing it also reduces the national welfare budget by several billion dollars per year.

Some means tests are inefficient. In AFDC, federal "quality control" standards do not address efficiency or effectiveness. They simply dock the state for giving any client more than his or her entitlement (but there is no penalty for giving less). This encourages states to divert tax dollars from benefits for the needy to the bureaucrats and lawyers who do the investigations, re-investigations, paper work, and litigation.

The purpose of a means test is to identify the "truly needy." What is the point of diminishing return, beyond which the investigatory costs and damage to clients outweigh its positive functions of meeting real needs on a priority basis, preventing seepage, and guarding against criminal fraud? How can it be made as compatible as possible with therapeutic and developmental goals for the client?

Reverse Means Test

The economic market has a reverse means test: If you do *not* have the means, you cannot get the service. Most people consider this reasonable for private providers of nonessential services. There is less consensus about its application to health and welfare programs that perform "public utility" functions. I will never forget the day I rushed my two-year-old son to a nearby "charitable" hospital after he drank paint remover. He nearly died when the emergency room refused to serve him until after I had completed arrangements with the business office! How can such incidents be prevented in a way that is also fair to the provider?

Diagnostic Evaluation: Noneconomic Need

Diagnostic intake determines your suitability for the specific benefits offered by a program. There are two basic selection criteria:

1. *Having the covered need or condition*. A Social Security orphan's pension requires a parent's death certificate. A community mental health clinic requires diagnosis of a disorder listed in the DSM-III.
2. *Ability to benefit*. A mental health clinic, having failed consistently in treating borderline personality disorders, may recognize the need, yet realistically reject such applicants.

When eligible applicants exceed the number a program can handle, diagnostic preference may be given either to those with the greatest need for the service or to those with the greatest ability to benefit from it.

Attributed Need: Group Eligibility

If most members of a group have the same condition, why check out every individual? Is it not simpler to blanket in the whole group as eligible?

During the War on Poverty, Project Headstart, located in ghettos, based eligibility on neighborhood residence, assuming (accurately) that (1) nearly all residents of poor neighborhoods are poor and (2) nearly all poor children are educationally deprived. In this case substituting attributed need for individual diagnostic and means testing had several advantages:

- *Efficiency.* What was saved by eliminating individual investigations exceeded the cost of serving the few who would not have qualified—and those few also benefited from the service.
- *Humaneness.* Means and diagnostic tests would require negative judgments about the adequacy of homes and children as a condition of eligibility. The neighborhood approach avoided such stigma and loss of self-esteem.
- *Effectiveness.* By eliminating the negative effects and deterrence of needs testing, it reached more of those who needed it and served them better.

A retired colleague of mine in San Francisco bragged about his dime-a-ride senior citizen BART transit pass. The taxpayers subsidized him because of an historic association of old age with poverty. However, *his* income was twice the national average. (Such public subsidies should not be confused with commercial senior discounts in motels and restaurants, which are offered to attract business from retirees with money to spend.) This raises the issue of *accuracy.* Although many are indeed poor, should the senior citizen group, whose poverty rate is below the national average, receive a subsidy that is withheld from single-parent households with a poverty rate three times as high?

Even when attributed need is cost-efficient and reasonably accurate, some people raise an *ideological* question: Is it acceptable for anyone who does not fit the intent to get needs-based benefits?

There is also such a thing as attributed non-need through the use of *categorical* criteria that blanket out categories of persons whose needs are otherwise the same as those of eligible recipients. A white male youth from an AFDC family may be as disadvantaged as his minority and female counterparts but is excluded from most affirmative action programs. An unskilled older worker with high blood pressure and some arthritis and a widowed homemaker, both aged fifty-eight, may be functionally unemployable despite impeccable character. Although they are "truly needy" and "worthy poor," they languish in no-man's land. They are too young for old-age benefits, too well for disability, and have no dependent children. They are covered by Social Security but cannot collect until they get older or sicker. In Sweden, by contrast, the social security program has the flexibility to allow for such circumstances.

Investment Return

A benefit may be provided not for the sake of the recipient but for its social and economic payoff to the larger society. This is true of medical education in Nebraska. Taxpayers pay a higher subsidy for the tuition of medical students than for other students in order to meet the state's need for physicians. Admission preference is given to residents because locals are most likely to practice in Nebraska after they graduate. The only nonresident in my son's class was engaged to marry a native. Supplementary financial aid was reserved for students who committed themselves to practice in an underserved rural area of the state.

Social policy and program goals need to be clarified and followed in practice. Either investment or individual benefit criteria can be legitimate and desirable if they are consistent with the stated program objectives.

Problems arise when mixed signals are given. Since 1965, there has been a trend toward evaluating individual-benefit programs in terms of economic payoff (cost-benefit analysis). This has led to inappropriate de facto goal displacement from user benefit to investment return. In other cases, where investment return is really a program's intent, official mission statements and selection criteria have failed to make it explicit.

In an individual-benefit program, investment-based preference violates the applicants' constitutional right to equal treatment under the law. Such was the case, declared the Supreme Court, when Allan Bakke was passed over for admission to medical school in favor of minority applicants who ranked lower according to the school's official admission criteria.[11] If California had followed Nebraska's example by stating its social purpose and designing its admission and financial aid policies accordingly, it probably would have been legal to include commitment to serve disadvantaged populations within the state as a selection factor.

Compensation Owed for Disservices

An individual may be given benefits to compensate for an undeserved diswelfare caused by society. Relocation assistance for inner-city families displaced by a new freeway for suburban commuters and disability pensions for soldiers wounded in combat are obvious examples.

A broader compensatory program was the original GI Bill of Rights after World War II. It provided funds to pursue higher education, low-cost loans to buy houses, and bonus points added to scores on civil service exams, all of which were intended to compensate for losing four years of career development as compared with those who stayed home.

Supreme Court Justice Thurgood Marshall applied the same principle in support of compensatory affirmative action in his Bakke case dissent.

After elaborating the history of unequal treatment and citing current statistics on the resulting inequality, Marshall concluded:

> The relationship between those figures and the history of unequal treatment afforded to the Negro cannot be denied. At every point from birth to death the impact of the past is reflected in the still disfavored position of the Negro.
>
> In light of the sorry history of discrimination and its devastating impact on the lives of Negroes, bringing the Negro into the mainstream of American life should be a state interest of the highest order. To fail to do so is to ensure that America will forever remain a divided society.
>
> I do not believe that the Fourteenth Amendment requires us to accept that fate. Neither its history nor our past cases lend any support to the conclusion that a university may not remedy the cumulative effects of society's discrimination by giving consideration to race in an effort to increase the number and percentage of Negro doctors.[12]

Earned Benefits and Deservingness

Occupational welfare provides *earned* benefits. Health insurance is a noncash wage payment for work performed. Pensions are deferred wages for that work. Social Security benefits are earned by paying a percentage of your earned wages into a public pension program. (Not all occupational welfare benefits are earned. Employee assistance plans are an investment in future productivity.)

Closely related to earned benefits is the *merit* criterion. A merit scholarship is given as a reward for high achievement without reference to financial need. (Sometimes this shades over into investment where a university's primary intent is to enhance its quality and reputation by recruiting exceptional students.)

Merit may be combined with other selective methods. My university, for instance, awards graduate scholarships competitively on merit—but only within the pool of students who have previously met the university's means test. Is this the best mix, or should it go the other way, giving priority to degree of need among students who meet a minimum merit standard?

Another deservingness criterion may be *moral judgment*. This seems to be a rationale for the difference between AFDC benefits for single parents "guilty" of a failed marriage or out-of-wedlock child and Social Security benefits for respectable widows. Such a moral distinction is ironic in light of another difference in policy toward the two groups. Before a 1968 court ruling, an AFDC mother could lose her grant for having unmarried sex, while Social Security permitted a widow to live out of wedlock with a man but took away her grant if she married him!

DEGREE OF CONTROL: CASH, KIND, AND VOUCHER

The final question is: How—and how much—does the giver control the receiver?

Cash

Cash gives the recipient the most freedom. The benefit may be related to specific needs and clear ideas on how the money should be spent. For instance, AFDC and SSI grants are supposed to be based on the cost of an adequate "package" of food, rent, utilities, clothing, and so on. Social Security insurance benefits are supposed to replace lost earnings in order to maintain a former standard of living. Tax welfare deductions for dependents or blindness assume special expenses. However, once received, the money is legal tender for whatever you choose to spend it on, however wisely or foolishly.

Kind

In-kind benefits are the most controlling. Someone else decides, bureaucratically or diagnostically, what is right for you and offers it on a take-it-or-leave-it basis. In-kind *goods* have included surplus government cheese, Christmas baskets, shelter and meals for homeless persons, uniforms for residents of certain institutions, and public housing apartments. Examples of in-kind *services* are medical services provided by a public clinic, social services given by United Way agencies, care in state mental hospitals, and public school education.

Voucher

Vouchers are promises by a third party to pay for designated goods and services purchased from a choice of approved providers. In their traditional form they use *coupons*, as in food stamps, or *charge cards*, as in Medicare. A variation is *tax credits*, which refund money spent for specified services, such as daycare.

Vouchers are a compromise between cash and kind. On the one hand, the payer controls what may be received. On the other hand, the voucher permits some flexibility within those limits. Instead of being restricted to surplus peanut butter and corn meal, food stamps may be used for any U.S.-grown food product; but unlike cash, they cannot be used for nonfood needs. Medicaid can be used only for certain health needs, but the patient can choose among competing providers instead of being limited to a specified government clinic.

Which Is Best?

Many of us have ideological preferences. Cash is most compatible with negative freedom goals of individual self-determination and minimum government interference. If they cannot avoid social welfare altogether, classical economists prefer cash because it is less disruptive to the free-market system of buying and selling than are alternatives.

A pessimistic view of human nature may support in-kind benefits. If clients cannot be trusted to make good decisions, Big Brother will do it for them. A harsher reason to use them is the ability to impose ''less eligibility'' by deliberately providing inferior goods and services in a manner that demeans the recipient.

Vouchers are a compromise choice for those who want to control beneficiaries while maximizing the market freedom of providers.

There may be an appropriate place for each. Perhaps the method of provision should vary with the characteristics of the beneficiary, the environmental circumstances, and the objectives of the social program—if we could only agree on just what those characteristics, circumstances, and objectives are.

SUMMARY

Social welfare programs may be designed to provide material assistance, therapeutic services, or development and empowerment opportunities.

The institutional approach provides social welfare as a basic function of society to meet common human needs and compensate for the diswelfares that occur in a capitalist industrial society. The residual approach provides a reluctant safety net for individual and family failures and exceptional bad luck.

Universal social welfare programs are institutional. They are made available to nearly everyone to meet common material and developmental needs. Selective programs target specific categories of people or problems. A common selection criterion is need, either assessed via individual means and diagnostic testing or attributed collectively to members of groups that have a high incidence of the problem. Other selective criteria include probable investment return, earnings from employment, rewards for achievement or good behavior, and compensation for diswelfares.

Cash is the form of benefit that least interferes with the freedom of both the individual and the economic market. In-kind goods and services are the most controlling. Vouchers control the benefit while allowing some consumer choice and provider competition.

NOTES

1. Peter Townsend, *Sociology and Social Policy* (London: Allen Lane, 1975), p. 15.

2. Harold Wilensky and Charles Lebeaux, *Industrial Society and Social Welfare*, 2nd ed. (New York: Free Press, 1965), p. 140.

3. Ibid., p. 139.

4. Franklin Roosevelt, "Message to Congress Reviewing the Broad Objectives and Accomplishments of the Administration," June 8, 1934.

5. *Omaha World Herald*, December 7, 1986. From a Report of the Council on Economic Priorities.

6. *New York Times*, March 30, 1990.

7. Richard Titmuss, *Commitment to Welfare* (London: George Allen & Unwin, 1968), pp. 129–30.

8. *Washington Post*, April 27, 1990.

9. Alfred Kahn, *Social Policy and Social Services*, 2nd ed. (New York: Random House, 1979), p. 78.

10. Ibid., p. 79.

11. *Regents of the University of California v. Allan Bakke*, 435 US 265 (1978).

12. Ibid.

Chapter 11

Rights and Entitlement

Does every American deserve a high school education, medical care, and a retirement pension? Should a university education be within reach of every academically qualified citizen? Do we have a right to life that includes protection from starvation? Does society have a responsibility for its mentally ill members? If yes to any of these questions, to what extent is it the responsibility of our government, as an agent of the people, to guarantee this as a *legal* right? Subject to what conditions? Given the existence of human sin and error, how can we make sure that these rights are protected?

LEGAL AND MORAL RIGHTS

Entitlement: Legally Guaranteed Rights

Some programs entitle you to benefits under one or more of the following forms of law:

- *constitutional* rights to equal treatment and due process
- *statutes* officially passed by a legislative body
- *regulations* and other administrative rules that elaborate and apply a statute; for instance, specifying that "handle promptly" means within thirty days of application

- *common law*, "the unwritten law based on custom, usage, and the decisions of law courts, as contrasted with statutory law"
- *equity*, "a system of rules and doctrines supplementing common and statute law and superceding such law when it proves inadequate for a just settlement"

This right is *justiciable*, "subject to court jurisdiction; liable for trial in court," if you believe you are not getting what you are entitled to.

Full entitlement guarantees the benefit to which each eligible person is legally entitled. Many full-entitlement programs are universal, like public education and the British National Health Service. Those that are selective meet Elizabeth Wickenden's definition: "Any program of governmental benefits to be acceptable must be based on criteria of eligibility that are objective, clearly defined, generally understood, well administered, and considered to be fair."[1]

Conditional entitlement, on the other hand, does not guarantee that you will get the benefit. It assures only equal consideration under official selection criteria for whatever is available. The Fourteenth Amendment guarantees conditional entitlement to all publicly funded programs. What you can challenge in court, as Allan Bakke did, is (1) whether the criteria are reasonable and (2) whether they were applied even-handedly.

Wickenden compares full and conditional entitlement:

Social insurance benefits are based on objective and hence readily recorded data: amount of wages in a covered occupation (virtually all) over a period of time. The amount of the benefit and the data that justifies it come out of a computer: a formula determines the amount of the benefit based on average earnings and, where indicated, the number of dependents.

Consider, by contrast, the number of variables and the judgments involved in a means-tested benefit. Someone must determine the standard of need that will apply and the availability of appropriated funds to sustain it. Typically this involves uncertainties and competitive fiscal pressures on the legislative body at that particular time. For example, it is a well-documented fact that the pressure to reduce Federal taxes while increasing military expenditures has taken a heavy toll of means-tested programs like public assistance, Medicaid, and food stamps.[2]

Another condition affecting eligibility may be *quality*. Nebraska's otherwise strict licensing of psychological services exempts public agencies. State law guarantees certain psychological services to school children and mental patients but does not guarantee that these services will meet normal professional standards. A similar quality condition occurs de facto when child protection services are mandated by law but a low level of funding overloads the workers to the point that they cannot do justice to each case.

Moral Rights

On another level, many of us believe in human rights derived from natural law, humanitarian ethics and/or religious belief, as expressed in the Declaration of Independence, the United Nations International Declaration on the Rights of Children, and the 1986 Bishops' Pastoral Letter on *Economic Justice for All*. Do not confuse this with a legal right, however. In our country, this belief in human rights has not stopped war, ended capital punishment, provided health care to 38 million uncovered citizens, or raised AFDC benefits to the poverty line.

On the other hand, moral rights can make a difference. When they are aggressively pursued by advocacy groups and accepted by politicians, they may be enacted into public social policies and programs. Before Roosevelt proclaimed that a minimum standard of living was a basic human right, there was no public assistance at all except the notorious poorhouse and a few meager state pensions for widows and the aged.

Moral rights often carry weight in the private sector. My father, like many physicians of his day, believed his Hippocratic oath required him to give medical care to whoever needed it, whether they could pay or not. The Salvation Army, believing in their inherent worth as God's children, care for people whom public policy ignores.

No Rights at All

Needs exist for which there is neither legal provision nor moral advocacy. If you are seventy-five and need a new kidney, neither Medicare nor your insurance company will pay for it, and your medical center may give a "moral" priority for available organs to younger patients. In such cases, there is still an economic market—assuming you have the money and can find someone willing to provide the service for profit.

ACCESSIBILITY

Sometimes, even though you have full entitlement on paper, it may not be accessible to you. Because of a shortage of surgeons, the British National Health Service has long waiting lists for nonemergency surgery. The wait can last a lifetime for some older patients. In other cases, a service may be available, but in a time, place, and form you cannot use.

Among the factors that affect the accessibility of services and benefits are the following:

- *Quantity.* Is there enough to go around, or will some come away empty?
- *Quality.* Are the standards such that you actually get what was promised?

- *Location*. Can clients get to it with the transportation available to them and in their physical condition?
- *Schedule*. Can ordinary people use it without risking loss of their jobs?
- *Information*. Do people understand what is available and how to apply?
- *Affordability*. Can all eligible people meet the costs of getting a service, including fees, transportation, baby sitting, and lost wages? If not, can such barriers be worked out on an individualized basis?
- *Usability*. Is help offered in the client's language? Is the food kosher? Are there ramps and elevators for disabled users?
- *Acceptability*. Is it provided without stigma in a respectful, supportive manner compatible with the client's culture?

Sheila Kammerman and Alfred Kahn have proposed a network of special access services to assure that people get what they need and are entitled to:

Access services include all arrangements which inform people about the availability of rights, benefits, or services; clarify eligibility (connect the rights, benefits, and services to people's particular situations); help them establish eligibility; refer them to appropriate offices and services; get them physically to appropriate offices and facilities; help assure responsiveness on the part of benefit providers or service providers to the needs of applicants.[3]

Accessibility makes a difference. In the Harlem welfare center where I worked, clients who were aged, disabled, or had small children with them had to walk through a crime-ridden warehouse area, climb to the third floor, and wait for hours in a dingy lobby to see workers who openly despised them. By contrast, when I was widowed, a Social Security worker, routinely informed by the funeral director, called me within a week, expressed sympathy, and reviewed all possible benefits to which I might be entitled. Based on my answers, she filled out the application form for me and mailed it out with a return envelope for my signature. One of these financial aid programs reaches nearly 100 percent of eligible persons; the other, less than 50 percent. Guess which?

ADMINISTRATIVE APPEALS

How It Is Supposed to Work

In the ideal entitlement program, there are few occasions for appeal. People know what they are entitled to and receive it in an atmosphere of mutual respect and courtesy. Eligibility decisions are largely routine, based on impartial data. If a client questions the decision, it is usually resolved in one of three ways through an amicable, routine review:

(1) The agency satisfactorily explains its decision. (2) The agency discovers and corrects its error with a courteous apology. (3) The client supplies missing information.

The Human Factor

As subjective elements come into play, the impartiality of administration and the effectiveness of friendly appeals diminish. Where the rules are less precise, interpretation of the intent of the law becomes more of an issue, particularly when the political climate is antiwelfare or the agency staff have ethnic, class, or gender prejudices against their clients. Both workers and their supervisors have a career self-interest in denying or covering up errors caused by negligence, indifference, or incompetence.

When decisions are subject to diagnostic and/or evaluative judgments, there are gray areas that permit honest differences between the evaluator and the client. Administrators are reluctant to undercut staff confidence and morale by reversing debatable but defensible decisions.

Conflict of Interest

Typically, the first line of appeal is an internal agency review. In such a trial, the agency is both the defendant and the judge and jury. This conflict of interest is exacerbated by unequal power. An appealing AFDC mother probably

- needs the agency more than it needs her
- has a dilemma on how to make a strong case without offending her judges
- worries about potential future reprisals
- has less education and verbal skill than opponents
- has lower status
- has less technical knowledge about policy and her rights
- lacks legal counsel, while the agency routinely uses it

The conflict of interest can be reduced (but not eliminated) if the agency procedures call for a neutral third party to preside over the hearing and decision is made by a diverse appeals committee. For instance, a university grievance committee may include students, faculty, and community people.

The power imbalance can be lessened if the client is provided with a good lawyer and/or has the backing of a powerful advocacy group that can expose and challenge any deviation from impartiality. In a Bronx welfare center, grievances had been a futile exercise for clients. After the city welfare director permitted the National Welfare Rights Organization to place a trained volunteer advocate at a table in the lobby, nearly all grievances were settled quickly and fairly. (A ripple effect of the successful appeals was that supervisors leaned on staff to get it right the first time.)

A similar effect resulted from the "poverty lawyers" programs of the 1960s. However, public agencies are unenthusiastic about outside interference. In the 1980s, the government terminated legal aid to the poor on the grounds that it was improper to finance complaints against itself. (A counterview is that legal aid to poor clients benefits the government by improving its performance in carrying out legislative mandates.) Low-income clients who cannot afford expensive attorney fees continue to encounter the problems described above. Most do not even try to appeal, regardless of the merit of their case.

COURT ADJUDICATION

Public agency policies and practices affecting rights and entitlement stand unless challenged in court. Challenges may be made in three areas: (1) interpretations and applications of the law, (2) procedures for determining eligibility and benefits, and (3) findings of "fact" in a given case.

Determining Facts

Courts decide disputed facts. A kitchen worker left her job and applied for unemployment benefits. These were denied because her employer said that she quit without provocation. She said that she had been forced out because the chef sexually harassed her and threatened her with violence when she refused his advances. The State Employment Service rejected her appeal. She went to court to obtain her entitlement. It was an issue of fact. Whose version was true? The court decided hers was. Is that what really happened? Probably, but it no longer matters. Legally, the "facts" are not necessarily what actually occurred but whatever the court decides they are. Thus, accurate or not, the factual issue is settled once and for all.

Due Process

Under the Constitution, your house and bank account cannot be taken from you without *due process* protections because they are *property rights*. A social welfare entitlement is also a dollars-and-cents property right backed by the full force and faith of the government. It cannot be taken away from you without due process. You can challenge whether agency procedures conform to the right of due process, whether they are carried out properly by the staff, or whether all applicants and clients receive equal treatment under the law.

Under the law, a diagnostic examination determines eligibility for a Social Security disability benefit. This eligibility continues indefinitely unless a reexamination determines that the disability no longer exists. In the early 1980s, the Social Security Administration abruptly terminated tens of thousands of disabled persons without any reexamination. The court found that they had been denied due process, ordered their reinstatement, and reprimanded the agency for willfully violating citizen rights.

Points of Law: Interpretation and Application

If you and the agency disagree on the interpretation of the law, you may ask the court to decide which one is right. Title IX of the Higher Education Act barred sex discrimination in colleges that receive federal funds. A recipient college discriminated against a female student in an unaided program area. There was no issue of fact. The college agreed that it was treating her differently because she was female but said it was none of the government's business, since the law applied only to the specific programs aided by the tax dollars, leaving the college free to do what it pleased in all other areas of its program. She claimed their action was illegal because the law barred *all* sex discrimination by a college that accepted *any* Federal aid. The court had to decide which was the correct interpretation.

The *intent of the legislators* is a key factor in the court's decision. What did the sponsors say they intended when they wrote it? What did the committee report say? What was assumed about the bill in arguments for and against it in the debate? In the Title IX case, despite testimony to the contrary by the original sponsors of the law, the court ruled that the college was right about the original intent. As with facts, whether or not it is historically accurate, the intent is whatever the court decides it was. (Congress responded by passing a new law that explicitly prohibited all discrimination by recipient colleges.)

Another possible point of law is its *constitutionality*. For decades, most states required a year or more of residence to qualify for AFDC. This was legal until a client challenged it. The Supreme Court decided it was unconstitutional because the Constitution gives us instant citizenship in a state the moment we make it our legal home and because the Fourteenth Amendment requires a state to treat all of its citizens equally. Meanwhile, unchallenged comparable residence requirements to qualify for in-state tuition at state universities continue to be legal.

Points of Law: Conflicts between Rights

The rights of individuals may conflict, where both cannot be maximized at the same time. For instance, courts may have to decide the balance between parental rights and children's rights in cases involving child abuse, custody, or visitation.

Courts also referee conflicts between the rights of individuals versus the rights of society. This was the case in a 1986 Supreme Court decision:

The U.S. Supreme Court has resolved a disturbing conflict between states' environmental laws and Federal bankruptcy law by deciding that bankrupt companies retain an obligation to safeguard the public safety after they go broke. The case concerned the bankrupt Quanta Resources Corp., a waste-disposal firm that had abandoned its PCB-contaminated sites in New Jersey and New York. PCB is a cancer-causing chemical.

Federal bankruptcy laws permit failed businesses to walk away from contaminated property by dictating that any remaining assets be dispersed among creditors instead of being used in clean-up efforts.

Some state laws, in contrast, are written to force *all* polluters to clean up their toxic messes. In the case of Quanta, New York and New Jersey contested the bankruptcy court's decision, which allowed the company to bypass state clean-up orders by abandoning the property. . . .

Wrong, said the High Court in a 5-4 decision written by Justice Lewis F. Powell Jr. The Federal bankruptcy code is not meant to allow property to be abandoned in violation of state health laws, Justice Powell wrote.[4]

Precedents

When interpretations and applications of points of law or due process are challenged, the court tends to be guided by precedents from past judicial decisions in similar or analogous cases. Generally higher court precedents carry more weight than those of lower courts. If the precedents are *strong in one direction*, the court usually follows them unless there is a persuasive argument for change. If there is a *trend* over time, the court tends to lean toward the emerging directions and rationales. If the precedents are *mixed*, the court may be more open to equity and social arguments.

Although the judge is expected to do his or her own homework, the lawyers for each side search out the precedents most favorable to their side and cite them to "help" the judge decide in their direction.

Note: Legislators, administrators, professionals, and the general public are also inclined to be influenced by precedents. In nonjudicial arenas, social policy advocates would do well to emulate their legal colleagues by researching precedents, both for their own insight into current policy and for strategic purposes.

WHICH COURT?

Federal courts handle issues involving federal laws, the Constitution, interstate matters, and international affairs. Under the Tenth Amendment, everything else belongs to the state courts. Occasionally, as in the bankruptcy/toxic waste case, different aspects of a dispute may be tried in each system. If state and federal laws conflict, the ultimate arbiter is the U.S. Supreme Court.

Within the federal system and each state there are trial courts and appeals courts. (There may also be "inferior" courts, such as traffic and justice of the peace, which dispose of minor cases in which there is no contention.) All disputed cases go to a trial court. A *trial* is "the formal examination of the facts of a case by a court of law to decide the validity of a charge or claim." The decision is binding on the parties.

Litigants cannot appeal the finding of facts. However, they may appeal alleged errors in due process or points of law. There are three categories of appeals court response:

1. *Refuse to review* because the appellant failed to establish reasonable doubt about the interpretation of law or due process. The trial decision stands.
2. *Review points of law*, and either affirm the earlier interpretation or reverse the decision based on a different interpretation.
3. *Review due process*, and either affirm the trial court action or vacate the decision due to procedural errors. The case may be retried under the corrected procedures dictated by the appeals court.

In the federal system and most states, there are two levels of appeal. The lower level settles most cases. The state and U.S. supreme courts tend to focus on conflicting decisions among lower appeals courts and broad issues that need to be clarified. Each appeals court interpretation of the law guides future court trials within its own jurisdiction (a region, a state, or the nation) unless and until superseded by a subsequent ruling.

SOCIAL POLICY AND THE COURTS

Impact on Social Policy

Courts and judges are supposed to be detached, objective arbiters, above the turmoil of ideology and politics. Theoretically they do not make social policy. They merely resolve disputes by finding the true intent and application of policies made by others. However, these decisions may in fact have a powerful impact on social policy in such ways as the following:

- *Changing the operation of existing programs.* Both de jure and de facto school segregation patterns were dramatically changed by a 1954 decision that separation on the basis of race was inherently unequal.

- *Changing what is legal and illegal.* Abortion became legal, and capital punishment became for a period illegal, because the Supreme Court found that existing state laws failed to meet constitutional fairness tests.
- *Abolishing social programs.* In 1934 and 1935, Roosevelt's New Deal was nearly dismantled by a series of Supreme Court decisions that declared his aid to farmers, businesses, and labor to be unconstitutional and threatened a similar fate for the Social Security Act.

Appointment of Judges

In theory, judges are selected exclusively for their ability to be wise and detached. They are given long-term appointments, even lifetime, to insulate them from political pressures and career temptations. While some are ideological activists, most judges sincerely try to be objective and fair according to precedent and their own best lights. In practice, of course, they are products of their particular class and ethnic backgrounds, education, previous career experiences, personal experiences, religious beliefs, and the prevailing social perspectives of their time and place in history.

All federal and many state judges are appointed by politicians, who naturally prefer judges who share their own ideologies and special interests. Roosevelt and Truman appointees moved the courts in social justice, prolabor, and positive freedom directions. Eisenhower's Warren Court stressed negative freedom and civil liberties. Nixon and Reagan appointments redirected the courts toward pre-Roosevelt positions on business and unions and pre-Warren positions on civil liberty and civil rights. In the following news item, lawyers on opposite sides of an issue acknowledged the impact of such selection:

Burning from a U.S. Supreme Court opinion early in 1984 [*National Labor Relations Board v. Bildisco & Bildisco*] that gave reorganizing companies wide discretion in throwing out union contracts, labor unions successfully lobbied Congress to tighten up the statute. . . .

In July, 1984, the Congress passed a law that forbids companies to unilaterally impose new work rules after filing for Chapter 11 [bankruptcy]. . . .

"The company just has to go through a few more hoops to prove it is in the interest of the company to break the collective bargaining agreement," says [management-side] bankruptcy attorney Scott Baena.

Labor lawyers doubt that the stronger language will change the outcome in many cases. "The four or five bankruptcy judges that are for unions will continue to rule that way, and the other 250 will continue to side with companies," says one [union-side] labor lawyer. "It's business as usual with a different set of rules."[5]

Presidents Roosevelt and Reagan were particularly controversial in their attempts to change social policy through selective appointment of judges.

After his 1934–35 Supreme Court setbacks, President Roosevelt, complaining about "nine old men" (appointed by his Republican predecessors), tried to "pack the court" by proposing a law that added a new justice to the Supreme Court for every one who was over age seventy. This would have given him six new appointees, enough to create a majority who leaned in his social policy direction. In the 1980s, President Reagan attempted to stack the court in the opposite direction through openly ideological choices.

Both were partially thwarted by Congress, which rejected Roosevelt's bill and Reagan's most extreme nominees. However, in the long run, each still achieved major social policy reversals in the courts through appointment of judges whose views coincided with their aims.

One way to change public social policy is to pass laws. Another is to control the administration of laws and programs through regulations and de facto practices. Obviously, a third way is to reinterpret laws and the Constitution through judicial appointments and test cases.

SUMMARY

Entitlement is a legal right to specified benefits under defined eligibility conditions. Full entitlement guarantees the benefit to everyone who meets the eligibility conditions. Where there is not enough to go around, conditional eligibility assures equal consideration under established selection criteria for what is available. You can go to court to enforce entitlement rights.

Moral rights are not enforceable but they may influence both public and private social policy.

A frequent problem in getting the services to which you are theoretically entitled is whether it is accessible to you in practice.

The first line of appeal for persons who feel they are not getting their fair entitlement is usually an internal agency review. Although this often resolves the issue in a mutually satisfactory way, many agency appeal systems are subverted by conflict of interest, unequal power relationships, or lack of due process.

Trial court adjudication of disputes involves determining the facts and interpreting the law as it applies to the case. Appeals courts may be asked to review the trial court's interpretations and/or its due process.

Although theoretically neutral, courts inevitably have a major impact on social policy through their interpretation of the Constitution and other laws. Because of this, politicians and interest groups attempt to get judges appointed whose ideology and interests coincide with their own.

NOTES

1. Elizabeth Wickenden, "Social Security—Why Not a Means Test?" Study Group on Social Security, Fact Sheet 13, New York, August 1984.

2. Ibid.

3. Sheila Kammerman and Alfred Kahn, *Social Services in the United States: Policies and Programs* (Philadelphia: Temple University Press, 1976), p. 436.

4. *Miami Herald*, February 3, 1986.

5. *Miami Herald*, February 23, 1986.

Chapter 12

Public, Voluntary, or Commercial?

In a market economy, there is a presumption in favor of competitive, for-profit free enterprise. Exceptions have to be justified. Whose turf is human service? Should it be within the commercial sphere, or is it different from "normal" business? Should the government "of the people, by the people, and for the people" do it? Should private altruists do it through voluntary nonprofit charities? In the United States, there is no clear, simple consensus, but there are some traditional patterns.

TRADITIONAL DISTINCTIONS

Service providers fall into three categories: *commercial business* (private for-profit), *public* (government), and *voluntary* (charitable not-for-profit). The legal distinctions among these sectors are clear and mutually exclusive.

Businesses operate for profit. Corporate hospital chains, proprietary nursing homes, and private practice professional corporations (PCs) are commercial human service agencies. A traditional American perception has been that business is more efficient because it must survive the crucible of competition, but that its profit and competitive priorities make the client's best interest secondary and encourage it to cut corners on quality of care.

Public agencies are owned and operated by government. *Line agencies,* such as a county health department or a state employment service, have authority delegated from, and are accountable to, the elected chief executive (mayor, governor, president). Where a buffer from partisan politics is desired, the legislature may authorize *autonomous public agencies* governed by independent elected or appointed boards of directors, such as a local school board or the Fed.

Traditionally, the government has been perceived to be in the best position to finance and guarantee universalistic entitlements such as Social Security, but to suffer from impersonal, bureaucratic rigidities that make it less effective for personal social services. It is also seen as limited in its ability to provide innovative, controversial, or low-priority services.

Voluntary charities are defined by Section 501 (c) (3) of the Internal Revenue Code as not-for-profit organizations that use all their income for public-interest educational, cultural, social, and health services. They are accountable to the general public through an annual outside audit of their finances and must conform to constitutional civil rights standards. Section 501 (c) (3) also includes religious bodies that may not meet all of these conditions.

Charities cannot engage in partisan political activity. In practice, this has been extended by Internal Revenue Service interpretations to prohibit "significant" nonpartisan public-interest lobbying in such areas as services to children, welfare reform, civil rights, and environmental protection. (A commercial provider is not subject to this restriction. The costs of nonpartisan lobbying, especially in its own self-interest, are subtracted from taxable income as a proper business expense.)

Voluntary organizations engaged in social policy advocacy are placed in a separate category, Section 501 (c) (4), which exempts them from paying taxes on contributions but denies their donors the personal tax deductions that donors to charities receive. The differentiation between nonprofits engaged in direct services to individual hosts and those engaged in agent or environment interventions reflects a traditional conservative U.S. social policy preference for adjusting people to the status quo as opposed to reforming it.

If an organization wishes to operate in more than one sector, it must make a clear separation. A public university incorporates a separate charitable foundation to receive and administer alumni gifts and endowments. A nonprofit religious order establishes a subsidiary business corporation for its winery. Failure to do so can lead to misunderstandings as noted in the following *Omaha World Herald* editorial:

Nebraska's three members of Congress have agreed to help pickle-card [a gambling device] charities that are being billed for federal income taxes that the groups said they didn't know they owed.

The law says that the churches and other charitable organizations must pay taxes on income from unrelated business activities. If operating a gambling game can legitimately be "related" to the activities of a church or youth organization, or the University of Nebraska at Omaha's athletic department, words have lost their meaning. . . .

The law that is causing the problem was passed in 1986. It was aimed at organizations such as the Unification Church, which runs businesses ranging from a Washington newspaper to a Massachusetts fish cannery. The provision on unrelated business income was designed to address the fact that such businesses have an unfair advantage if their profits are tax-free.[1]

Traditionally, voluntary agencies have been perceived to be best for personalized and caring services and to have the flexibility to be pluralistic and innovative. They can meet needs ignored by other sectors due to controversy, unwanted clients, low priority, or unprofitability. On the negative side they have sometimes been seen as "soft" in administrative and disciplinary areas.

IDEOLOGIES

There are a number of conflicting ideologies about the role of each sector in social welfare. In U.S. social policy, these coexisting currents sometimes create a *riptide*, "a tide opposing another tide or other tides, thus producing a violently disturbed area of water."

Classical Liberalism and Free-Market Economics

"Society in every state is a blessing, but government, even in its best state, is but a necessary evil; in its worst state it is an intolerable one."[2]

"The major threats to individual freedoms are seen to stem from concentrations of political and economic power."[3]

"You cannot extend the mastery of government over the daily lives of the people without at the same time making it the master of their souls and thoughts."[4]

Classical liberalism opposes any concentration of government power. Society operates best through a free market regulated by supply and demand, with open, profit-oriented competition among suppliers/sellers and freedom of choice for consumers/buyers. Why should social welfare be an exception? If someone wants a benefit enough to buy it, someone else will find it worth supplying. If there are safety net gaps, social welfare should be provided in ways that minimize concentrations of power and least disturb the free market. One way is open and equal competition among a diversified mix of voluntary and business providers. Another way is maximum financing of services from personal income, private insurance systems, and charitable contributions.

If unavoidable, there is also public welfare provision through mechanisms such as tax welfare, cash benefits, and vouchers, which maximize consumer choice and provider competition.

Pluralism

"If a man does not keep pace with his companions, perhaps it is because he hears a different drummer. Let him step to the music which he hears, however measured or far away."[5] Pluralism affirms Henry David Thoreau's "different drummer" and recognizes, with John Stuart Mill, the fallibility of the majority. Multiple cultures and lifestyles are a permanent and desirable characteristic of American life. Social welfare must relate to diverse groups on their own grounds and avoid imposing on others any one group's "right way."

This calls for a diversified system of providers that serve cultural and lifestyle minorities as well as the mainstream. Public, voluntary, and business providers are all welcome as parts of this mix. The best form of public social welfare is unrestrictive financing of private sector benefits through tax welfare, purchase of service, and flexible subsidy.

Limitations of Capitalism

The foundation of capitalism, by its own definition, is the profit motive. Richard Tawney distinguished between the businessperson and the professional: "Both provide service and get a reward for doing so, but the professional puts the emphasis on the service, while the businessman puts his on the reward."[6]

Many who advocate capitalism in general believe that commercialism does not belong in social welfare services. Neil Gilbert makes such a distinction:

The structure of governance in nonprofit organizations traditionally involves boards of directors and advisory groups composed of people expected to promote the social welfare interests of the community. . . .

In contrast to nonprofit organizations, the directorship of profit making agencies is concerned with protecting the financial interests of the ownership group to which they usually belong. This is as it should be. Investors, staff, and the general public *expect* the governing bodies of profit making agencies to act in their self-interest. This is not to say that these bodies are oblivious to community welfare or devoid of public spirit. At the bottom line, however, abstract considerations of these sorts rarely take precedence over the hard and clear requirements of profit-and-loss statements.[7]

Institutional Primacy of Government

In this view, government as the primary institution in society for the mutual support function, has bottom-line responsibility "to promote the general welfare." Other rationales for this role include its fiscal power and an ethical belief in universal human rights. About the same time that President Hoover (quoted earlier) rationalized nonintervention in the Great Depression, New York's Governor Franklin Roosevelt expressed an institutional view to his legislature: "Modern society *acting through its government* owes the definite obligation to prevent the starvation or dire waste of any of its fellow men and women who try to maintain themselves but cannot" (emphasis added).[8]

Some would add a religious imperative: "A magistrate is a minister of God for those doing good unto praise."[9] "Under God's law and subject to His authority, the state's necessary and appropriate role is to support good and curb evil. To this end, it establishes and maintains structures to achieve justice and order and to promote the general welfare."[10]

Applications of these beliefs may include

- bottom-line public responsibility for planning, guaranteeing, funding, and assuring standards for basic social welfare services and benefits
- a central public role in funding and/or direct provision of benefits
- an independent voluntary sector that serves as a gadfly and critic, provides controversial services, fills gaps, and pioneers services for later public adoption
- a supplementary role for the commercial sector, to provide "second tier" nonessential services on a "private pay" basis
- pragmatic partnerships of government with the voluntary and business sectors in specific areas

Sphere Sovereignty

Nineteenth-century Dutch Neo-Calvinists asserted that God had established separate spheres, notably the family, the church, and the state. Within its own sphere, each is sovereign; that is, each has God-given functions, responsibility, and authority. It is improper for one sphere to interfere with another. In the Netherlands, sectarian programs provide most personal social services with government funding. A modified version of this can be found in several northeastern states that choose, wherever possible, to purchase adoption and foster care services from sectarian agencies in lieu of direct provision.

Problems arise when citizens disagree on spheres. Nebraska law made education of children a government sphere and set standards for curriculum and teachers. A rural "evangelical" school refused to follow the state curriculum or to hire certified teachers, arguing that education was inseparable from religion and therefore in the family and church spheres. (The court affirmed the state's sovereignty, after which the legislature pragmatically changed the rules to accommodate pluralism.)

Social welfare application of sphere sovereignty can take as many forms as there are viewpoints. Three traditional views have been that

1. all economically viable provisions belong to the business sphere, while residual "charity" is the responsibility of public and voluntary spheres
2. "objective" financial benefits (Social Security, AFDC, etc.) are in the public sphere whereas "personal" services belong to the voluntary
3. delivering child, family, and aging services is a sectarian sphere, while financing them is in the public sphere

Subsidiarity

Although few Americans have heard of subsidiarity, it may be our most popular de facto ideology. It views society as organized in successive levels from the smallest and most primary groupings to the broadest formal structures. Each "higher" (broader) level is *subsidiary* ("acting as a supplement, especially in a secondary capacity") to the smaller and more personalized ones. Applied to social welfare, the order of preference is something like this:

1. informal assistance from relatives, friends, and neighbors
2. mutual assistance and support groups
3. voluntary agencies, preferably nonbureaucratic and decentralized
4. independent business enterprises
5. public financing of other sectors
6. direct public services, as decentralized as circumstances permit
7. central government interventions in the overall social environment

When Pope Pius XI enunciated the principle in 1931, he stressed the negative freedom values of classical liberalism and classical economics:

It is a fundamental principle of social philosophy, fixed and unchangeable, that one should not withdraw from individuals and commit to the community what they can accomplish by their own enterprise and industry.

So too, it is an injustice, a grave evil, and a disturbance of right order for a larger and higher organization to arrogate to itself functions which can be performed by smaller and lower bodies.[11]

Thirty years later, Pope John XXIII further developed subsidiarity by elaborating the responsibility of higher levels to perform the positive freedom and social justice functions that lower levels cannot adequately carry out:

The state should leave to these smaller groups the settlement of business of minor importance. It will thus carry out with greater freedom, power, and success the tasks belonging to it, because it alone can effectively accomplish these, directing, watching, stimulating, and restraining, as circumstances suggest or necessity demands.[12]

It is therefore necessary that the administration give wholehearted and careful attention to the social as well as the economic progress of citizens, and to the development, in keeping with the development of the productive system, of such essential services as the building of roads, transportation, communications, water supply, housing, public health, education, facilitation of the practice of religion, and recreational facilities.

It is necessary also that governments make efforts to see that insurance systems are made available to the citizens, so that, in case of misfortune or increased family responsibilities, no person will be without the necessary means to maintain a decent standard of living.

The government should make similarly effective efforts to see that those who are able to work can find employment in keeping with their aptitudes and that each worker receives a wage in keeping with the laws of justice and equity.

It should be equally the concern of civil authorities to insure that workers be allowed their proper responsibility in the work undertaken in industrial organization, and to facilitate establishment of intermediate groups which will make social life richer and more effective.

Finally, it should be possible for all the citizens to share as far as they are able in their country's cultural advantages.[13]

BLURRING OF DISTINCTIONS

Traditionally the three sectors have been legally and ideologically distinct. However, trends over the past few decades have gradually blurred these differences in practice.

Commercialized Charity

In the past, because they cost more than their users could pay, most human services were provided by subsidized public and voluntary agencies. Obviously, you cannot run a business at a loss—at least, not for long!

Beginning in the 1930s and accelerating after 1950, unions spearheaded a movement that made health insurance standard for all large employers and many smaller ones. In 1965, public insurance was added for the aged (Medicare) and poor (Medicaid).

As public and private insurance began to pay in full for their clients, health care was transformed from a money loser to a potential profit center. It did not take long for alert businesses to begin serving insured patients, and they tended to behave like traditional voluntary agencies. Because insurers used cost reimbursement as the basis for payment (similar to the method used in setting public utility rates), costs and revenues went up and down together. Cutting corners did not increase profits, and providing more expensive services did not reduce them. Under these circumstances, a business could afford to be as patient oriented as a charity. In fact, it paid to be.

Meanwhile, nonprofit and public hospitals became *quasi-commercial*. They were also being paid in full. Contributors and legislators, expecting them to "pay their own way," reduced or ended operating subsidies. Naturally, as they became dependent on sales revenue, they became "businesslike" in their charges and collection practices. They refused service to persons who could not guarantee payment and often discharged or transferred patients who could no longer pay their bills.

Similarly, homes for the aged became commercialized. Traditionally, they were religious charities for indigent widows, but Social Security and private pension plans created a new market of retirees who could pay their own way. Re-created as "retirement communities," businesses moved into the field—and the traditional religious sponsors shifted to more luxurious, self-supporting retirement homes that limited their caring services to paying customers.

The bottom line: In areas where consumers pay the bill directly or through insurance, you may have trouble telling, from its services and business practices, whether an agency is public, voluntary, or commercial.

Quasi-Public Voluntary Agencies

Broad-based voluntary organizations like a community hospital or the United Way have always had public characteristics due to their commitment to serve the entire community, their expectation of general community support, indirect public funding through tax exemption and tax-deductible gifts, and their pragmatic accommodation to the priorities and biases of the majority (or of the local power structure).

The boundary has been further blurred by another trend over recent decades. Many of those agencies now receive a substantial percentage of their operating income both from purchase of service and from public project grants. Ironically, the latter was a response to two opposite ideologies: government control and government divestiture. In the 1960s, the motive was to co-opt the voluntary sector into federal social policy priorities in health, mental health, child welfare, housing, poverty programs, affirmative action, special education, rehabilitation, and many other areas. In the 1970s and 1980s, the primary objective of grants was a shift of social responsibility and decision making from the government to the private sector. To what extent have these voluntary agencies taken on both the positive attributes and the liabilities of the public sector?

Comprehensive Community Mental Health Centers are a classic case of quasi-public agencies. They were authorized by public legislation to achieve public objectives through a government-planned national network of catchment areas. The centers were set up and maintained with public subsidies, subject to public regulation, and even had a requirement that local public officials be on their boards. They tend to receive little or no charitable subsidy. Yet each center is legally incorporated as a voluntary charity!

While they tend to lack some of the unique qualities attributed to voluntarism, these hybrids seem to function successfully in broad, mainstream service areas.

Professionalism Crosses the Lines

Traditionally, voluntary agencies are expected to operate with high standards of staff altruism, individualized caring, self-direction, and professional competence. Public agencies are expected to be standardized, bureaucratized, and less professional. Businesses are expected to give profit precedence over service. Overall, there is a significant thread of truth in these sector distinctions.

However, in real life, it is not that simple and clearcut, particularly where there are dominant professional cultures. Are public university professors less dedicated, less competent, less free academically, less collegial in governance—or less idiosyncratic and persnickety—than in private universities? Not in my experience with both sectors! In good ways and bad, they have more in common with their peers in another sector than with other staff within their own programs.

Similarly, management priorities may vary somewhat according to sector, but I have personally encountered little difference among public, voluntary, and commercial hospitals in the competence, dedication, and patient care provided by the direct-service nurses, physicians, and social workers whom they employ. Have you?

Exceptions to general sector patterns are common in direct medical care, counseling, and psychotherapy. I have known many cases where middle-class clients received more dedicated service at less cost, and with a gentler approach to fee collection, from a private practitioner (a small business) than from a nonprofit clinic or agency—and many of those private practitioners quietly give charitable service at their personal expense.

CHURCH AND STATE RELATIONSHIPS

Because so many voluntary health, education, and welfare agencies have some sectarian identification, church-state questions are inevitably tied to the subject of public-voluntary relationships.

There are three basic patterns of church-state relationship: domination, partnership, and separation. Before discussing them, it may be useful to identify major organizational and ideological differences within the term *sectarian*, which loosely refers to any agency, program, or activity identified with a particular religion or religious group.

- *Sects*, such as the Amish, the Pilgrims, and some modern evangelical churches, are "called apart" through strict membership qualifications and practices.
- *Churches* are more inclusive, often blanketing people into membership by birth or even nationality—indeed, *catholic* means "all inclusive"—and integrated into the larger society as basic functional institutions.
- *Associational* organizations have no formal religious auspice but may have a general identity with beliefs or members of a religious body. Examples are Jewish community services and liberal arts colleges founded by such Protestant denominations as Episcopal, Presbyterian, and the United Church of Christ.

Domination

Church and state may be merged in a *theocracy*, a "government by priests claiming to rule with divine authority," such as the Massachusetts Bay Colony under the Puritans or Iran under its Ayatollah. This tends to be associated with dominant sects.

A *secular creed* may operate the same way. Since it has no "theo" (God), perhaps we should call it *credocracy*. In the Soviet Union from 1920 to 1990, Communist party "priests" ruled with the transcendent authority of Marxist ideology. Traditional religions were suppressed and persecuted as competitors that were inherently subversive to the True Faith and its dominance.

A more subtle domination, associated with churches, is *nonsectarian sectarianism*, in which de facto religiocultural content is consistently followed and even imposed, sometimes unwittingly, through secular programs that have no formal religious connection at all. While nineteenth-century U.S. Catholic and Jewish minorities were developing extensive sectarian social welfare systems, mainline middle-class Anglo-Protestant churches were not. Why should they? Basic social institutions such as public schools, child welfare, and charity organization societies already embodied *their* beliefs and values. The school prayer controversy relates to this pattern.

Partnership

Religions that believe that both the church and the state are instituted by God to carry out divine purposes in society lean toward one of the following forms of partnership and collaboration:

- *An established church,* as in many Catholic and Lutheran countries, has special privileges and responsibilities. It often receives public subsidies for its education and social welfare programs. Other religions may be either tolerated without special benefits or repressed.

- *Multiple establishment* evolved as a compromise approach in Germany and the Netherlands. Divided on whether to establish a Catholic or a Protestant church, they established both.

- *Nonestablishment* permits a friendly, cooperative attitude between church and state with neither privileges nor restrictions. Religious bodies have the same right as secular organizations to advocate economic justice, "right to life," or any other social policy. Sectarian agencies have no more nor less access to public subsidy than nonsectarian ones.

Separation

By contrast, separation calls for church and state to have as little to do with each other as possible. It may be advocated from opposite directions. Sects want separation of church and state to protect their sovereign sphere from government intrusion. On the other side, antireligion activists want separation because of their conscientious objection to any use of their tax dollars for religious purpose.

Another reason for separation is purely pragmatic. A religious group, unable to prevail, may opt for separation to prevent any other church from being established or exerting influence over the government. Pragmatic separationists, should they gain sufficient power, may shift their policy preference to partnership or domination. John Robinson, pastor to the Pilgrims, observed with candor: "Protestants living in the countries of the papists [Roman Catholics] commonly plead for toleration of religions: so do papists that live where Protestants bear sway: though few of either, especially of the clergy . . . would have the other tolerated where the world goes on their side."[14]

PUBLIC FUNDING OF SECTARIAN SERVICES IN THE UNITED STATES

The First Amendment

At one time or another, several colonies had established churches: Congregational in several New England states, Reformed in New York and

New Jersey, Anglican in Virginia, Roman Catholic in Maryland. Others, founded by and for victims of persecution (Quakers in Pennsylvania, Baptists in Rhode Island), distrusted any established church. Unable to agree on one religion for the United States as a whole, they compromised on neutrality: "Congress shall make no law respecting an establishment of religion, or prohibiting the free exercise thereof."

What did they intend in 1789, nonestablishment or "wall of separation"? What should it mean now? The Supreme Court itself cannot seem to decide. Its decisions have gone both ways, leaving an unsettled and ambiguous gray area.

Content, Impact, or Auspice?

A central issue around public funding for sectarian health, education, and welfare services is whether "religion," for First Amendment purposes, is determined by specific religious *content*, the general religious *impact*, or *structural* church-relatedness. In each case, there are gray areas which make the exact boundary of "fundability" uncertain.

The content approach is least restrictive. The government will not subsidize chaplaincy services in a Catholic hospital but sees no problem with paying for an appendectomy. Sometimes the boundary is elusive. In a parochial school, Bible study is religious and math is not, but what about a literature course that excludes censored writings or a social studies course taught from the value orientation of the religion?

A stricter test is probable religious impact. Is there a difference between a nun teaching arithmetic to first graders in a room that displays a crucifix and a professor teaching statistics in a Baptist college? Court decisions have tended to take impressionability of the student into account, applying more restrictive standards to elementary schools than to universities whose students are presumably sophisticated adults.

The most restrictive approach may be auspice, on the premise that the simple fact of being related to a religious body makes every activity inherently religious, regardless of content, objectives, or impact. (Critics counter that discriminating among otherwise identical nonreligious services solely on the basis of auspice violates equal protection under the law.) Even here there are gray areas. Is there a difference between a parish-owned parochial school and a Jewish community center that is an autonomous secular corporation?

A related issue has been how the First Amendment applies to public employment of ordained clergy and members of religious orders. Since separation of church and state prohibits the government from legally recognizing internal church status, those individuals have a constitutional right to equal treatment under the law, without discrimination related to their free exercise of personal religion outside the job. Thus a minister can be president, a nun can teach in a public school, and a priest-psychologist can be reimbursed for psychotherapy services. However, no one, lay or ordained, can act as an agent of a church or perform religious functions in his or her capacity as a government official, and the priest-psychologist cannot be reimbursed for spiritual counseling.[15]

Kind of Funding

In practice, the rigor with which "separation" is applied varies with the funding method. *Direct subsidy* of an agency budget is scrutinized the most. Any or all of the three criteria may be applied. Once a boundary is established, whatever it may be, direct subsidy seldom crosses it.

For *purchase of service*, on the other hand, auspice alone is seldom a legal issue. Government third-party payments for health and social services tend to use a content approach exclusively. In education, impact seems to be the key factor.

Church and state issues are often ignored entirely in areas of *tax welfare*. This applies both to *indirect public purchase* (e.g., tax credits for payments to sectarian daycare centers) and to *indirect subsidy* (matching tax-deductible contributions to religious groups). Most people do not realize that such tax welfare is a government subsidy. Others point out that even though the sectarian provider benefits, the official transaction is between the government and the individual. Besides, they add, it is a long-established and popular practice.

Government aid to church-related services does not come without strings. To be eligible, a sectarian health and welfare agency must agree to meet the same professional standards and Section 501 (c) (3) requirements as nonsectarian charities. Both the subsidy and the accompanying regulation are compatible with "nonestablishment" but a breach of "separation."

There is another, seldom recognized consideration in this partnership: If the government payment for service is less than the agency's cost, the sectarian agency is actually subsidizing the state, which would otherwise have to bear the full cost of providing the service itself.

WHO IS RIGHT?

How do you decide who should do what? On the average, each sector—sectarian, nonsectarian voluntary, business, and public—has certain assets and liabilities. Yet as we have seen, in any given case, "It ain't necessarily so." It may be useful to look at it from three different angles before deciding which way to go.

1. *Ideology*. Do you, or someone else who matters, have ideological objections to some auspices and relationships or preferences for others? How important are they?

2. *Pragmatism*. How well does each get the job done, with what costs and drawbacks? The answer may be different for different agencies, different regions, and/or different program areas.

3. *Legality*. What you consider to be ideologically and/or pragmatically desirable may be legal in another nation but unconstitutional in your own.

And then again, there is the traditional U.S. approach to these questions: muddle through.

SUMMARY

There are three sectors of human service providers. Traditionally, the public sector has been seen as appropriate for broad, expensive, and impersonal social welfare functions and for funding other sectors. The commercial sector has been seen as more efficient but suspect in its service priorities. The voluntary sector has been seen as appropriate for personalized caring; for cultural, sectarian, and other subgroup services; and for creative innovations.

These generalizations were always only partly true. In recent decades, the growth of public grants and purchase of service have blurred some of the old distinctions. Businesses have expanded into traditional charity domains, and charities have become more businesslike. In another direction, as public dollars have become a primary source of revenue for all sectors, voluntary and commercial providers have become more standardized and public-like. The growth of accreditation and licensing has further reduced the sector differences.

A variety of ideological perspectives are active in this area. There are pro- and anticommercial views, and there are pro- and antigovernment views. Two ideologies propose systematic divisions of labor: a horizontal one (sphere sovereignty) and a vertical one (subsidiarity). Pluralistic views support a potpourri with no sector or ideology in control.

In the United States, a major sector issue is between government and sectarian voluntary agencies. Church-state relationships can involve dominance by a religious body or a secular creed; partnership; or separation. The First Amendment and related court decisions are ambiguous as to whether church and state should have an open border or an iron curtain.

Separation is most strict regarding symbolic actions and programs affecting children. Nonestablishment cooperation without favoritism tends to prevail in health, higher education, and adult services. Tax welfare policy leans toward multiple establishment, including a number of special privileges and indirect subsidies.

NOTES

1. *Omaha World Herald*, April, 11, 1990.

2. Thomas Paine, *Common Sense*, 1776.

3. Charles Rowley and Alan Peacock, *Welfare Economics: A Liberal Restatement* (London: Martin Robertson, 1975), p. 90.

4. Herbert Hoover, quoted in Walter Trattner, *From Poor Law to Welfare State*, 4th ed. (New York: Free Press, 1989), p. 252.

5. Henry David Thoreau, *Walden*, 1854, "Conclusion."

6. Richard Tawney, *The Acquisitive Society*, New York: Harcourt Brace, 1921.

7. Neil Gilbert, *Capitalism and the Welfare State* (New Haven, CT: Yale University Press), 1983, p. 14.

8. Quoted in Trattner, *From Poor Law to Welfare State*, p. 254.

9. John Calvin, *Institutes of the Christian Religion*, IV, 20, 4.

10. "Church Hospitals and the Hill-Burton Act: A Statement Approved at the 1961 Annual Meeting of the National Lutheran Council," mimeographed.

11. Pope Pius XI, Encyclical "Quadragesimo anno," 1931.

12. Pope John XXIII, Encyclical "Mater et magistra," 1961.

13. Pope John XXIII, Encyclical "Pacem in terris," 1963.

14. Quoted in *Relations between Church and State*, published by the Massachusetts Council of Churches for the Association of Council Secretaries, 1961, p. 10.

15. An exception to this is military and prison chaplains, who are paid by the government to provide religious services to "captive" citizens in order to protect their right to religious freedom.

Chapter 13

Who Pays the Piper?

A social welfare service is not created out of thin air. Someone pays for it. This is done in many ways, but it boils down to two basic approaches: economic market (*sell* the product) and social market (*subsidize* the producer).

SUBSIDIES

A subsidy is given to the agency to cover the cost (fully or partially) of providing a service or material aid. It may be public money, directly from an appropriation or grant or indirectly through tax welfare. It may be charitable gifts, bequests, or endowments. It may in the form of in-kind goods and volunteer services. Some subsidies are available for any legitimate agency activity. Others are narrowly designated for a specific purpose.

Restricted

Donor-restricted subsidies are earmarked by the giver for specific purposes, such as landscaping the campus or training social workers to work with the chronically mentally ill. They apply Saul Alinsky's golden rule: "He who has the gold makes the rule."

Through restricted funding a private donor persuades an agency to give priority to his or her special interest, be it research on a rare disease,

abortion counseling, or building up the football team. The federal government achieves national priorities with decentralized administration by offering grants to states, localities, and nonprofit organizations willing to
do the job through their own programs.

In-kind gifts may be donated goods, such as food for a pantry service
or used dental equipment for a neighborhood clinic. They may be free
use of equipment, such as a loaned van for transporting clients or access
to a mainframe computer. Volunteers donate work as scout leaders or
hotline counselors, or by giving free legal and financial counsel to the
agency. An in-kind contribution is inherently restrictive. You cannot feed
a volunteer to hungry clients nor use a donated typewriter for crisis
intervention.

There are partial in-kind contributions. If a shopping mall invites a family service agency to set up a branch for a token rent, the difference between the commercial value of the space and the rent actually charged
is an in-kind gift. So is 50 percent of the service performed by a teaching
sister who voluntarily works for half the regular salary of lay teachers.

Most agencies would prefer *cash gifts* to in-kind subsidies. The volunteer
or equipment may not be as satisfactory as what the agency could have
bought. However, like other restricted giving, it is probably a take-it-or-
leave-it choice. Volunteers may have time but not money to offer. Donors
of equipment may be motivated by a tax or business advantage that an
equivalent cash gift does not offer. From an agency perspective, the ideal
in-kind subsidy is one that substitutes for an otherwise necessary cash
expenditure. If the agency has to transport clients, a loaned van directly
saves the cost of buying one. The teaching sister's salary reduction saves
part of the cost of the lay teacher who would otherwise have had to be
hired.

For the donor, control is an obvious advantage of restricted giving. From
the agency perspective, there are several disadvantages. The biggest one
is lack of flexibility. The agency does not necessarily get what it needs
most. An alumni gift for a new football team weight room, however
welcome, cannot be used to upgrade an inadequate library.

"Following the money" changes agency priorities, not infrequently at
the expense of its primary mission. A school of social work on which its
region depended for professional practitioners obtained several worthwhile research and community service grants, each of which required
allocation of time from full-time faculty members. Many programs carry
enough faculty to handle both teaching and grants projects. In this case,
however, the school was understaffed and overextended to begin with.
Like an anemic blood donor, it further depleted its degree program to
provide transfusions to grant projects. Before long, 40 percent of its courses
were being taught by part-time instructors who lacked full academic
credentials. When accreditation questions were raised, the school chose

to curtail its primary mission by dropping a branch used by students from underserved rural areas rather than reduce its restricted funding.

A similar displacement of goals occurred in the late 1960s when expansion of restricted direct-service grants diverted most Community Action Programs from their original social development priority.

Restricted subsidies usually cost more to administer. There may be extra costs to train and supervise volunteers, prepare proposals, maintain separate accounting, and prepare reports to the donor. Nevertheless, it can be a great benefit to agencies when it (1) coincides with agency objectives, (2) adds to rather than displaces agency priorities, and/or (3) forces greater accountability upon a sloppy agency.

Unrestricted

Unrestricted subsidies give an agency the flexibility to use the money wherever it will do the most good, within the legal boundaries of its charter. Agencies usually prefer this. Donors who agree with the agency mission and trust its leadership usually allow this flexibility. Because unrestricted money could legally be retained by the owner as profit, commercial human services rarely seek or receive unrestricted contributions.

Moral Restrictions?

For an auditor there is no middle ground. Either the funds are legally restricted or they are not. However, within the legally unrestricted category, there may be some quasi-restrictive internal practices. A sometimes misunderstood category is *board-designated funds*. This is unrestricted income that has been set aside by the agency board for an earmarked purpose. However, the agency can "unrestrict" it again if and when it chooses.

There may be a nonbinding *understanding* between agency and donor on how legally unrestricted money will be used. At its simplest level, an agency leans toward honoring a funder's preferences, especially if it plans to ask for money again next year.

More shrewdly, unwritten understandings have been used to get around Internal Revenue Service regulations that deny tax deductions for contributions to support social advocacy. A wealthy supporter of a social justice movement found that direct contributions were not deductible. A right-wing ideologist encountered the same problem in promoting his economic policies. The first made an unrestricted contribution to her church mission board, whose executive informally assured her that an equal or greater amount from another part of the board's budget would be allocated to that cause. The other endowed a professorship of economics that the university "coincidentally" offered to an apologist for the donor's viewpoint.

Complicating the issue of moral restrictions is the dilemma of multiple accountability. Which takes precedence, the preferences of direct donors; the values of indirect donors, such as the taxpayers who provide the tax welfare share of a deductible gift; the well-being of those served; or the best interests of collective society? There may not be one universal right answer. According to situational ethics, it depends on many variables in any given situation. If so, one needs to develop principles and guidelines to help sort out those variables.

INDIRECT GOVERNMENT SUBSIDY

Tax Exemption

Nonprofit social welfare organizations are tax exempt. The government does not collect income taxes on the agency's program-related revenue, including service fees, contributions, and income from endowments. Many states and cities waive property and sales taxes as well. This is tax welfare: Any taxes forgiven have the same effect on net usable income as a government cash contribution in that amount.

Tax Deductibility

The charitable deduction is another tax welfare subsidy. If there were no deduction, a donor with $100 available would first pay the tax on it and then donate the remainder. Instead, the government contributes its tax share on that $100. Here is how it works.

A lower-middle-income taxpayer pays $15 per $100 of income to the federal government plus about 1/5 of that amount ($3) in state income taxes. The government gets $18; he keeps $82 after taxes. When he makes a $100 deductible gift, he gives his $82 share, and the government gives its $18 share. (Dividing $18 by $82, we find the government is donating $.22 for each after-tax net dollar he contributes out of his own pocket.)

An upper-income taxpayer in the 28 percent bracket pays $28 to the federal government plus $5.60 to the state. Her deductible $100 gift costs her a net of $66.40, which the government matches with its $33.60 tax share.

There is more. If your gift is cash, you get the regular deduction. If you give it in appreciated stock, real estate, or other investments, you get the full regular deduction and, *in addition*, a second deduction on the capital gains due on those securities. Whereas few working-class wage earners can take advantage of this option, the upper-income giver usually can. If she gives $100 in stock she bought for $50, she saves the income tax ($16.80) on the $50 capital gain. Added to the $33.60 calculated above, the government's share of the contribution has increased to $50.40, and her net share is reduced to $49.60. The government is donating more than a dollar for each after-tax dollar she contributes out of her own pocket, nearly five times the matching rate for the modest income giver.

Everybody likes the charitable deduction. Agencies get more dollars. Givers like it because it increases the impact of their gifts. Humanitarians applaud its social benefits and its encouragement of the spirit of giving and caring. Libertarians associate it with freedom, pluralism, and individualism. Those who distrust big government like the idea of diverting taxes from public welfare to private charities.

So who could criticize it? Well, it *is* regressive redistribution.[1] In the illustration above, for every net dollar from the giver's pocket, the government added $.22 to the lower giver's charity but over $1.00 for the higher giver's one. (This is on purpose to encourage philanthropy by those who can afford large gifts. In contrast, on political contributions where it wishes to encourage many small gifts, it uses a tax-credit system that provides the same benefit to both givers.) And where did those gifts go? Primary recipients of the small, lower-matched gifts are churches and social services. Major recipients of the large, higher-matched gifts are private universities, prep schools, and the fine arts. Thus, most of the government's subsidy through the charitable deduction goes for services used primarily by upper-income persons.

A further effect, which is desirable or not according to your ideology, is that by decentralizing social welfare choices to affluent taxpayers, this indirect tax welfare subsidy method retards the development of national public social welfare priorities.

Other Subsidies

Largely unnoticed are other odds and ends of government subsidy. An example is the following snippet, buried in a lengthy report on the federal budget: "The Treasury and Postal Service appropriations bill ran over budget chiefly because an extra $820 million was provided the Postal Service to subsidize lower [postage] rates for charities."[2]

Although commercial human services do not have tax exemption or deductibility, they do have access to a different set of government subsidies. Unable to afford an operating deficit in its church-related teaching hospital, a medical school sold the hospital to a business corporation. *Accelerated depreciation* (allowing a tax deduction greater than the actual decrease in the value of capital equipment) created paper losses that the corporation used to reduce taxes on earnings in its other enterprises. The tax benefit more than offset a small, real operating loss. Thus, a complicated tax welfare subsidy available only to commercial enterprises enabled the community to retain a needed community service.

SALES REVENUE

Historically most social welfare services had to be subsidized because they cost more than their users could afford. In recent years, however, as both employers and government have turned to purchase of services instead of direct provision, sales revenue has replaced subsidy as the primary source of income in many service areas.

This is popular for several reasons. It offers an alternative to large civil service bureaucracies. It reduces administrative headaches for large employers and enables smaller ones to offer competitive benefit packages. Unions like the fact that employers are less able to dispense benefits in controlling ways. Free-enterprise supporters accept it as a compromise that preserves a competitive economic market in the "human service business." Users like the greater freedom of choice it offers.

There are two obvious methods for buying services. The traditional method is *payment for services received*. After your car gets repaired, you receive and pay a bill for parts and labor. After you get repaired, you receive and pay a medical bill for parts and labor.

The other is *prepayment* for future benefits. Some contracts specify the benefit. Students pay tuition in advance for a designated course. Other prepayments buy variable benefits. The fee paid in advance to a Health Maintenance Organization (HMO) buys whatever medical services become needed.

SETTING THE PRICE

If social welfare services are to be sold, how should the price be set?

Maximizing Profit

Business (including private professional practice) is expected to maximize profit by charging the highest price the traffic will bear. Nonprofit agencies in such areas as adoption and health care may also follow this principle in order to earn "operating surpluses," which they may apply to money-losing services or capital improvements.

In a free market, competition among sellers and bargaining by buyers who have a choice of providers keep prices under control. However, social welfare seldom meets free-market conditions. A sick patient may have little or no choice of hospital. His physician will probably tell him where to go. And the last thing on his mind is to haggle over price. Even where there is choice and time to make it, the average patient does not have the information or technical competence to evaluate and compare hospitals. The hopeful adoptive parent, in a "seller's market" (in this case, a shortage of available babies) is in no position to argue about fees. Under these circumstances, "what the traffic will bear" can exploit vulnerable clients and patients.

Audited Cost

For private utilities and other situations where free-market competition is not practical, the government counters the monopoly effect by fixing a *cost-plus* "fair price." This is based on the audited cost of producing the product plus an extra percentage to provide a fair profit. The government and insurance companies use the audited-cost approach in negotiating the price for the hospital services they purchase.

The basic building block is an *itemized* bill. A service is broken into its component parts (a drug dose, an hour of therapy). The direct cost of each item is calculated, and a pro rata share of "overhead" (administration, depreciation, and utilities) is added in.

This is cumbersome to administer, open to frequent errors, and difficult to check. A compromise has been to *cluster* items into a standard package with a set price based on the average total of all items. Per diem rates for basic room, board, and care in a hospital, nursing home, or institution are clusters.

Later, Medicare came up with the idea of a *supercluster* prospective pricing system. It analyzed the average cost in all hospitals in a region for an average cluster of items required in a total treatment package for each of several hundred diagnostically related groups (DRGs), such as appendicitis, normal childbirth, and open heart surgery. Based on this data, a set price was fixed for each DRG.

Client Ability to Pay

Social welfare programs that have both sales and subsidy income may set fees based on what the client can afford. The following are three common approaches:

1. *Attributed general ability to pay.* A state college that serves middle-income students sets an "affordable" tuition rate (price) at 1/3 the actual cost, subsidizing the rest from taxes.
2. *Attributed differences in ability to pay.* A YMCA has above-cost "businessmen's memberships" to subsidize below-cost "youth memberships."
3. *Sliding scale.* A family service agency charges its audited cost to affluent clients. Using a means test, it individually reduces this fee to what each lower-income client can afford.

Symbolic

In some well-subsidized programs that could offer the service free, a symbolic price may be charged for its effect on the user, unrelated to cost. Our society puts a stigma on receiving charity, and we also tend to assume that what is free "can't be worth much." Even a token payment may improve client self-esteem and respect for the service, as well as create a motivation "to get my money's worth" by making good use of the service.

A Shot in the Dark

A hallowed method used to be the ignorant guess. Before nonprofit programs were required to do program accounting, many of them had no idea what any specific service actually cost. Fees were simply a shot in the dark or a number off the top of their heads.

The image of human service administrators as soft hearted and soft headed is now in disrepute. In the businesslike atmosphere of the United States in the late twentieth century, funders and active boards of directors want to know actual costs and require explicit justification for any below-cost prices. It is still okay to be soft hearted, but not to be soft headed.

THIRD PARTY PAYMENTS

The most significant funding development of the second half of the twentieth century in the United States has been the growth of third-party payments. There are always at least two parties to a service, a provider and a user. Traditionally, the first party (provider) subsidized it and/or the second party (user) bought it. If someone else purchases the service for the user, a *third party* is introduced.

Among the largest third-party purchasers of service are employers, public and private health insurance, the military, and such public social service programs as vocational rehabilitation, child welfare, and Title XX of the Social Security Act.

This started in the private insurance field.[3] The traditional insurance method was *indemnity*, a cash payment to the insuree (or survivor) to compensate for a loss after it has occurred. This is still common in life, homeowner's, disability, and unemployment insurance.

However, in health insurance the indemnity approach presented problems for both the patient and the provider. The patient had a financial crisis. He did not have the cash flow to pay the bill first and wait for reimbursement. Sometimes he went without. Other times the doctor and hospital provided the service anyway. If he did have insurance, likely as not he was no longer sick when he finally received the insurance check, so he spent it for something he needed or wanted at that time, leaving the bill still unpaid.

Hospitals solved these problems by creating their own insurance company, Blue Cross, which made the payments directly to them, instead of to the patient. This both freed the patient from financial anxiety and guaranteed that the hospital would get paid. Everybody was happy. Physicians (Blue Shield), the government, and other insurance companies soon followed suit.

A problem with third-party payments has been cost control. Consumers who do not pay their individual bills ask for the best care available regardless of cost. The providers want to maximize service and revenue. The third party that pays the piper (and the employer or taxpayer who foots the bill) is "stuck" with health care inflation.

One response to rising costs has been *withdrawal* from social responsibility. In the United States, Medicaid, private insurance, and Medicare made a variety of incremental cutbacks in services covered, the share of costs paid, and eligibility. Asked about unmet needs, they shrugged sympathetically.

Private insurance tends to restrict coverage by itemizing exclusions. Medicaid takes the other approach of itemizing what *is* covered. A procedural method to limit coverage makes payment for nonemergency surgical and hospital services conditional upon a separate review and written preapproval by the payer.

Another response is to *increase control* over services, providers, and price. Eschewing the central command approach of a single national health service, third-party payers have used lesser-control approaches. One is to set a ceiling on what they will pay for a given service. One variation of this, the DRG prospective pricing system, adds a capitalist twist to price control by offering profit incentives to providers who spend less on treatment.

A third cost reduction device is the *preferred provider system*: "I can get it for you wholesale." The payer negotiates a discount from one provider in return for guaranteeing a large volume of business. Insurees can use the preferred provider and have their full bill paid or exercise their freedom of choice by absorbing the retail markup (the price difference between the preferred provider and what their independent doctor charges).

Provider-Insurers

Occupying the middle ground are HMOs. A comprehensive HMO is a private version of the universal British health care model. It collects premiums like an insurance company but provides all needed health services directly instead of buying them from others. Thus it combines in one organization the provider's interest in service and the payer's concern for cost control. It promises the patient security, convenience, and efficiency in exchange for freedom of choice.

Obviously, a full HMO requires a large membership base. A compromise for smaller memberships has been the hybrid prospective payment group (PPG), which provides basic medical services directly but purchases specialized hospital services.

Theoretically, where there are competing autonomous HMOs within a regional market, the opportunity to shop among HMOs maintains economic-market checks and balances. In practice, it appears that large, comprehensive, carefully planned and professionally managed HMOs have had notable success for half a century, while many smaller and newer ones, especially for-profit PPGs, have been criticized by their insurees for alleged reluctance to authorize (and purchase) appropriate services from medical specialists and hospitals.

Economizing versus Maximizing Services

Incentives may be developed either to maximize services or to economize. Maximum utilization is encouraged by prepaid HMOs and full third-party reimbursement because it does not cost the patient any more to do so.

Economizing incentives discourages unnecessary (as well as necessary) demands for services by making it unpleasant or costly for the patient to seek service. The standard methods are

- *Deductibles.* The initial burden is on the consumer. For instance, you pay the first day's hospitalization or the first $100 of medical fees.
- *Coinsurance.* You pay 20 percent (or some other percentage) of all costs.
- *Red tape.* Time-consuming, unpleasant, and frustrating procedures, such as lengthy forms, second opinions by insurance company physicians, and written preapproval, deter patients from seeking care.

On the provider side, audited-cost reimbursement is an incentive to maximize services. The more providers provide, the more they get paid. On the other hand, *prepayment* (as in HMOs) and *prepricing* (as in DRGs) are incentives to economize because providers are paid the same for extensive or the minimum service.

OLD AND NEW FEDERALISM

One of the hottest policy issues for centuries has been nationalism versus localism. What is the responsibility of the national government for social welfare? When should it provide benefits directly? When should it finance social welfare without running it? What should be left strictly to state and local government? To the private sector? To individuals? How can you allow local variations yet protect the equal rights of all citizens?[4]

There are several centralizing imperatives. Advanced technology creates needs for both public and private sector coordination of production, distribution, and the monetary system. We band together for mutual protection from foreign threats, both real and imagined. Those who have experienced race, gender, age, or lifestyle discrimination turn to the Constitution, Congress, and the federal Department of Justice for protection against localized and private sector injustices.

There also seems to be an innate decentralizing spirit in humans, which even seventy years of repressive central control could not stamp out in the Soviet Union. For all our centralization needs, we want to protect ourselves from becoming victims of our protectors, keep our individual identity and freedom within a mass society, and preserve the rich subcultural heritage of our roots.

Our federal system under the Constitution is a conscious attempt to set up checks and balances. Yet it is an uneasy, never quite settled, compromise. There has always been a tension between centralization and decentralization with a "moving equilibrium" that flows back and forth. Some of us who see human fallibility as universal may not want this tension ever to be fully resolved.

Origins: A Limited Federal Role

In 1789, the Constitution created a federated national government to which formerly independent member states delegated certain specified functions and authority to carry them out. These included

1. interstate and international commerce
2. military defense
3. foreign relations
4. immigration and citizenship
5. the general welfare.[5]

States' Rights and the Pierce Veto

In the early years, what public social welfare existed at all was generally at the local and state level, with a few exceptions such as veterans' pensions and landgrants[6] for education.

In 1854, Dorothea Dix persuaded Congress to authorize landgrant subsidies for state mental hospitals. In his veto of the bill, President Pierce (who was elected by a coalition that included the slave states) made a strong case against any federal support for social welfare. The Union is a federation of sovereign states voluntarily banded together for limited purposes, he said, not a nation in its own right. In support, he cited the Tenth Amendment, which reserved to the states everything not specifically delegated to the federal government or forbidden to them. He dismissed the clause "to provide for the common defense and general welfare of the United States" as vague rhetoric:

Indeed, to suppose it susceptible of any other construction would be to consign all the rights of the States and of the people of the States to the mere discretion of Congress, and thus to clothe the Federal Government with authority to control the sovereign States, by which they would have been dwarfed into provinces or departments and all sovereignty vested in an absolute consolidated central power, against which the spirit of liberty has so often and in so many countries struggled in vain.[7]

He added a pragmatic fiscal argument. Federal support for the mentally ill would set a precedent that by extension could make all illness, poverty, and need a federal responsibility. This, he warned, could overwhelm the government.

Ebb and Flow

Since the Pierce veto, the tide of national versus decentralized responsibility has ebbed and flowed several times. Several "sovereign states," using the Pierce rationale, tried to quit the Union. Their interpretation was overruled by superior fire power in the War between the States. Immediately after the Civil War, three amendments expanded federal power to intervene internally within the states: the Thirteenth abolished slavery, the Fourteenth mandated equal protection under state laws, and the Fifteenth guaranteed voting rights to black men (but not to women or Indians). In addition, the Freedman's Bureau was established as a direct federal education and social service program for freed slaves.

These increases in federal power and responsibility were reversed or subverted by the courts, state legislatures, Congress, and large corporations after 1870, ushering in an era of laissez-faire government, robber baron capitalism, and Jim Crow racism.

In the Progressive Era, from about 1901 to 1920, the federal government expanded its power and aggressiveness, especially in the established areas of military action, foreign affairs, and interstate commerce, but also to a lesser degree in social welfare. The U.S. Children's Bureau was established as a national social welfare advocate. Labor laws were passed to protect women and children. States established pensions for destitute widows and the aged. A federal maternal and child health program was passed. The Nineteenth Amendment at last extended voting rights to women. About the same time, the Eighteenth Amendment, Prohibition, set a radical precedent for central social control by intervening in the private behaviors of individuals within the states.

Although perhaps not recognized at the time, a pivotal event in 1912 was the Sixteenth Amendment, authorizing an income tax, which ultimately eliminated Pierce's second argument by giving the federal government the ability to finance a welfare state.

The "normalcy" era of the 1920s largely returned the nation to the decentralized policies and practices of the nineteenth century. This included the termination of most federal and state social welfare programs.

A New Deal: Providing for General Welfare

In 1933, Franklin Roosevelt rejected the Pierce arguments by responding to massive suffering with massive federal interventions. In 1937 the Supreme Court affirmed federal social welfare under the "general welfare" clause. In the first of two Social Security Act decisions, it said, in reference to unemployment benefits:

The fact developed quickly that the states were unable to give the requisite relief. The problem had become national in area and dimensions. There was need of help from the nation if the people were not to starve. It is too late today for the argument to be heard with tolerance that in a crisis so extreme the use of the moneys of the nation to relieve the unemployed and their dependents is a use for any purpose narrower than *the promotion of the general welfare*.[8]

In the second decision, the scope of "general welfare" was broadened further to include noncrisis social welfare:

The scheme of benefits created by the provisions of Title II [old-age and survivor insurance] is not a contravention of the limitations of the Tenth Amendment. *Congress may spend money in aid of the "general welfare"*, Constitution, Art. I, section 8. . . . The line must still be drawn between one welfare and another, between particular and general. . . . The discretion, however, is not confided to the courts. *The discretion belongs to Congress*, unless the choice is clearly wrong, a display of arbitrary power, not an exercise of judgment (emphasis added).[9]

CURRENT METHODS OF FEDERAL FINANCING AND CONTROL

Since 1937, the federal government has been "here to stay" in the business of providing and/or financing social welfare benefits. The extent and nature of that participation, however, has responded to the continuing ebb and flow of ideology and policy on the proper federal, state, and private sector balance.

The federal government participates in social welfare through direct administration, purchase, restricted grants, open grants, and indirect subsidies.

Direct Federal Administration

In the United States, there has been a traditional reservation about federal administration of direct services due to such factors as historical compromises between state and federal roles, ideological fears of centralized power, and a widely held (and widely disputed) premise that locally controlled social programs are more caring and responsive to individual human needs.

Several direct programs evolved from constitutional military functions. The most obvious is the Veterans Administration. Another large social welfare program provides direct-health, mental health, and social services for active military personnel and their dependents.

Less obvious are programs that are extensions of foreign policy. The Bureau of Indian Affairs and the Indian Health Service began as part of the administration of *occupied nations* (defeated Indian tribes confined to reservations). More recently, direct federal welfare and resettlement programs were provided for Cuban refugees of U.S. foreign policy toward Castro and later for Southeast Asians who were displaced allies from a foreign war. By contrast, there was no federal program for Haitians because their refugee status, however compelling, was not caused by U.S. foreign policy.

After "general welfare" became a basis for federal involvement, direct administration tended to develop for practical reasons of effectiveness and/or efficiency especially where there was a focus on

- *universalism*, such as old-age, retirement, and disability insurances
- *equal treatment*, such as SSI for needy aged and disabled persons
- *objective and impersonal* eligibility and benefits (as opposed to individualized diagnostic or "investment" evaluation)

Purchase

Purchase from contractors is an alternative to direct federal provision that retains desired controls over eligibility, utilization, standards, and priorities while permitting some flexibility and pluralism. Because purchase involves a negotiated price, there need be no intrinsic preference among public, nonprofit, and commercial providers. The reasons for purchase instead of direct provision tend to fall into three categories:

1. *Economic*. It is cheaper to buy small quantities of services than to provide them directly over a dispersed geographic area. The military buys health services for its dependents located at bases that do not have full-service health installations.

2. *Political*. Supporters of a social program may buy off opposition by making the program profitable for them. Medicare and Medicaid were passed only after writing in an expensive fee-for-service system which raised physicians' incomes.

3. *Ideological*. Purchase in the free market is preferred over direct public provision by those who stress individualism, pluralism, freedom of choice, and/or capitalist free enterprise.

Restrictive Grants

Grants are donor-restricted subsidies. Roosevelt initially developed a grant system because it was quicker to expand existing state emergency relief programs than to develop a huge new federal bureaucracy. It also served to co-opt the states into partnership instead of political opposition. Once started, it was sufficiently rewarding to both sides that it became the new traditional way of operating.

Grants combine advantages of both centralization and decentralization. They enable the central government to plan, implement priorities, and assure minimum standards. They tap the stronger federal revenue capability (due to the Sixteenth Amendment) as compared with local government and charity. The federal government can make efficient use of expertise through a small staff that provides technical assistance to all fifty states.

From a state and local perspective, it provides resources to do things they could not otherwise afford and permits flexible response to local conditions and subcultures. The partnership is a check and balance against error, prejudice, corruption, and misuse of power by either partner.

Decentralization is often advocated as a means to increase administrative efficiency through smaller, less bureaucratic organizations. (My own personal experience suggests just the reverse. I found the U.S. Department of Health, Education, and Welfare in the 1960s to be far more competent and efficient, and less bureaucratic, than New York City's Welfare Department in the 1950s or Nebraska's Department of Social Services in the 1970s and 1980s.)

Grants vary in their degree of control. The most controlled is the *project grant*, which is usually made to public or nonprofit agencies for time-limited periods in areas such as research, training, demonstration, and start-up of new programs. The grantor typically puts out a statement of its objectives and invites proposals that detail (1) the applicant's concrete project and how it furthers the grantor's objectives, (2) how the results will be measured and evaluated, (3) a plan of operation, often quite detailed, and (4) an itemized budget.

Categorical grants are usually given to state or local governments for ongoing programs. Their objectives are broader than project grants but still targeted to a defined need and population. There are hundreds of categorical grant programs in such areas as public assistance, child welfare, rehabilitation, employment services, agricultural extension, education, and public health. The federal government publishes guidelines on program objectives, priorities, and standards. It requires from the grantee (1) a state plan compatible with the guidelines that spells out programs and selection criteria, (2) financial and program accountability to the grantor, and often (3) commitment of matching funds.

Most categorical grants distribute funds among the states through a formula based on population and/or relative need. A few programs like AFDC, which meet a critical need that is variable and unpredictable, may be open ended, with no ceiling on the federal commitment.

Permissive Grants

A *block grant* is simply a broader category with looser conditions. It offers greater flexibility and self-determination at the expense of weaker control over priorities, standards, and consistency. Advocates of block grants tend to give higher priority to individualism and pluralism than to universalism. They may also have more confidence in state and local than in central government.

In 1967, the pioneer block grant combined nine existing categorical public health "disease" grants, permitting each state to allocate among the nine purposes according to its own particular regional problems and priorities. In the 1970s and 1980s there was a major ideological shift from the categorical to block philosophy in social services, urban development, and education.

The ultimate block grant is *revenue sharing*. Taxes are collected centrally and disbursed on a formula basis as an unrestricted subsidy to state or local governments. When President Nixon began dismantling the poverty program in the early 1970s, states and cities lost big chunks of money. Opposition was neutralized by partially replacing lost grants with general revenue sharing. Carried to its logical extreme, revenue sharing could shift the social welfare system from a somewhat universalistic national pattern to a patchwork quilt of local choices. This appears also to have been an intent of 1980s block grants.

A permissive grantlike approach is indirect subsidy through tax welfare and "freebies." Among the most permissive are the tax exemption, charitable deduction, and subsidized postage discussed earlier in this chapter.

SUMMARY

Two basic methods of paying for social welfare services are to subsidize the producer or buy the product.

Subsidies may be restricted, in cash or kind, to specific purposes or unrestricted and available for any legitimate agency function. Restricted funding offers more control to the giver. Unrestricted funds can be used by the agency wherever they are most needed. Indirect government subsidy is provided through tax exemption, the charitable deduction, and other means.

Agencies increasingly sell their services. Due to the unique circumstances of social welfare, economic market pricing is not reliable. The favored methods are variations on an audited-cost approach. Subsidized agencies may use other pricing methods such as ability to pay or symbolic charges.

A popular method of paying for health and welfare services has become third-party purchases by the government, insurance companies, and employers on behalf of their people. Especially in the health field, conflicting interests among consumers, providers, and payers have created a somewhat chaotic situation regarding cost controls and assurance of needed services that have led to both withdrawal of responsibility and efforts to impose central controls. Provider-insurers, such as HMOs, combine the functions of financing and delivering services.

Throughout history there has been a tension between centralized coordination and decentralization. The nation's ideology and policies on this have been cyclical, with an apparent long-term trend toward incremental centralization. Federal patterns of providing for social welfare needs reflects this ambivalence. Some programs, like Social Security, are directly administered. Others, like AFDC and Medicaid, are provided through categorical grants to the states. Still others target project grants to public and nonprofit agencies. In the past quarter century, a decentralization trend has been implemented through block grants, third-party purchase of service, and withdrawal of federal responsibility.

NOTES

1. In economics, *regressive* means increasing the inequality between upper- and lower-income groups.
2. *Omaha World Herald*, November 16, 1985.

3. Child welfare has a long purchase-of-care tradition that had a different origin (sectarian issues) and predates the pattern described here.

4. See the discussion of subsidiarity in Chapter 12.

5. See Article I, Section 8, of the U.S. Constitution.

6. A landgrant is a block of federal land given to a state or private corporation for resale, the proceeds of which finance the intended purpose.

7. Franklin Pierce, veto message, "An Act Making a Grant of Public Lands to the Several States for the Benefit of Indigent Insane Persons," May 3, 1854.

8. *Steward Machine Co. v. Davis*, reproduced in National Conference on Social Welfare, *The Report of the Committee on Economic Security of 1935, 50th Anniversary Edition* (Washington, DC, 1985), p. 118.

9. *Helvering v. Davis*, ibid., p. 128.

Chapter 14

Choice

No matter how qualified or deserving we are,
we will never reach a better life
until we can imagine it for ourselves
and allow ourselves to have it.[1]

NO HIDING PLACE

A word processor offers two methods of selecting a format. You can set your own margins, type size, spacing, and so on. If you do not, it automatically selects its own standard "default format" for you. Like the computer format, we cannot avoid social policy choices. Choices have been and will again be made explicitly or through de facto practice. If *you* do not make them, you have selected *someone else's* policy as your default choice, which is probably different from what you would have preferred. "We design our lives through the power of our choices. We feel most helpless when we've made choices by default, when we haven't designed our lives on our own."[2]

Some of those choices may be outright *bad* social policy, harmful to people individually and collectively. The slogan of the 1960s social justice movement, "If you're not part of the solution, you're part of the problem," was not idle rhetoric. Institutionalized racism, sexism, and classism were so embedded in the fabric of society's beliefs, culture, relationships, statuses, and legal structure that they were being perpetuated, often unwittingly, by well-meaning fellow citizens in their everyday patterns of work and life. Personal accountability is not diminished by denying reality, minding our own business, washing our hands like Pilate, or retreating into private piety and micromoralism.

The following are some of the common—and correctible—sources of bad policy choices:

- *Bad purpose.* South Africa's policy of apartheid was designed to favor the interests of a minority at the expense of everyone else.

- *Other priorities.* In his 1854 veto of aid to mental health, President Pierce affirmed "the duty incumbent on us all as men and citizens, and as among the highest and holiest of our duties, to provide for those who, in the mysterious order of Providence, are subject to want and to disease of body or mind"—but not as high and holy as states' rights.

- *Ignorance.* President Hoover, a compassionate man who had led a hunger relief effort that reputedly saved millions of Russian lives after the Communist revolution, took a hard line against hunger relief for his own American people in 1930–33. Incredible as it may seem, he was so out of touch that he literally did not know they were suffering.

- *Inaccurate premises.* Historians June Axinn and Herman Levin found a second contributing factor: "Trapped by the hope of his own prediction of an early return to economic normalcy . . . Hoover was reluctant to have the federal government assume new responsibilities and powers."[3]

- *Ideology.* According to a Social Darwinist, "Society is constantly excreting its unhealthy imbecile, slow, vacillating, faithless members to leave room for the deserving. A maudlin impulse to prolong the lives of the unfit stands in the way of this beneficent purging of the social organism."[4]

INTENT

The heart of social welfare policy is its intent:

It is the *objectives* [emphasis added] of these services, transactions, and transfers in relation to social needs, rather than the particular administrative method or institutional device employed to attain objectives, which largely determine our interests. The study of welfare objectives thus lies at the centre of our focus of vision. We may bring to this focus, singly or in combination, the methods, techniques, and insights of the historian, the economist, the statistician, the sociologist, or, on occasion, some of the perspectives of the philosopher.[5]

The intent of a social policy may be self-serving, altruistic, or both. The Food Stamps program was both. Farmers were looking for a market for their chronic agricultural surpluses. Over 80 percent of Americans were already buying as much as they needed. Where was there potential for increase? Answer: the poor who could not afford to buy an adequate diet. Proposal: Put food money in their pocket, but be sure it can be used only for U.S. farm products. The agriculture lobby was joined, for entirely different reasons, by humanitarian liberals concerned with the well-being of poor Americans.

Manifest and Covert Intents

In the best of all possible worlds, intents would be rational, explicit, and open for all to see. In reality, they are often hidden, ambiguous, or fuzzy. The chart below may be useful in sorting out social policy positions, decisions, and alternatives. One dimension is whether the advocates and policy makers are aware of their own intent and what it is based on. The second is whether the intent of the advocates is known to other interested parties.[6]

AWARENESS OF INTENT

		Advocates and Policy Makers	
		AWARE	UNAWARE
Other			
Interested	AWARE	Overt	Unwitting
Parties	UNAWARE	Covert	Unperceived

What is the real purpose of a policy? *Manifest* intents are out in the open for all to see. As comedian Flip Wilson used to say, "What you see is what you get." If you propose a flat income grant to each citizen, to be financed by progressive income taxes, your equalization, redistribution and antipoverty intents are obvious. Interested parties can respond accordingly.

Policy advocates may fear that if their true intent were known, it would be rejected by the general public or by powerful interest groups. So they keep their intent *covert*, "hidden, secret, concealed, disguised, deceitful." The simplest covert method is the Pearl Harbor approach: Keep it secret until you are ready to strike so that the opposition will be caught unprepared.

A *hidden agenda* is more subtle. When psychologists sought licensure restrictions, their stated intent was to protect clients. Although this was indeed true, their primary intent may have been covert: increased income and security for guild members.

In other cases, the stated intent is a *lie*. A few years ago, lobbyists sought to replace progressive income tax brackets with a flat percentage rate for everyone. Their stated intent was simplification. Their covert aim was to reduce taxes for their upper-income clients by shifting a greater share of the burden to middle-income taxpayers. If simplification had honestly been an intent, they would not have included in the same "reform" bill a set of tax credits and exclusions for their clients that increased the complexity of the tax law.

Misdirection is another strategy. In a football draw play the quarterback, by pretending to set up for a pass, draws the defenders into rushing him while handing the ball covertly to a running back who slips through the hole this creates. A head of state, intent on reducing the national role in social welfare, first reduced taxes, creating a large budget deficit. This deficit "regrettably" made human service cuts "imperative." This strategy is reminiscent of the traditional illustration of *chutzpah*: A man on trial for murdering his parents asks for mercy on the grounds that he is an orphan.

In addition to raising ethical questions, covert strategies have practical liabilities. *Strategically*, if the deceit is discovered, a backlash may defeat the policy and destroy the deceiver's future credibility. *Substantively*, the policy may be poorer without the constructive criticism that overt scrutiny would have provided. *Procedurally*, covert behavior undermines the give and take essential to the health and stability of democratic systems.

On the other hand, are some ends important enough to satisfy the ethics and warrant the risk? Are there circumstances where unjust misuses of power justify covert counterstrategies on behalf of oppressed groups?

Unrecognized Intents

Advocates and decision makers may be unaware of the real intent of their policies due to vagueness, self-deception, and/or internal disagreements.

Vague good intentions, "soft hearted and soft headed," occur when advocates do not have a sound grasp of the existing situation or clarity about their values, interests, and ways of thinking. These lead to ambiguities, confusion, and contradictions regarding the specific intent of specific policies.

In one local community, an intense emotional conflict developed between supporters and opponents of sex education. Each piously mouthed its own catchwords and emotionally attacked the other's slogans, yet both groups genuinely wanted healthier attitudes toward sex and fewer teen pregnancies. Perhaps if their real intents had been clearer, they could have worked together to find a mutually agreeable way to achieve them.

Self-deception is a particular problem for righteous people, such as clergy, social workers, feminists, liberals, and evangelical Christians. When activist young faculty members gained control of a faculty union, they legally represented the interests of all faculty. Against management protestations, they adamantly bargained for a new salary policy that raised their own junior faculty salaries to parity with comparable universities at the expense of senior faculty, whose already wider parity gap was further increased. Claiming that this was an act of general social justice for an "oppressed class" (assistant professors), they indignantly denied any self-interested intent. Further, despite their research PhDs, they appeared to be incapable of understanding the statistical documentation presented by their critics.

Two problems with unwitting actors are illustrated here. First, the unwitting actor is vulnerable. In a hotly contested vote, the union had narrowly won its right to represent all faculty. Their self-righteous self-deception created an anti-union faculty majority. Second, it is difficult to reason or negotiate with naively zealous policy advocates. Sociologist Marion Levy once said, "Always hope that your opponents be evil, for in evil there is a strain of rationality and therefore the possibility of out-thinking them. Good intentions randomize behavior. When good intentions are combined with stupidity, it is impossible to out-think them."[7]

Like the blind men and the elephant, advocates of a policy or program may have *different interpretations* of its intent. Such ambiguity may get a policy passed but endow it with a legacy of inconsistency in application, problems of evaluation, and alienation of those whose expectations are not met. In the Economic Opportunity Act of 1964 (War on Poverty), community action was interpreted in four distinct ways.

1. Social planners, impressed by the success of Ford Foundation "Gray Cities" projects, saw it as *reorganizing services* to aid the poor more effectively.
2. The president's top poverty aide, who had a collective bargaining background, stressed "maximum feasible *participation* of the poor" in decision-making structures that affected them.
3. Community organizers and civil rights leaders focused on *empowerment* of oppressed groups.
4. Mayors saw it as a vehicle to *make city governments more effective* in solving urban problems.[8]

In a traditional or homogeneous setting, no one may even be aware that a choice has been made. Because it is not recognized at all, *unperceived intent* carries an extra risk of being bad policy. In the 1960s U.S. Welfare Administration, with its history of dynamic female leadership since the founding of the Children's Bureau a half century earlier, titles of address were the same for men and women. When I transferred from there to NIMH (the National Institute of Mental Health), which was culturally identified with male-dominant psychiatry and clinical psychology, I encountered a de facto policy whereby men were formally addressed by their titles, whereas their female peers were first-named. When I raised the issue, the typical response from both male and female staff was a blank stare. This may seem to be only symbolic, but it correlated with differences between the two agencies on gender equality in employment, promotion, rank, and power.

Covertness may at times be tactically advantageous. However, it is always desirable to maximize your own awareness in dealing with covert, unwitting, and unperceived intents of existing or proposed policy. This improves your ability both to make wise choices and to gain strategic advantage.

Behind the Intent: Facts

To understand the intent of a policy, you must learn two things about its supporters' perspectives: (1) what they think the situation *is* and (2) what they believe it *should be*. In the context of the analysis of ways of thinking in Chapter 2, a few suggestions of what to look for may be useful.

Where do the supporters' facts come from?

- *Empirical data*: What sources? How accurate? How complete?
- *Projection*: From what experiences are they projecting? Do projections coincide with other available information?
- *A priori belief*: What premises about reality do they take for granted? Are conclusions logically and consistently related to the premise? To what extent are they compatible with available data?

A common error is to treat an a priori belief as if it were empirical data. There is documented evidence that many welfare mothers are eager to get off welfare through employment. For investment return, the best use of limited education, training, and support services is to give priority to volunteers who are already motivated to make best use of them. This was successful in the 1960s (and again in a 1980s Massachusetts project), yet federal legislation in the 1970s and 1980s repealed these policies in favor of punitive approaches. Why? The policy makers, ignoring the weight of empirical evidence, accepted as fact an a priori belief, rooted in Calvinism and its grandchild the Protestant Ethic, that all paupers are inherently lazy and shiftless.

Similar errors occur when empirical data are incorrect due to selection, biasing, and methodological error, or when personal experiences are inaccurately generalized to a group of people, the economic system, or society as a whole: ''The poor don't . . . '' ''Anyone with gumption can . . . '' ''Profit-oriented entrepreneurs always . . . ''

Behind the Intent: Interests and Values

What is the source of policy objectives? They can usually be traced either to self-interest or to a priori values.

Most policies that claim to promote the common good benefit one particular interest group more than others. A secretary of defense said in the 1950s, "What is good for General Motors is good for the nation." Is it? Trickle-down benefits will raise the standard of living for workers, said the advocates of supply-side tax cuts for owners in 1981. Did they? Policies that reduce poverty and discrimination create trickle-up benefits for the white middle class in the form of a more productive, gentler, and safer society, say social justice liberals. Do they?

Is a proposed policy truly win-win, whereby advancing the interests of one group benefits the larger society? Or is it zero sum, by which one's gain is another's loss? Who stands to gain the most? Do they especially need or deserve to gain? At whose expense? How well can the loser afford that cost?

What explicit values are stated in relation to the policy? Are they consistent with the values implicit in the specific provisions of proposals and how the policy is carried out? If not, look further to discover why the discrepancy exists. Is it deliberate hypocrisy or misdirection? Is it pious self-deception? Does it stem from the ambiguity of a value conflict in which the issue of transcendent versus subordinate values has not been clearly resolved?

Jesus may have suggested the best clue to the real intent of a policy: "Beware of false prophets who come to you in sheep's clothing but inwardly are ravenous wolves. You will know them by their fruits. Are grapes gathered from thorns, or figs from thistles? So every sound tree bears good fruit, but the bad tree bears evil fruit.[9]

Diversion of Intent: Implementation Processes

"There is many a slip twixt the cup and the lip."[10] Original good intentions are usually compromised and watered down by the time they have run the gauntlet of legislative, political, and economic realities and been implemented by less-than-perfect agencies and individuals. In 1964, President Johnson declared war on poverty. However, underlying systemic causes of poverty were addressed more in rhetoric than in concrete actions. As enacted, the antipoverty programs were not all-out war but a collection of skirmishes that provided compensatory training and education to individual victims of poverty. Its idealistic community action empowerment tended to be diluted when it threatened the status quo. Many of the "warriors" were limited by inadequate professional competence and diverted by their own political or personal agenda.

Nevertheless, these programs contributed to an unprecedented reduction in poverty during the five-year war. Yet many critics called it a failure. Why? Because (1) its limited real successes bore little resemblance to its grandly proclaimed original intent and (2) poverty increased again after a new administration reversed its policies and dismantled its programs.

Intents themselves may be reversed along the way. The author of the Nixon Family Assistance Plan (FAP) to nationalize AFDC says he proposed it as an antipoverty program. After the White House had reworked it, administrative goals of uniformity, control, and cost reduction had taken priority over reduction of poverty. The original intent was further eroded by punitive antirecipient amendments in the Senate. As it came out the other end, it would have reduced aid to 3/4 of current recipients and further restricted eligibility. When many early FAP supporters repudiated the revised version, its originator publicly castigated them for deserting his brainchild. Their response: It is a wise father who knows his own child after it has been through the policy mill![11]

Diversion of Intent: Evaluation Processes

Social policy intent may also be diverted by technical tools. When the president of Ford Motor Company became secretary of defense in 1961, he brought with him a successful industrial efficiency approach called *cost-benefit analysis*. The essence of this is to convert all results (benefits) into a common denominator so that they can be compared with each other and with the costs. In our society, the only accepted common denominator universal enough to do this is market price; that is, dollars. This works well for business, where dollars are the ultimate objective.

Within five years, cost-benefit analysis had become the primary analytical tool for choosing among social policy and program alternatives and for evaluating their effectiveness. The problem is that many aspects of human well-being are literally priceless. It is difficult to put a dollar price on self-esteem, satisfaction, physical and mental health, liberty, happiness, life itself—or Faust's soul.

Conversion to dollars gradually but inexorably displaces original intents. It works like this:

1. Unable to measure directly the individual well-being objective of rehabilitation, evaluators select earnings of rehabilitated persons as the closest available economic indicator of well-being.
2. Soon the economic indicator replaces the overall well-being intent as the working objective in planning and administration.
3. Eventually, policy and program people forget the original intent and begin to think exclusively in terms of the indicator. Meeting the needs of disabled individuals is subtly but surely displaced by a goal of maximized aggregate

earnings. Needs-based selection is replaced by investment-based selection. The "easiest" cases are given preference, for they offer a bigger payoff at a lower cost. Those with the greatest need for rehabilitation become the least desirable clients.

EFFECTS

Effects are the bottom line.

What does it profit, my brethren, if a man says he has faith but has not works. . . . If a brother or sister is ill-clad and in lack of daily food, and one of you says to them, "Go in peace, be warmed and filled," without giving them the things needed for the body, what does it profit? So [a good intent] by itself, if it has no works, is dead.[12]

Social policy is "a society's purposes and practices as they affect the social welfare of persons individually and collectively." Obviously, it is important to know what the actual effects of existing policies are, so that we know whether to keep or change them and, based on experience, can predict the effects of proposed new policies. In Don Quixote's words, "The proof of the pudding is in the eating." Unfortunately, for a variety of reasons, the effects may not be fully and accurately identified.

Manifest Effects

Manifest effects are ones where there is available, open, and objective information about them and some basis for assuming a connection between the cause (policy) and the effect.

A manifest effect of Social Security, predicted in advance by its designers and verified by subsequent data, has been the reduction of poverty among retirees. As the program took effect, the poverty rate for the aged fell steadily, from an estimated 70 percent in 1935 to 40 percent in 1960 and 11 percent in 1987, by which time it was below the poverty rate for the general population. Former Social Security commissioner Robert Ball used Census Bureau income data to document the causative connection:

If there were no social security, there would be about 3.5 elderly poor persons for every one now below the poverty level. Social security cuts the incidence of poverty among the elderly by over 70%. Nine to ten million people above 65 are kept above the rock bottom poverty level by social security, and four to five million other social security beneficiaries are also kept above the poverty level by their benefits. Millions more would have incomes only slightly above poverty if it were not for social security.

Cutting social security will reverse the progress that has been made and plunge additional people into the poor and near-poor category.[13]

There may be manifest side effects, expected results that are not part of the policy intent. For instance, the intent of Medicare and Medicaid was to improve the welfare of patients, but a predicted—and documented—byproduct was to increase the income of physicians and hospitals by reducing the incidence of unpaid bills and free service.

Some manifest effects were *unforeseen*. Based on the history of third-party purchase in child welfare, Medicare and Medicaid were expected to expand nonprofit programs in lieu of public services. Apparently no one predicted that commercial health care would expand instead. As it turned out, the new programs helped create both the incentive (potential for profit) and the opportunity (erosion of uniquely voluntary characteristics in nonprofit hospitals and clinics) for business to enter the field.

Obscured Effects

To *obscure* is "to conceal from view; to hide; to make less conspicuous; to make less intelligible; to confuse." *Direct falsification* may be used. Despite extensive documentary evidence from his own government agencies showing large increases in the poverty rate, an antiwelfare president proclaimed in a nationally broadcast speech, "There is no hunger in America."

It may be more subtle. It has been said, "There are three kinds of lies: lies, damned lies, and statistics." In 1984, the government cut the poverty count by 1/3 by counting as personal income of poor persons all fees paid to physicians and hospitals on their behalf. Thus an elderly SSI recipient who had been hospitalized became statistically upper middle income for the year—while her manifest poverty was unchanged.

Effects can also be obscured by *diverting attention*. A school board, responsive to childless taxpayers, enacted an economy budget that eliminated the lunchroom, free textbooks, music, and extracurricular activities. By focusing public attention on tax savings of $100 per family, it obscured the much larger new costs that would be imposed on parents for books and supplies, higher-priced commercial lunches, fees paid to participate in "self-supporting" school sports and clubs, and private lessons to replace the canceled music program.

Another ploy is to *create confusion*. Faced with overwhelming evidence on the health hazard of smoking, the tobacco industry used confusing technical criticism of the research studies to raise doubts and delay social policy changes.

Deception about social policy effects may backfire sooner or later. Let us look at the illustrations given above.

- The juxtaposition of highly visible unemployment and a homelessness crisis with the president's hunger statement aroused dramatic rebuttals that in turn reactivated social advocacy among unions and a new wave of middle-class volunteers who had "forgotten" about "the hidden Americans."

- Social scientists and others vociferously attacked the new poverty definition as misleading and invalid. The ensuing publicity about the effort to obscure the increase in poverty had the reverse effect: It brought it to the attention of millions of Americans who normally ignored such statistics.

- After experiencing the real cost of the school tax "saving," previously apathetic parents organized and elected a new school board that restored the old program and turned a deaf ear to subsequent economy proposals.

- Passage of antismoking policies was accelerated by the tobacco lobby's loss of credibility when exposure of internal correspondence showed that tobacco companies had privately accepted the truth of what they were publicly challenging.

Not all hidden effects are deliberately obscured. Some are obscured by *intervening variables*. The domestic economic policies of Presidents Nixon, Ford, and Carter appeared to cause inflation while those of President Reagan seemed to lower it. However, the actual effects, if any, of their policies (and those independently pursued by the Fed) were obscured by the overwhelming impact of a dramatic rise of world oil prices in the 1970s and an equally dramatic fall in the early 1980s.

Some effects may not be recognized at all, even after they occur. For instance, let us say that iatrogenic illness (disorders caused by medical treatment) is a major health hazard. In that case, an effect of comprehensive national health care might be to increase ill health. Unaware of this effect, the policy response to this increase might be to exacerbate the problem by adding still more iatrogenic services.

By keeping voters uninformed and reducing accountability, deliberate obscuring subverts democracy. Although there may be a proper time and place for it, most obscuring is a ploy to cover up errors or to promote special interests that could not survive the light of day. Opening both intents and effects to public scrutiny will probably improve social policies and programs in the long run. Desirable ones can be supported and enhanced on their merits. Ineffective or harmful ones can be revised or replaced: When in doubt, bring it out.

MAKING THE CHOICE

Every realistic social policy choice is a compromise that balances three key factors: *desirability, design,* and *feasibility*.

Desirability

Desirability is a mix of interests, values, and beliefs as discussed in Chapter 2. In whose *interest* is a policy objective: your own, your peer group, a client group, some other target group, or society as a whole? What *values* guide you in deciding whose interests take priority, what is "good" or "bad" for them, and what means are acceptable? Is there a universal meaning, value system, or guiding force? If so, what is it? What do you believe the facts are about specific needs, their relationship to the overall social system, and the probable effects of your proposed policy?

Design

Research uses the terms *necessary cause* and *sufficient cause*. Adapted to social policy, something is *necessary* if the objective cannot be achieved without it. Universal basic literacy is necessary for full employment, since nearly every job requires at least the ability to read instructions and signs. But it is not sufficient because most jobs require other education and skills too. Thus something is *sufficient* if it can achieve the objective. There may be "more than one way to skin a cat." For instance, in combating typhoid fever, either a clean water supply or vaccination may be sufficient. Either means-tested relief grants or universal old-age pensions, if adequate, could assure a guaranteed minimum income in old age. In such cases, you have a choice of options.

If no single intervention is sufficient, you may need to combine several. Even a superbly trained workforce will not guarantee full employment if the jobs are not there. You may also need policies for economic development, plus education and training, plus residual public works programs. A senior citizen "does not live by bread alone." For "quality of life" in old age, you may want policies that provide (1) a guaranteed minimum-income program, (2) wage-related social security above the minimum, (3) tax incentives for private pensions, (4) full-coverage Medicare, (5) meals on wheels and senior citizen centers, (6) medical research into Alzheimer's disease and arthritis, and (7) private sector religious services.

An ideal social policy design would incorporate all necessary elements in a package sufficient to fulfill the intent. Such packages are rare in the real world. A good design might be sufficient to meet a limited objective that contributes to —and does not preclude further progress toward— your long-range social policy goal.

Feasibility

A desirable intent plus a good design does not by itself get the job done. You still have to be able to carry the plan out. Intent and design must be adjusted to feasibility. Among factors affecting feasibility are

- *State of the art.* Can it be done at all? Can Bangladesh guarantee an adequate income for its people under any circumstance? Can an AIDS epidemic be ended by any existing means?

- *Resources.* Are the necessary funds attainable? If so, will qualified staff be available?

- *Motivation.* Will there be enough commitment to assure proper implementation? There was not on Prohibition. There was on voting rights.

- *Politics.* What will the traffic bear with those who have to approve, provide resources, implement, accept, cooperate with, or use the policy or program? Are there special obstacles or opportunities? In an earlier chapter, Gilbert was quoted as saying we *cannot* afford adequate health and welfare services—yet we have hundreds of billions of discretionary dollars for nonconsumption military pursuits and for private luxuries. It is more accurate to say we *choose not to* afford them due to other priorities?

In a diversified free society like the United States, social policy choices are seldom clear, decisive, and comprehensive. For better or for worse, most of our policy choices are imperfect compromises of intent and design with feasibility. With apologies to Alfred (Lord) Tennyson, we might describe the charge of the "policy light brigade" thus:

> "Half a loaf, half a loaf, half a loaf onward,
> Into the valley of *dearth* rode the six hundred."

SUMMARY

Social policy choice is unavoidable. The only options are actively to determine the social policies we desire or, by default, to accept another interest group's choice. The latter increases the risk of bad policies.

The most important single aspect of a policy is its purpose. The intent may be open and honest, a covert hidden agenda, or unwitting and unrecognized. To identify and understand intent, you must learn what the "intenders" bring with them in their beliefs about facts, their values, and their self-interests. Intents may be compromised or changed in the process of getting a policy accepted and implemented. They may be subverted or displaced by the technical measures used to evaluate results.

As with intent, the actual effects of a policy or program may be manifest, deliberately obscured, or unrecognized. All proposed policies should predict their direct effects and anticipate probable side effects. Accurate and open assessment of effects are a primary basis for revising policies and perhaps the most reliable basis for predicting the future effects of alternative policy choices.

Policy decisions are a compromise among the factors of desirability, design, and feasibility. Desirability without works is wishful thinking.

A design that is not feasible under existing circumstances is a failure. A successfully carried out design is a waste unless its results are worthwhile and desirable.

NOTES

1. Richard Bach, *One* (New York: William Morrow, 1988), p. 95.
2. Ibid., p. 98.
3. June Axinn and Herman Levin, *Social Welfare: A History of the American Response to Need*, 2nd ed. (New York: Harper & Row, 1982), p. 178.
4. Walter Trattner, *From Poor Law to Welfare State*, 4th ed (New York: Free Press, 1989), p. 83.
5. Richard Titmuss, *Commitment to Welfare*, 2nd ed. (London: George Allen & Unwin, 1976), p. 21.
6. This framework was adapted from Robert Merton's model of manifest and latent functions in *Social Theory and Social Structure* (Glencoe, IL: Free Press, 1961).
7. Quoted from classroom memory.
8. This analysis is based on my direct experience as a federal Economic Opportunity Act planner. Patrick Moynihan's personal observations in *Maximum Feasible Misunderstanding* (New York: Free Press, 1969) tend to support this analysis.
9. Matthew 7:15–17.
10. Palladas, ca. 400 B.C.
11. This analysis is based on direct experience as a lobbyist on the issue.
12. James 2:14–17.
13. Robert Ball, "Cutting or Skipping the Cost-of-Living Adjustment (COLA) for Social Security Beneficiaries Is Unwise and Unfair" (New York: Study Group on Social Security, 1985).

Chapter 15

A Framework for Analyzing
Social Policy

"Every day in every way" social policies affect you. Many of them are fine with you as they stand, or at least okay. For instance, you may be very pleased with the Bill of Rights and consider the Social Security retirement program to be generally good despite its faults. You are probably pessimistically resigned to a number of other policies you consider unwise or unfair but cannot change. But you feel strongly enough about a few things to want to *do* something. Perhaps you can!

Doing, of course, involves many practice activities beyond the scope of this particular book, such as political strategies, social action, organizing, conflict management, program planning, and administration. Before strategies and tactics can do you much good, though, you first have to identify your position and goals. This final chapter suggests a general approach for doing so, applying the insights from the rest of the book. There are four major steps:

1. Identify the *issue*
2. Analyze what *exists*
3. Determine what *should be*
4. Decide what is *possible*

WHAT'S THE ISSUE?

Defining Boundaries

In a *Peanuts* comic strip, Linus aspires to be "the world's greatest humble country doctor." Lucy tells him he cannot because he does not love mankind. He replies, "I love mankind, it's people I can't stand." Noble as it may be, loving mankind goes only so far. Eventually you have to narrow your general good intentions down to the specific situation/condition and the particular aspects that will be the focus of your energy and attention. Some boundary dimensions are the following:

1. *What*: the subject area or condition with which you are concerned. It can be a *problem*, such as acid rain or unwanted pregnancies, or a *well-being potential*, such as holistic health or higher education. Be clear. If your goal is equal treatment on pensions, do you mean vertical equality, which would give the company president and his secretary identical pensions, or temporal equality, which would maintain the (vertically unequal) standard of living each had during working years?
2. *Why*: your reasons for this particular concern, including your beliefs about relevant facts, values, and interests.
3. *Who*: individuals, organizations, or groups involved as
   • *hosts* who are affected by the conditions,
   • *agents* who affect the conditions, and/or
   • *actors* who do—or could—influence the relevant policy.
4. *Where*: geographical, political, or organizational boundaries. Is your focus the United States, Arkansas, the Lower East Side, the Ottumwa school district, or the community hospital? For practical reasons, boundaries are often adjusted to fit political jurisdictions, service catchment areas, or census data tracts.
5. *When*: time lines for long-term goals and immediate objectives.

What's the Difference?

If everyone agrees with an existing state of affairs, it receives little or no policy attention. An *issue* is "a point, matter, or question to be disputed or decided" among actors. A policy issue may involve differences about whether to change or preserve what currently exists, as well as differences about competing purposes (broad goals). Even when people agree about goals, they may differ on specific applications of a generally agreed-upon purpose (objectives), and on the means for achieving selected objectives.

What Is?

The roots of differences can usually be traced back to *perceptions of reality* (what is) and/or *normative premises* (what should be). As in court decisions, the "facts" that influence social policy are not what is but what actors think they are, influenced by inaccuracies and incompleteness of information and projections, and colored by their interests, beliefs, and other selective biases, as discussed in Chapter 2. Roosevelt and Johnson, perceiving widespread hunger, developed antipoverty and economic opportunity programs. Hoover and Reagan saw no hunger and so rejected such policies as wasteful and un-American. Each policy fitted the president's "facts."

An AFDC caseworker told me that where she saw vulnerable young women struggling to be adequate persons and mothers despite "the slings and arrows of outrageous fortune," her colleagues saw irresponsible, promiscuous, ne'er-do-wells. These "facts," by determining how clients were treated, became self-fulfilling: On the average, her clients lived up to her "reality" and the others lived down to her colleagues' "reality."

The following news item illustrates how the "fact factor" muddied groundwater policy. The pivotal issue was whether underground water is part of the privately owned land above it or a vast public sea:

PLAN TO SELL UNDERGROUND WATER
TO DENVER STARTS LEGAL FISTFIGHT

Bubbling beneath the surface [of San Luis Valley] is a liquid treasure, an enormous pool of underground water with a volume perhaps 70 times larger than Lake Mead. The tranquillity of the valley has been shattered by a plan to develop and export the water. Its instigators are entrepreneurs who plan to make some money.

The Denver-based American Water Development Inc. hopes to turn its Baca Ranch into what essentially would be a massive water farm. . . .The company plans to dig dozens of wells on the Baca ranch and draw up 200,000 acre feet of water a year, roughly 65,000,000 gallons worth or about half the present annual water demand in the Denver area.

"They are going to draw the water table down, and our wells are going to go dry," charged rancher Felix Gallegos, whose family has been running cattle in the valley for four generations. "It will probably all become a desert."

Even if it did [destroy farming in the valley], the company argues, it would still be entitled to exploit Baca water under property rights traceable to the original 1823 Spanish land grant for the ranch. Legal experts say that such a theory is untested. A coalition of community leaders and agricultural interests, backed by several state and federal agencies, has gone to court to stop the project.[1]

We can see in this case that one key fact is ecological effect. Farmers predict a desert; whereas the company's computer projections assert that the project would have "minimal impact." Another key fact is legal: whether the 1823 Spanish landgrant does or does not give a 1990 owner private property rights to water under its land. The final policy may depend on which "facts" are accepted.

Procedural "facts" also influence policy. Does commercial competition in human services improve effectiveness and efficiency, or does it lead to cutting corners at the expense of patients? Does unionization improve the operation of the free market by enabling a weak seller (worker) to bargain on a more equal basis with a powerful buyer (a large employer), or does collective bargaining subvert the free market by reducing price competition among sellers of labor?

What Should Be?

The other major source of policy difference has to do with intents, based on our values and interests. Normative issues may be as fundamental as whether there is an inherent right to life, liberty, and happiness.

Even where fundamental norms are shared, differences arise over specific *applications*. Granted a general right to life, liberty, and happiness, does society, acting through its government, have a clear responsibility to promote the general welfare by assuring that all citizens will have an adequate quality of life, positive freedom, and equal opportunity in the pursuit of happiness? Or is government responsible only to protect citizens from direct predators who would steal their life, liberty, and property? May the government itself, under any circumstances, deprive citizens of life, liberty and property? If so, for what reasons: criminal activity? unwillingness to work? political dissent? national defense? "the greatest good for the greatest number"?

Normative differences may arise over the right *means* for achieving an objective. Those who support death with dignity for the terminally ill may still disagree intensely about whether to permit lethal injections or only passive actions such as withholding life-support treatments. Those who favor a minimum adequate standard of living argue about whether to achieve this through universal social insurances or means-tested relief.

A more mundane basis for difference on what should be is *competing self-interests*. On the average, childless taxpayers favor lower school taxes than do parents. The 85 percent of employees who already have health insurance benefits differ from the unprotected 15 percent on the importance of universal health insurance. Electric utilities, auto makers, and the oil industry, on whom the costs would fall most heavily, lobby vigorously against certain environmental standards that are not cost-effective for their profits.

HISTORICAL PERSPECTIVE: SCROOGE'S THREE GHOSTS

In Charles Dickens's *A Christmas Carol*, Ebenezer Scrooge is visited on Christmas Eve by three ghosts, of Christmas present, past, and future, who in combination give him the full picture. Christmas Present shows what is happening this Christmas and Scrooge's contribution to it. Christmas Past gives Scrooge insight into how he came to be what he is today. Christmas Future shows Scrooge where he will end up if he does not change. Like Scrooge, we need to know *the present situation, how it got there,* and *where it's heading.*

Obviously, you have to know the present situation:

- *The condition.* In regard to the "what, who, and where" concerns identified in defining the issue, what is the current status? What are the problems and needs, strengths and opportunities?

- *Existing policies and programs.* How do they affect the condition? To what extent do they meet needs and solve or prevent problems? To what extent do they create or exacerbate them? What opportunities for well-being have they responded to? With what results? What are the deficiencies?

- *Issues.* What disagreements exist relative to the condition, present policies, and/or proposed policies? Who holds each view and why? What is the level of interest, power, and energy of each actor?

"What's past is prologue, what is to come is yours and mine to decide."[2] A perspective on the past can be important in several ways for understanding the present and predicting the future:

- *Etiology of conditions.* Etiology is "the assignment of causes or origins." In order to choose effective social policies for problems or unmet needs, it is important to know why they exist and how they came about, so that the intervention will either address the cause or provide benefits that will not be undermined by those causes. Taking a "history" is a standard diagnostic procedure before prescribing treatment.

- *Etiology of intents.* Understanding where policies came from, what the circumstances were at that time, what values and interests they were designed to serve, and how and why they were modified over time provides insight into their relevance today and whether to change them.

- *Precedents and Trends.* Court interpretations of de jure policy lean heavily on two historical factors: (1) the original intent, such as legislative history, and (2) precedents, which are past interpretations and any trend over time toward changes in them. These are prime considerations for policy makers as well.

- *Learning from experience.* By studying what has gone before, we can avoid repeating past mistakes or reinventing the wheel. "He gains wisdom in a happy way, who gains it by another's experience."[3]

- *Perspective.* An objective overview is difficult to achieve from the middle of a fray in which we are emotionally involved. A more detached perspective on the dynamics of comparable situations in the past may increase our awareness of the dynamics of the present.

- *Historical determinism.* Those who believe with Roman emperor and philosopher Marcus Aurelius that "each thing is of like form from everlasting and comes round again in its cycle,"[4] or with Arnold Toynbee that history tends to repeat itself with variations, may seek insight into the current situation by looking at its earlier prototypes. On the other hand, those who hold a linear view will base their future projections on past historical trends.

Combining past experience and current information is our best shot at making *contingent predictions* about the future: What will it be like if there is no change? How will it be different if this or that policy change is adopted? Indeed, past experience is the foundation of nearly all planning, budgeting, and policy making.

WHAT'S GOING ON HERE?

Key Elements

A typical social policy can, and should, be viewed from a number of different directions. Some of the more common ones are identified below. The relative importance of these several elements will vary with each situation. They may be subdivided or combined, depending on what fits the particular issue best.

1. *Description of the condition.* Sources may include
   - *collected data* from the census, public health records, agency records, and so on
   - *professional observation,* yours and others', including case records, papers, journal articles, and books
   - designed *social research*
   - *journalistic accounts* in newspapers, magazines, and television
   - *literary depictions,* such as Charles Dickens's *Oliver Twist* or John Steinbeck's *Grapes of Wrath*
   - *philosophical critiques,* such as those of theologian Reinhold Niebuhr or organizer Saul Alinsky

2. *Socioeconomic context.* Elements may include characteristics of the hosts, agents, and actors such as geographic setting, age, race, gender, socioeconomic class, ethnic identity, and how subgroups interact with each other. In the larger context are the effects on the issue of technological developments, patterns of distribution of the "good things" within the society, and how the overall economy is functioning.

3. *Cultural context.* This addresses beliefs, values, ways of thinking, and patterns of behavior. Is there consensus, imposition by those in power, a majority view with minority deviations, or egalitarian pluralism? Are the differences among subgroups compatible or conflicting? What are the specific beliefs, values, and ways of thinking of each important actor, and how do they affect this issue?

4. *Legal context*. This includes the Constitution, statutory laws, common law, entitlements, regulations, administrative directives and procedures, and judicial interpretations.

5. *Structures of provision*. This is chiefly related to service and benefit programs and to regulation of agents. It includes such things as

   - auspices, lines of authority, controls, accountability, and sources and levels of financing

   - intergovernmental (federal, state, local); intersectoral (public, voluntary, commercial; church and state); and interagency overlap, coordination, collaboration, and competition

   - planning and coordinating mechanisms

   - staffing types, sources, qualifications, and patterns of utilization

   - criteria and methods for selecting clients or targets

   - methods of provision—cash, kind, voucher, incentives, sanctions and so on

6. *Political context*. This includes two dimensions: the formal political system and the de facto operation of power and interests.

7. *What else?* In each policy situation it is useful to stop and say, "Is there anything important not already covered under one of the other categories?"

The Actor Factor

Who is currently involved in affecting the outcome? Who else could be? How, and how much, can each influence the policy? What is your ability to relate to each?

"Actor factor" analysis, which should be applied to each important active or potential actor, starts with such obvious characteristics as status, power, energy level, intensity of interest and commitment, styles of communication and action, individual personalities, and group or organizational characteristics. Obviously, each of these requires quite different information and ways of getting it. Some draw upon research and statistics. Other data can only be learned from the actors themselves.

A second key area is each actor's intent, as discussed in Chapter 14, and its sources, as discussed in Chapter 2. This enables us to evaluate the soundness of policy positions and to develop effective strategies for dealing with opponents, allies, and other potential actors. Biasing factors include such things as their actual and perceived self-interests; their "history," because it has shaped where they stand now; sources, accuracy, completeness, and slanting, of their information; and content, sources, and consistency of their beliefs and values.

The actor factor may be integrated into the analysis of each key element.

SETTING A HEADING

In navigation, setting a heading is the choice of a compass direction. Now that you have analyzed the existing situation, including how it got there, where it seems to be going, and where the actors are coming from, you are ready to become the navigator and set your heading. You need to determine (1) the starting point (current situation), (2) the destination (desired outcome), (3) the relationship between the two points (the gap), and (4) the course to get from starting point to destination.

What Should Be: The Desirable Situation ?

"What should be" is the situation or condition you believe ideally should exist. It always entails some *deduction*, "reasoning from the general to the specific, or from a premise to a logical conclusion," from a priori beliefs and values about what is good or bad and what things are more or less important. It may also involve some projection from comparative study of actual situations, past and present, that are considered to be relatively better or worse. Even if your ideal situation is not attainable, it is the lodestar by which you set your heading, the standard against which you compare available policy choices.

The Gap: Zero Base and Incremental Approaches

The gap is the discrepancy between what should be and what is. It is also called the problem, deficiency, disorder, unmet need, or unrealized potential. You can approach it from opposite directions: *Zero base* sets the destination from scratch, then compares it with the current situation. *Incremental* starts with what is, then considers what should be changed.

The zero-based wellness model identifies, a priori, the desirable condition (wellness). Robert Kennedy put it this way: "Some men see things as they are and say, why? I dream things that never were and say, why not?" Martin Luther King's civil rights crusade used a wellness model, as expressed in his famous "I have a dream" speech. It follows this sequence:

1. *Determine what should be.*
2. *Examine what is,* empirically.
3. *Identify the gap* by comparing step 2 with step 1.
4. *Set outcome goals* that are feasible steps toward what should be.

The incremental problem-solving approach is based on the medical model of diagnosis and treatment. It evolves as a response to recurring problem cases that become identified as patterns of dysfunction. Administrators and true conservatives ("persons who wish to preserve traditions or institutions and resist innovation or change") normally move incrementally from what is in a process Charles Lindblom calls "successive limited comparisons"[5]:

1. *Examine the problem* (what is).
2. *Define "health"* (the desirable situation) in relation to the problem, either negatively as absence of the condition or by comparing more healthy and less healthy existing situations.
3. *Diagnose the problem.* Infer from available data the probable causes of the deviance from step 2.
4. *Set corrective outcome goals,* also known as treatment goals, based on the diagnosis.

In real life, we often blend the two approaches. For instance, creative human service professionals may be led to a social policy concern by diagnosis of problem cases; but once "turned on" to the issue, they may move beyond problem solving to an I-have-a-dream wellness approach. Sometimes the dynamics of determining what is and what should be are so intertwined that it is difficult to tell which came first, the chicken or the egg. This is no problem—so long as you end up with both.

Outcome Goals

A goal is a long-term *end result* (condition) toward which a social policy is directed. It may be the ideal condition or, more often, something that partially fills the gap between "is" and "should be." For instance, given the gap between universal good health and current health conditions, one policy goal might be a nonpolluted environment; another, healthful eating and exercise habits by the population; a third, universal state-of-the-art health services. Although none of these goals completely achieves the ideal condition, each contributes toward filling the gap.

Long-term goals govern your selection of more immediate, concrete policy objectives.

WHAT CAN BE DONE?

Alternative Objectives [6]

It would be nice to achieve your goal in one step, with the one available means. Unless it is a very simple, concrete goal, "you should live so long!"

Social policy is like the wilderness sport of orienteering. Having set your heading, you still have to chart a specific course over hills, across streams, and around cliffs. You cannot just go as the crow flies. Your problem is how the crow would go if it had a broken wing and had to walk.

If you cannot achieve the goal all at once, identify possible *intermediate objectives* that may be achievable within a reasonable time under realistic circumstances. An objective may achieve a piece of the final goal, provide a stepping stone toward its eventual achievement, or both.

Skilled social policy planners may develop a strategy that involves a *sequential series of stepping stones* that eventually arrive at the goal. In the 1970s, a goal of the United Way of America was for its related social services to do cost effectiveness planning and evaluation. Its first objective, which it carried out jointly with other national voluntary agencies and the American Institute of Certified Public Accountants, was to develop a program accounting system that identified agency costs in relation to each separate service program (intended effect) within an agency. Having achieved the first step (technical capability), the second stepping stone was to make program accounting a condition of United Way funding. This took care of measuring the cost side. A logical third stepping stone objective should have been to develop valid and reliable measures of human service success (effectiveness) followed by a fourth that required all of its agencies to submit annual effectiveness reports. If all four had been carried out, the full goal would have been achieved.

Another astute social policy strategy is to design a *set of coordinated pieces*, each of which is independently achievable and worthy in its own right. Achievement of the whole set would accomplish the entire goal. Let us say the goal is universal comprehensive health care. One piece might be a comprehensive Medicare for all citizens over sixty-five (15 percent of the population). A second might be a comprehensive Medicaid for all citizens with incomes below the poverty line (another 15 percent). A third might be to require all employers of fifty or more workers to provide private family health insurance to their employees (55 percent). A fourth might be a mandatory government health insurance program for small employers (10 percent). At this point, the goal is 95 percent achieved.[7] The final piece might be achieved by extending Medicaid to cover all other nonemployed persons under sixty-five.

A piecemeal approach to social goals has been the American way. A coordinated and planned piecemeal approach has not been.

Alternative Means

For each objective, identify alternative means to get there. For instance, different nations achieved universal health care through such varied means as

- direct public provision of services
- universal public insurance, which purchases care from private providers
- compulsory private insurance by employers, with residual public insurance for those who fall between the cracks
- giving employers a Hobson's choice of paying taxes for the government insurance program or providing equivalent private insurance
- mandated provincial (state) plans that must meet national standards.

Logically, you first select the objective and then consider alternative means to get there. However, because the choice of means may greatly affect overall acceptability and effectiveness, it is often more realistic to deal with them together by identifying *object/means combinations* for evaluation and selection. A pragmatic method of keeping the number of combinations manageable is Amatai Etzioni's *mixed scanning*: Do a quick scan of possibilities, from which you select the most promising few for more comprehensive analysis.[8]

Analyzing the Opposition's Alternatives

Among the alternatives to be reviewed and analyzed are those your opponents and others have proposed, or reasonably could propose. Whether you like them or not, you will have to be prepared to deal knowledgeably with them.

- *Recognize their merits.* You may want to modify your objective and/or means to incorporate their good points.
- *Identify their weaknesses.* Prepare rebuttals to use for persuasion and/or contention.
- *Identify possible compromises.* If you cannot prevail, it is useful to know where you can "give a little" and where you should not.

Selecting the Practical Policy

Chapter 14 identified three criteria for selecting the specific objective/means combination: desirability, design, and feasibility. Unfortunately, there is no simple one-size-fits-all formula. How you balance desirability and feasibility, benefits and costs, effectiveness and efficiency, long-term and short-term results, direct and indirect effects, and so forth, will involve value judgments, weighing priorities, and imprecise estimates.

You can go to extremes. You can accommodate to feasibility to the point that the original purpose is forgotten, as in the case of the proposed Family Assistance Plan (FAP) described in an earlier chapter. (Ironically, the FAP concessions to feasibility made it *infeasible* by losing it the votes of liberal senators.)

At the other extreme, the goal may be important enough to disregard conventional feasibility considerations. Two of the best-known expressions of this relate to waging war and spreading love. In 1864 in Mobile Bay, Admiral Farragut said, "Damn the torpedoes! Captain Drayton, go ahead! Jouett, full speed!" Eighteen centuries earlier, the apostle Paul said, "We have become a spectacle to the world. . . .We are fools for Christ's sake. . . .We hunger and thirst; we are ill-clad and buffeted and homeless . . . reviled . . . persecuted . . . slandered; we have become, and are now, as the refuse of the world, the offscouring of all things."[9]

Most of us, most of the time, follow a middle road:

1. Eliminate objectives that turn out to be *undesirable* because they have unacceptable side effects, are too vague, or preclude further steps.

2. Eliminate means that appear to be *unworkable*. Sometimes rejection of means due to effectiveness problems may lead to selecting instead a *prerequisite stepping stone* such as research, training, or electing new representatives.

3. Eliminate means that are *unacceptable* because of cost, negative side effects, or ethical problems. However effective they might be for reducing acid rain, you probably would not choose terrorist attacks against public utilities as your means.

4. Eliminate or compromise combinations that, whatever their intrinsic merit, will be blocked by "the powers that be" or resisted by the target hosts. (Of course, pessimistic projections are not always accurate. Farragut and Paul both won. A World War II U.S. Army Air Force slogan asserted, "The difficult we do immediately. The impossible takes a little longer.")

5. Finally, from what is left, choose the combination that for that specific case best reflects *your* relative weighting of desirability, design, and feasibility— seasoned with a dash of "gut feeling."

CONCLUDING OBSERVATIONS

Extent of Analysis

Think about all the dimensions and elements outlined in this chapter. Be aware of the many factors and choices discussed throughout this book. Then be practical. The relative comprehensiveness of your *actual* analysis will depend on the importance of the issue, how much you need to know to deal with other key actors, what data are available, and how much time, energy and resources you can afford. There is a point of diminishing returns beyond which, you will decide, the gains in knowledge are not worth the additional cost.

Social Policy Is Always Evolving

There is a logic to the sequence of analysis outlined in this chapter. In practice, however, we tend to jump around. It is normal to anticipate later steps in earlier decisions and to go back to revise earlier ones in light of later considerations. In social policy, nothing is etched in stone. It is always imperfect, evolving, and contingent upon circumstances. In the words of that baseball savant Yogi Berra, "It ain't over until it's over."

Even if there are absolute values and principles (as I believe), their application in specific social policies of specific societies at specific times is always *imperfect* (due to incomplete knowledge, limited self-awareness, and rationalizations of self-interests) and *impermanent* (due to changing social, economic, geophysical, technological, and other circumstances).

What you write on a typewriter is set. Any significant change requires retyping the whole page. By contrast, what you write on a word processor is entered on a memory disk you can reedit any number of times. When you go back and change something, everything subsequent automatically adjusts. Each printout, however final it appears, is a draft relative to the continuing, flexible memory disk. Although social policy has specific printouts, it is *always a working draft*, always subject to review and possible revision, never a final solution.

An old pastor once confided to me that his was the most secure profession in the world. Our mission, he said, is to fight sin, and there is no danger of ever working ourselves out of a job. Involvement in social policy offers such security!

SUMMARY

The first task in social policy analysis is to define the subject you are addressing: what? why? who? where? when? Next, identify the differences among actors in perception of facts and premises about what should be. On what level do these differences occur, broad general purpose, specific objectives, or means?

Second, analyze the existing situation, including social, economic, cultural, legal, and political factors. To fully understand the situation you must bring in a historical perspective: how it came to be the way it is and where it is likely to go depending on what policy choices are made.

Third, determine what should be and set outcome goals in relation to it. This can be done through a zero-base approach that starts with the desirable and works back or an incremental approach that starts with what is and works forward.

Fourth, identify possible limited, concrete objectives and evaluate them in terms of their contribution toward achieving the goal. Identify possible alternative means for viable goals. Select the optimum objective-means combination in light of desirability, design, and feasibility.

"When thou has done, thou hast not done, for I have more."[10] Social policy is forever evolving.

NOTES

1. *Los Angeles Times*, March 10, 1990.
2. William Shakespeare, *The Tempest*, Act 1, Scene 2.
3. Plautus, second century B.C.
4. Marcus Aurelius Antoninus, *Meditations*, A.D. second century, II, 14.
5. Charles Lindblom, "The Science of 'Muddling Through,' " *Public Administration Review*, vol. 19, spring 1959, pp. 79–88.
6. The dictionary defines *alternative* as "a possibility of one out of two (or less strictly more) things." The "less strictly" version is used here.
7. Percentages used are illustrative, not precise.
8. Amatai Etzioni, *The Active Society* (New York: Free Press, 1968).
9. First Letter to the Corinthians, 4:9–13.
10. John Donne. *A Hymn*, 1622.

Bibliography

Acton, H. B. *The Morals of the Market: An Ethical Exploration*. London: Longman, 1971.

Alinsky, Saul. *Rules for Radicals*. New York: Vintage, 1972.

Altmeyer, Arthur. *The Formative Years of Social Security*. Madison: University of Wisconsin Press, 1966.

Axinn, June, and Herman Levin. *Social Welfare*. 2nd ed. New York: Harper & Row, 1982.

Axinn, June, and Mark Stern. *Dependency and Poverty*. Lexington, MA: Lexington Books, 1988.

Ball, Robert. *Social Security Today and Tomorrow*. New York: Columbia University Press, 1978.

Bell, Winifred. *Contemporary Social Welfare*. New York: Macmillan, 1983.

Beveridge, W. H. *The Pillars of Society*. New York: Macmillan, 1943.

Beveridge, W. H. *Why I Am a Liberal*. London: Jenkins, 1945.

Blumberg, Paul. *Inequality in an Age of Decline*. Oxford: Oxford University Press, 1980.

Boulding, Kenneth. "The Boundaries of Social Policy." *Social Work*, vol. 12, no. 1, January 1967.

Burns, Eveline. *Social Security and Public Policy*. New York: McGraw-Hill, 1956.

Caplow, Theodore. *How to Run Any Organization*. Hinsdale, IL: Dryden, 1976.

Carnegie, Andrew. *The Gospel of Wealth*. New York: The Century Company, 1900.

Chadwick, Edwin. *The Report of His Majesty's Commissioners for Inquiring into the Administration and Practical Operation of the Poor Laws*, 1833.

Chambers, Donald. *Social Policy and Social Programs*. New York: Macmillan, 1986.

Cohen, Wilbur, and Milton Friedman. *Social Security: Universal or Selective?* Washington, DC: American Enterprise Institute, 1972.

Colby, Ira. *Social Welfare Policy: Perspectives, Patterns, Insights*. Chicago: Dorsey, 1989.

Communist Party of Great Britain. *People before Profits*, 1970.

Constitution of the United States.

De Schweinitz, Karl. *England's Road to Social Security*. New York: A. S. Barnes, 1961.

De Toqueville, Alexis. *Democracy in America*. New York: Alfred E. Knopf, 1980.

Declaration of Independence.

Dobelstein, Andrew. *Politics, Economics, and Public Welfare*. Englewood Cliffs, NJ: Prentice-Hall, 1980.

Dye, Thomas. *Understanding Public Policy*. Englewood Cliffs, NJ: Prentice-Hall, 1981.

Elman, Richard. *The Poorhouse State*. New York: Pantheon, 1966.

Etzioni, Amatai. *The Active Society*. New York: Free Press, 1968.

Friedman, Milton. *Capitalism and Freedom*. Chicago: University of Chicago Press, 1972.

Fromm, Erich, ed. *Socialist Humanism*. London: Allen Lane, 1967.

Gailbraith, J. K. *The Affluent Society*. Boston: Houghton Mifflin, 1958.

George, Vic, and Paul Wilding. *Ideology and Social Welfare*. London: Routledge & Kegan Paul, 1976.

Gil, David. *Unraveling Special Policy*. Cambridge, MA: Schenkman, 1976.

Gilbert, Neil. *Capitalism and the Welfare State*. New Haven, CT: Yale University Press, 1983.

Gilbert, Neil, and Harry Specht. *Dimensions of Social Welfare Policy*. Englewood Cliffs, NJ: Prentice-Hall, 1974.

Gilder, George. *Wealth and Poverty*. New York: Basic Books, 1981.

Glasser, Ira, Willard Gaylin, S. Marcus, and David Rothman. *Doing Good: The Limits of Benevolence*. New York: Pantheon, 1978.

Hamilton, Alexander, James Madison, and John Jay. *The Federalist Papers*. New York: Mentor, 1961.

Hansmann, Henry. "The Role of Nonprofit Enterprise." *Yale Law Review*, vol. 8, no. 5, April 1980.

Harrington, Michael. *The New American Poverty*. New York: Holt, Rinehart & Winston, 1984.

Haskins, Ronald, and James Gallagher. *Models for Analysis of Social Policy*, Norwood, CT: Ablex, 1981.

Hayek, Friedrich. *The Road to Serfdom*. London: Routledge, 1944.

Hayek, Friedrich. *Individualism and Economic Order*. London: Routledge & Kegan Paul, 1949.

Hayek, Friedrich. *The Constitution of Liberty*. London: Routledge & Kegan Paul, 1971.

Hill, Michael. *Understanding Social Policy*. Oxford: Basil Blackwell, 1980.

Hobbes, Thomas. *Leviathan*, 1651.

Hofstadter, Richard. *Social Darwinism in American Thought*. Boston: Beacon Press, 1944.

Howe, Irving, ed. *Beyond the Welfare State*. New York: Schocken, 1982.

Hume, David. *Treatise of Human Nature*. 1740.

Kahn, Alfred. *Social Policy and Social Services*. 2nd ed. New York: Random House, 1979.

Kahn, Alfred, and Sheila Kammerman. *Not for the Poor Alone*. Philadelphia: Temple University Press, 1975.

Kammerman, Sheila, and Alfred Kahn. *Social Services in the United State: Policies and Programs*. Philadelphia: Temple University Press, 1976.

Keith-Lucas, Alan. *The Poor You Have with You Always*. St. Davids, PA: North American Association of Christians in Social Work, 1989.

Kennedy, Gerald. *Of Heroes and Hero Worship*, 1943.

Kramer, Ralph. "Public Fiscal Policy and Voluntary Agencies in the Welfare State." *Social Service Review*, vol. 53, no. 1, March 1979.

Kramer, Ralph. *Voluntary Agencies in the Welfare State*. Berkeley: University of California Press, 1981.

Lampman, Robert. *The Share of Top Wealth Holders in the National Wealth*. Princeton, NJ: Princeton University Press, 1962.

Leftwich, Richard, and Ansel Sharp. *Economics of Social Issues*. 5th ed. Plano: Business Publications Inc., 1982.

Leiby, James. *A History of Social Welfare and Social Work in the United States*. New York: Columbia University Press, 1978.

Leiby, James. "Moral Foundations of Social Welfare and Social Work: An Historical View." *Social Work*, vol. 30, no. 4, July 1985.

Levin, Henry. *Cost-Effectiveness*. Beverly Hills, CA: Sage, 1983.

Levitan, Sar. *The Great Society's Poor Law*. Baltimore: Johns Hopkins University Press, 1969.

Lindblom, Charles. "The Science of 'Muddling Through.' " *Public Administration Review*, vol. 19, spring 1959.

Locke, John. *Two Treatises of Government*. 1690.

Lowell, James Russell. "New England Two Centuries Ago." 1888.

Magill, Robert. *Social Policy in American Society*. New York: Human Sciences Press, 1984.

Malthus, Thomas. An Essay on Population, 2nd. Ed., 1803.

Marshall, T. H. *Social Policy*. 4th ed. London: Hutchinson, 1975.

McCarthy, Michael. *The New Politics of Welfare: An Agenda for the 1990s?* Chicago: Lyceum, 1989.

Meenahan, Thomas, and Robert Washington. *Social Policy and Social Welfare*. New York: Free Press, 1980.

Mill, John Stuart. *On Liberty*. 1859.

Morris, Robert. *Social Policy of the American Welfare State*. New York: Longman, 1985.

Morris, Robert. *Rethinking Social Welfare*. New York: Longman, 1986.

Morris, Robert, ed. *Testing the Limits of Social Welfare*. Hanover, NH: University Press of New England, 1988.

Moynihan, Daniel. *Maximum Feasible Misunderstanding*. New York: Free Press, 1969.

Myers, Robert. *Social Security* 3rd ed. Homewood, IL: Richard D. Irwin, 1985.

National Conference of Catholic Bishops. *Economic Justice for All*. Washington, DC: 1986.

National Conference on Social Welfare. *The Report of the Committee on Economic Security of 1935, Fiftieth Anniversary Edition*. Washington, DC: 1985.

Neuman, Franz. *The Democratic and Authoritarian State*. New York: Free Press, 1957.

Okum, Arthur. *Equality and Efficiency: the Big Tradeoff*. Washington, DC: Brookings Institution, 1975.

Paine, Thomas. *Common Sense*. 1776.

Perkins, Frances. *The Roosevelt I Knew*. New York: Viking Press, 1946.

Pierce, Franklin. Veto message: "An Act Making a Grant of Public Lands to the Several States for the Benefit of Indigent Insane Persons." 1854.

Pinker, Robert. *The Idea of Welfare*. London: Heinemann, 1979.

Piven, Frances, and Richard Cloward. *Regulating the Poor*. New York: Pantheon, 1971.

Piven, Frances, and Richard Cloward. *The New Class War*. New York: Pantheon, 1982.

Pope John XXIII. Encyclical "Mater et magistra." 1961.

Pope John XXIII. Encyclical "Pacem in terris." 1963.

Pope Pius XI. Encyclical "Quadragesimo anno." 1931.

Rawls, John. *A Theory of Justice*. Cambridge, MA: Harvard University Press, 1971.

Rein, Martin. *Social Policy: Issues of Choice and Change*. New York: Random House, 1970.

Rein, Martin. *Social Science and Public Policy*. New York: Penguin, 1976.

Rein, Martin. "Equality and Social Policy." *Social Service Review*, vol. 51, no. 4, December 1977.

Roosevelt, Franklin. "Message to Congress Reviewing the Broad Objectives and Accomplishments of the Administration." June 8, 1934.

Rousseau, Jean Jacques. *The Social Contract*. 1762.

Rowley, Charles, and Alan Peacock. *Welfare Economics: A Liberal Restatement*. London: Martin Robertson, 1975.

Ryan, William. *Blaming the Victim*. New York: Pantheon, 1971.

Sampson, Timothy. *Welfare: A Handbook for Friend and Foe*. Philadelphia: United Church Press, 1972.

Schlesinger, Arthur. *The Age of Roosevelt*. Vol 2, *The Coming of the New Deal*. New York: Houghton Mifflin, 1959.

Schorr, Alvin. *Slums and Insecurity*. London: Nelson, 1964.

Schorr, Alvin. *Poor Kids*. New York: Basic Books, 1966.

Schorr, Alvin. *Explorations in Social Policy*. New York: Basic Books, 1968.

Scott, Gordon. *Welfare, Justice, and Freedom*. New York: Columbia University Press, 1980.

Sharp, Gene. *Social Power and Political Freedom*. Boston: Porter Sargent, 1980.

Smith, Adam. *The Wealth of Nations*. 1776.

Sowell, Thomas. *Civil Rights: Rhetoric or Reality?* New York: Quill, 1984.

Spencer, Herbert. *Social Statics and Man versus the State*. 1884.

Swift, Jonathan. *Gulliver's Travels*. 1727.

Swift, Jonathan. *A Modest Proposal for Preventing the Children of Poor People in Ireland from being a Burden to Their Parents or Country, and for Making Them Beneficial to the Public*. 1729.

Tawney, Richard. *The Acquisitive Society*. New York, Harcourt Brace, 1921.

Tawney, Richard. *Religion and the Rise of Capitalism*. New York: Mentor, 1926.

Tawney, Richard. *The Radical Tradition*. London: Penguin, 1964.

Theobold, Robert. *Free Men and Free Markets*. New York: Potter, 1963.

Thoreau, Henry David. *Walden*. 1854.

Titmuss, Richard. *Essays on the Welfare State*. London: George Allen & Unwin, 1958.

Titmuss, Richard. *Income Distribution and Social Change*. London: Allen & Unwin, 1962.

Titmuss, Richard. *Commitment to Welfare*. London: George Allen & Unwin, 1968.

Titmuss, Richard. *The Gift Relationship*. New York: Pantheon, 1971.

Titmuss, Richard. *Social Policy*. New York: Pantheon, 1974.

Townsend, Joseph. *A Dissertation on the Poor Laws by a Well-Wisher to Mankind* (1786). Berkeley: University of California Press, 1971.

Townsend, Peter. *Sociology and Social Policy*. London: Allen Lane, 1975.

Trattner, Walter. *From Poor Law to Welfare State*. 4th ed. New York: Free Press, 1989.

Tropman, John, Milan Dluhy, and Roger Lind, eds. *New Strategic Perspectives on Social Policy*. New York: Pergamon, 1981.

Tuchman, Barbara. *The March of Folly*. New York: Ballentine, 1984.

Veblen, Thorstein. *The Theory of the Leisure Class*. New York: Macmillan, 1899.

Warren, Roland. *Truth, Love, and Social Change*. Chicago: Rand McNally, 1971.

Warren, Roland. *The Community in America*. 2nd ed. Chicago: Rand McNally, 1972.

Waxman, Chaim. *The Stigma of Poverty*. 2nd ed. New York: Pergamon, 1983.

Weber, Max. *The Protestant Ethic and the Spirit of Capitalism*. New York: Charles Scribner's Sons, 1958.

West, Guida. *The National Welfare Rights Movement: The Social Protest of Poor Women*. New York: Praeger, 1981.

Wickenden, Elizabeth. "Social Security—Why Not a Means Test?, Fact Sheet #13," New York: Study Group on Social Security, 1984.

Wilensky, Harold, and Charles Lebeaux. *Industrial Society and Social Welfare*, 2nd ed. New York: Free Press, 1965.

Index

ABOUT THE AUTHOR

HOBART A. BURCH is Professor and past Director of the School of Social Work, University of Nebraska at Omaha, teaching social policy, planning, administration, and community organization. He has served as the Secretary of Labor's Special Assistant for Legislation to develop youth manpower programs under Title I of the Economic Opportunity Act of 1964, as Special Assistant to the U.S. Commissioner of Welfare, and as Deputy Director of Program Liaison for the National Institute of Mental Health.